ANNUAL EDITIONS

P9-BHS-808

Aging 13/14
Twenty-Sixth Edition

EDITOR

Harold Cox
Indiana State University

Harold Cox, professor of sociology at Indiana State University, has published several articles in the field of gerontology. He is the author of *Later Life: The Realities of Aging* (Prentice Hall, 2006). He is a member of the Gerontological Society of America and the American Sociological Association's Occupation and Professions Section and Youth Aging Section.

*Connect
Learn
Succeed*™

The McGraw·Hill Companies

Mc Graw Hill

Connect
Learn
Succeed™

ANNUAL EDITIONS: AGING, TWENTY-SIXTH EDITION

1 2 3 4 5 6 7 8 9 0 QDB/QDB 1 0 9 8 7 6 5 4 3

ISBN 978-0-07-813608-5
MHID 0-07-813608-3
ISSN 0272-3808 (print)
ISSN 2158-3528 (online)

Acquisitions Editor: *Joan L. McNamara*
Marketing Director: *Adam Kloza*
Marketing Manager: *Nathan Edwards*
Developmental Editor: *Dave Welsh*
Senior Project Manager: *Joyce Watters*
Buyer: *Nichole Birkenholz*
Cover Designer: *Studio Montage, St. Louis, MO.*
Senior Content Licensing Specialist: *Shirley Lanners*
Media Project Manager: *Sridevi Palani*

Compositor: Laserwords Private Limited
Cover Image Credits: Design Pics/Kristy-Anne Glubish (inset); Glow Images (background)

Editors/Academic Advisory Board

Members of the Academic Advisory Board are instrumental in the final selection of articles for each edition of ANNUAL EDITIONS. Their review of articles for content, level, and appropriateness provides critical direction to the editors and staff. We think that you will find their careful consideration well reflected in this volume.

ANNUAL EDITIONS: Aging 13/14
26th Edition

EDITOR

Harold Cox
Indiana State University

ACADEMIC ADVISORY BOARD MEMBERS

Editors/Academic Advisory Board continued

Preface

In publishing ANNUAL EDITIONS, we recognize the enormous role played by the magazines, newspapers, and journals of the public press in providing current, first-rate educational information in a broad spectrum of interest areas. Many of these articles are appropriate for students, researchers, and professionals seeking accurate, current material to help bridge the gap between principles and theories and the real world. These articles, however, become more useful for study when those of lasting value are carefully collected, organized, indexed, and reproduced in a low-cost format, which provides easy and permanent access when the material is needed. That is the role played by ANNUAL EDITIONS.

The decline of the crude birth rate in the United States and other nations, combined with improving food supplies, sanitation, and medical technology, has resulted in an ever-increasing number and percentage of people remaining alive and healthy well into their retirement years. The result is a shifting age composition of the populations in these nations—a population composed of fewer people under age 20 and more people 65 and older.

In 1900 in the United States, approximately 3 million Americans were 65 years old and older, and they composed 4 percent of the population. In 2000, 36 million persons were 65 years old and older, and they represented 13 percent of the total population. The most rapid increase in the number of older persons is expected between 2010 and 2030 when the baby boom generation reaches the age of 65. Demographers predict that by 2030, there will be 66 million older persons representing approximately 22 percent of the total population. The increasing number of older people has made many of the problems of aging immediately visible to the average American. These problems have become widespread topics of concern for political leaders, government planners, and average citizens. Moreover, the aging of the population has become perceived as a phenomenon of the United States and the industrialized countries of Western Europe—it is also occurring in the underdeveloped countries but in fact of the world. An increasing percentage of the world's population is now defined as aged. Today, almost all middle-aged people expect to live to retirement age and beyond. Both the middle-aged and the elderly have pushed for solutions to the problems confronting older Americans. Everyone seems to agree that granting the elderly a secure and comfortable status is desirable. Voluntary associations, communities, and state and federal governments have committed themselves to improving the lives of older persons. Many programs for senior citizens, both public and private, have emerged in the last 50 years.

The change in the age composition of the population has not gone unnoticed by the media or the academic community. The number of articles appearing in the popular press and professional journals has increased dramatically over the last several years. Although scientists have been concerned with the aging process for some time, the volume of research and writing on this subject have expanded in the last three decades. This growing interest has resulted in this twenty-sixth edition of *Annual Editions: Aging 13/14*.

This volume represents the field of gerontology in that it is interdisciplinary in its approach, including articles from the biological sciences, medicine, nursing, psychology, sociology, and social work. The articles are taken from the popular press, government publications, and scientific journals. They represent a wide cross-section of authors, perspectives, and issues related to the aging process. They were chosen because they address the most relevant and current problems in the field of aging and present a variety of divergent views on the appropriate solutions to these problems. The topics covered include demographic trends, the aging process, longevity, the quality of later life, social attitudes toward old age, problems and potentials of aging, retirement, death, living environments in later life, and social policies, programs, and services for older Americans.

The articles are organized into an anthology that is useful for both the student and the teacher. Two new learning features have been added to this edition to aid students in their study and expand critical thinking about each article topic. Located at the beginning of each unit, the *Learning Outcomes* feature outlines the key concepts that students should focus on as they read the material. *Critical Thinking* questions located at the end of each article allow students to test their understanding of the key concepts. A *Topic Guide* assists students in finding other articles on a given subject within this edition, and a list of recommended *Internet References* guides them to the best sources of additional information on a topic. The goal of *Annual Editions: Aging 13/14* is to choose articles that are pertinent, well written, and helpful to those concerned with the field of gerontology. Comments, suggestions, and constructive criticism are welcome to help improve future editions of this book. Any anthology can be improved as will this one—annually.

Harold Cox

Harold Cox
Editor

The Annual Editions Series

VOLUMES AVAILABLE

Adolescent Psychology

Aging

American Foreign Policy

American Government

Anthropology

Archaeology

Assessment and Evaluation

Business Ethics

Child Growth and Development

Comparative Politics

Criminal Justice

Developing World

Drugs, Society, and Behavior

Dying, Death, and Bereavement

Early Childhood Education

Economics

Educating Children with Exceptionalities

Education

Educational Psychology

Entrepreneurship

Environment

The Family

Gender

Geography

Global Issues

Health

Homeland Security

Human Development

Human Resources

Human Sexualities

International Business

Management

Marketing

Mass Media

Microbiology

Multicultural Education

Nursing

Nutrition

Physical Anthropology

Psychology

Race and Ethnic Relations

Social Problems

Sociology

State and Local Government

Sustainability

Technologies, Social Media, and Society

United States History, Volume 1

United States History, Volume 2

Urban Society

Violence and Terrorism

Western Civilization, Volume 1

World History, Volume 1

World History, Volume 2

World Politics

Contents

UNIT 1
The Phenomenon of Aging

Unit Overview   xx

The concepts in bold italics are developed in the article. For further expansion, please refer to the Topic Guide.

UNIT 2
The Quality of Later Life

UNIT 3
Societal Attitudes toward Old Age

The concepts in bold italics are developed in the article. For further expansion, please refer to the Topic Guide.

UNIT 4
Problems and Potentials of Aging

UNIT 5
Retirement: American Dream or Dilemma?

The concepts in bold italics are developed in the article. For further expansion, please refer to the Topic Guide.

UNIT 6
The Experience of Dying

The concepts in bold italics are developed in the article. For further expansion, please refer to the Topic Guide.

UNIT 7
Living Environment in Later Life

UNIT 8
Social Policies, Programs, and Services for Older Americans

The concepts in bold italics are developed in the article. For further expansion, please refer to the Topic Guide.

The concepts in bold italics are developed in the article. For further expansion, please refer to the Topic Guide.

Correlation Guide

The *Annual Editions* series provides students with convenient, inexpensive access to current, carefully selected articles from the public press. **Annual Editions: Aging 13/14** is an easy-to-use reader that presents articles on important topics such as *living longer, retirement, health care, dying,* and many more. For more information on *Annual Editions* and other *McGraw-Hill Contemporary Learning Series* titles, visit www.mhhe.com/cls.

This convenient guide matches the units in **Annual Editions: Aging 13/14** with the corresponding chapters in two of our best-selling McGraw-Hill Aging textbooks by Quadagno and Ferrini/Ferrini.

Annual Editions: Aging 13/14	Aging and the Life Course: An Introduction to Social Gerontology, 6/e by Quadagno	Health in the later Years, 5/e by Ferrini/Ferrini
Unit 1: The Phenomenon of Aging	**Chapter 1:** The Field of Social Gerontology **Chapter 2:** Life Course Transitions **Chapter 3:** Theories of Aging	**Chapter 1:** Our Nation's Elders: The Facts **Chapter 2:** Biologic Aging: Theories and Longevity **Chapter 3:** The Body and Its Age Changes
Unit 2: The Quality of Later Life	**Chapter 6:** Biological Perspectives on Aging	**Chapter 2:** Biologic Aging: Theories and Longevity **Chapter 3:** The Body and Its Age Changes **Chapter 9:** Physical Activity **Chapter 11:** Sexuality
Unit 3: Societal Attitudes toward Old Age	**Chapter 7:** Psychological Perspectives on Aging	**Chapter 1:** Our Nation's Elders: The Facts
Unit 4: Problems and Potentials of Aging	**Chapter 6:** Biological Perspectives on Aging **Chapter 7:** Psychological Perspectives on Aging **Chapter 8:** Family Relationships and Social Support Systems **Chapter 11:** Health and Health Care **Chapter 12:** Caring for the Frail Elderly	**Chapter 2:** Biologic Aging: Theories and Longevity **Chapter 3:** The Body and Its Age Changes **Chapter 4:** Chronic Illnesses: The Major Killers **Chapter 5:** Other Chronic Diseases and Conditions **Chapter 6:** Acute Illness and Accidents **Chapter 7:** Mental Health and Mental Disorders **Chapter 8:** Medication Use **Chapter 9:** Physical Activity **Chapter 11:** Sexuality
Unit 5: Retirement: American Dream or Dilemma?	**Chapter 10:** Work and Retirement **Chapter 14:** The Economics of Aging	
Unit 6: The Experience of Dying	**Chapter 13:** Death, Dying, and Bereavement	**Chapter 15:** Dying, Death, and Grief
Unit 7: Living Environment in Later Life	**Chapter 8:** Family Relationships and Social Support Systems **Chapter 9:** Living Arrangements **Chapter 12:** Caring for the Frail Elderly **Chapter 15:** Poverty and Inequality	**Chapter 13:** Medical Care **Chapter 14:** Long-Term Care
Unit 8: Social Policies, Programs, and Services for Older Americans	**Chapter 4:** Demography of Aging **Chapter 5:** Old Age and the Welfare State **Chapter 11:** Health and Health Care **Chapter 14:** The Economics of Aging **Chapter 15:** Poverty and Inequality **Chapter 16:** The Politics of Aging	

Topic Guide

This topic guide suggests how the selections in this book relate to the subjects covered in your course. You may want to use the topics listed on these pages to search the Web more easily.

On the following pages a number of websites have been gathered specifically for this book. They are arranged to reflect the units of this Annual Editions reader. You can link to these sites by going to www.mhhe.com/cls

All the articles that relate to each topic are listed below the bold-faced term.

Internet References

The following Internet sites have been selected to support the articles found in this reader. These sites were available at the time of publication. However, because websites often change their structure and content, the information listed may no longer be available. We invite you to visit www.mhhe.com/cls for easy access to these sites.

Annual Editions: Aging 13/14

General Sources

Alliance for Aging Research
www.agingresearch.org

The nation's leading nonprofit organization is dedicated to improving the health and independence of Americans as they age through public and private funding of medical research and geriatric education.

ElderCare Online
www.ec-online.net

This site provides numerous links to eldercare resources. Information on health, living, aging, finance, and social issues can be found here.

FirstGov
www.firstgov.gov

Whatever you want or need from the U.S. government is on FirstGov.gov. You'll find a rich treasure of online information, services, and resources.

UNIT 1: The Phenomenon of Aging

The Aging Research Centre
www.arclab.org

This organization is dedicated to providing a service that allows researchers to find information related to the study of the aging process.

Centenarians
www.hcoa.org/centenarians/centenarians.htm

There are approximately 70,000 centenarians in the United States. This site provides resources and information for and about centenarians.

National Center for Health Statistics
www.cdc.gov/nchs/agingact.htm

NCHS is the federal government's principal vital and health statistics agency. It is a part of the Centers for Disease Control and Prevention, U.S. Department of Health and Human Services.

UNIT 2: The Quality of Later Life

Aging with Dignity
www.agingwithdignity.org

This nonprofit was established to provide people the practical information, advice, and legal tools needed to help their loved ones get proper care.

The Gerontological Society of America
www.geron.org

This organization promotes the scientific study of aging and fosters growth and diffusion of knowledge relating to problems of aging and of the sciences contributing to their understanding.

The National Council on the Aging
www.ncoa.org

This organization is a center of leadership and nationwide expertise in the issues of aging. This private, nonprofit association is committed to enhancing the field of aging through leadership, service, education, and advocacy.

UNIT 3: Societal Attitudes toward Old Age

Adult Development and Aging: Division 20 of the American Psychological Association
www.iog.wayne.edu/APADIV20/APADIV20.HTM

This group is dedicated to studying the psychology of adult development and aging.

American Society on Aging
www.asaging.org/index.cfm

This organization is the largest and most dynamic network of professionals in the field of aging.

Canadian Psychological Association
www.cpa.ca

This is the contents page of the Canadian Psychological Association. Material on aging and human development can be found at this site.

UNIT 4: Problems and Potentials of Aging

AARP Health Information
www.aarp.org/bulletin

This site offers information on a BMI calculator, the USDA food pyramid, healthy recipes, and health-related articles can be found.

Alzheimer's Association
www.alz.org

This not-for-profit organization is dedicated to researching the prevention, cures, and treatments of Alzheimer's disease and related disorders and providing support and assistance to afflicted patients and their families.

A.P.T.A. Section on Geriatrics
http://geriatricspt.org

This organization is a component of the American Physical Therapy Association. At this site, information regarding consumer and health information for older adults can be found.

Caregiver's Handbook
www.acsu.buffalo.edu/~drstall/hndbk0.html

This site is an online handbook for caregivers. Topics include nutrition, medical aspects of caregiving, and liabilities of caregiving.

Internet References

Caregiver Survival Resources
www.caregiver.com

Information on books and seminars for caregivers can be found at this site.

International Food Information Council
www.ifi c.org

Here you can find information regarding nutritional needs for aging adults. The site focuses on publications with nutritional information for educators and students.

University of California at Irvine: Institute for Brain Aging and Dementia
www.alz.uci.edu

This organization is dedicated to the study of Alzheimer's and the causes of mental disabilities for the elderly.

UNIT 5: Retirement: American Dream or Dilemma?

American Association of Retired People
www.aarp.org

AARP is the nation's leading organization for people 50 and older. It serves their needs by providing information, education, advocacy, and community service.

Health and Retirement Study (HRS)
www.umich.edu/~hrswww

The University of Michigan Health and Retirement Study surveys more than 22,000 Americans over the age of 50 every two years. Supported by the National Institute on Aging, the study paints an emerging portrait of an aging America: physical and mental health, insurance coverage, financial status, family support systems, labor market status, and retirement planning.

UNIT 6: The Experience of Dying

Agency for Health Care Policy and Research
www.ahcpr.gov

Information on the dying process in the context of U.S. health policy is provided here along with a search mechanism. The agency is part of the Department of Health and Human Services.

Growth House, Inc.
www.growthhouse.org

This award-winning website is an international gateway to resources for life-threatening illness and end-of-life care.

Hospice Foundation of America
www.HospiceFoundation.org

On this page, you can learn about hospice care, how to select a hospice, and how to find one near you.

UNIT 7: Living Environment in Later Life

American Association of Homes and Services for the Aging
www.aahsa.org

This is a not-for-profit organization dedicated to providing high quality health care, housing, and services to the nation's elderly.

Center for Demographic Studies
http://cds.duke.edu

This organization is located in the heart of the Duke University campus. The primary focus of its research is long-term care for elderly populations, specifically those 65 years of age and older.

Guide to Retirement Living Online
www.retirement-living.com

An online version of a free publication, this site provides information about nursing homes, continuous care communities, independent living, home health care, and adult day care centers.

The United States Department of Housing and Urban Development
www.hud.gov

News regarding housing for aging adults can be found at this site sponsored by the U.S. federal government.

UNIT 8: Social Policies, Programs, and Services for Older Americans

Administration on Aging
www.aoa.dhhs.gov

This site, housed on the Department of Health and Human Services website, provides information for older persons and their families. There is also information for educators and students regarding the elderly.

American Federation for Aging Research (AFAR)
www.afar.org

Since 1981, this organization has helped scientists begin and further careers in aging research and geriatric medicine.

American Geriatrics Society
www.americangeriatrics.org

This organization addresses the needs of our rapidly aging population. At this site, you can find information on health care and other social issues facing the elderly.

Community Transportation Association of America (CTAA)
www.ctaa.org

This is a nonprofit organization dedicated to mobility for all people, regardless of wealth, disability, age, or accessibility.

Consumer Reports State Inspection Surveys
www.ConsumerReports.org

To learn how to get state inspection surveys and to contact the ombudsman's office, click on "Personal Finance" and then select "Assisted Living."

Medicare Consumer Information from the Health Care Finance Association
http://cms.hhs.gov/default.asp?fromhcfadotgov_true

This site is devoted to explaining Medicare and Medicaid costs to consumers.

National Institutes of Health
www.nih.gov

Information on health issues can be found at this government site. It contains quite a bit of information relating to health issues and the aging population in the United States.

The United States Senate: Special Committee on Aging
www.senate.gov/~aging

This committee deals with the issues surrounding the elderly in America. At this site, you can download committee hearing information, news, and committee publications.

UNIT 1

The Phenomenon of Aging

Unit Selections

1. **Elderly Americans,** Christine L. Himes
2. **America's Old Getting Older,** Associated Press
3. **Living Longer: Diet and Exercise,** Donna Jackson Nakazawa and Susan Crandell
4. **How to Live 100 Years,** Alice Park
5. **Will You Live to Be 100?** Thomas Perls, MD and Margery Hutter Silver, EdD
6. **Long Live . . . Us,** Mark Bennett

Learning Outcomes

After reading this Unit, you will be able to:

- Describe the age composition of the U.S. population.

- Identify what makes the age composition of the current U.S. population different from previous generations.

- Identify two major problems that confront the population 90 and over.

- Identify the factors that demographers believe lead to an increase in the population 90 and older.

- Identify the foods you can eat to increase the antioxidants in the human body.

- Describe the effect of caloric restriction on the body's free radicals.

- Describe the advantages that older persons seem to have in dealing with health problems.

- Categorize the percentage of the health of persons who are older that is based on genetics and on lifestyle.

- Identify the health problems that may increase if one consumes a high fat and high protein diet.

- List the risk of various diseases that are associated with being obese.

- Identify the life expectancy in the United States for all persons regardless of sex in 2009.

- List the life expectancy of men and women in the United States in 2009.

Student Website

www.mhhe.com/cls

Internet References

The Aging Research Centre
www.arclab.org
Centenarians
www.hcoa.org/centenarians/centenarians.htm
National Center for Health Statistics
www.cdc.gov/nchs/agingact.htm

The process of aging is complex and includes biological, psychological, sociological, and behavioral changes. Biologically, the body gradually loses the ability to renew itself. Various body functions begin to slow, and the vital senses become less acute. Psychologically, aging persons experience changing sensory processes; perception, motor skills, problem-solving ability, and drives and emotions are frequently altered. Sociologically, this group must cope with the changing roles and definitions of self that society imposes on individuals. For instance, the role expectations and the status of grandparents differ from those of parents, and the roles of retirees are quite different from those of employed persons. Being defined as "old" may be desirable or undesirable, depending on the particular culture and its values. Behaviorally, aging individuals may move more slowly and with less dexterity. Because they are assuming new roles and are viewed differently by others, their attitudes about themselves, their emotions, and, ultimately, their behavior can be expected to change.

Those studying the process of aging often use developmental theories of the lifecycle—a sequence of predictable phases that begins with birth and ends with death—to explain individuals' behavior at various stages of their lives. An individual's age, therefore, is important because it provides clues about his or her behavior at a particular phase of the lifecycle—be it childhood, adolescence, adulthood, middle age, or old age. There is, however, the greatest variation in terms of health and human development among older people than among any other age group.

Although every 3-year-old child can be predicted to have certain developmental experiences, there is a wide variation in the behavior of 65-year-old people. We find that by age 65, some people are in good health, employed, and performing important work tasks. Others of this cohort are retired but in good health or are retired and in poor health. Still others have died prior to the age of 65. The articles in this section are written from biological, psychological, and sociological perspectives. These disciplines attempt to explain the effects of aging and the resulting choices in lifestyle as well as the wider, cultural implications of an older population.

In the article "Elderly Americans," Christine L. Himes delineates the increases in life expectancy and the aging of the U.S. population that has occurred during the last century. The article "America's Old Getting Older" points out the ever-increasing number and percentage of the population living to 90 years of age and more as well as the reasons for this increase in longevity. In "Living Longer: Diet and Exercise," Donna Jackson Nakazawa and Susan Crandell discuss how the research findings in the areas of diet and exercise, if followed, could increase an individual's life expectancy by a number of years. In "How to Live 100 Years," Alice Park presents two of the current reasons given

© Hill Street Studios/Blend Images LLC

for living a longer life—lifestyle and genetics—and attempts to determine which are the best explanations for longevity. In "'Will You Live to Be 100?'" Thomas Perls and Margery Hutter Silver report on a study of long-living individuals conducted at Harvard Medical School. Following their research, they created that included dietary and lifestyle choices as well as family histories to help an individual determine what his or her probability of living to a very old age is. In "Long Live . . . Us," Mark Bennett points out how much the life expectancy had increased in the United States by 2009 as well as the difference in life expectancy for men and women.

Elderly Americans

CHRISTINE L. HIMES

The United States is in the midst of a profound demographic change: the rapid aging of its population. The 2000 Census counted nearly 35 million people in the United States 65 years of age or older, about one of every eight Americans. By 2030, demographers estimate that one in five Americans will be age 65 or older, which is nearly four times the proportion of elderly 100 years earlier, in 1930. The effects of this older age profile will reverberate throughout the American economy and society in the next 50 years. Preparing for these changes involves more than the study of demographic trends; it also requires an understanding of the growing diversity within the older population.

The lives and well-being of older Americans attract increasing attention as the elderly share of the U.S. population rises: One-fifth will be 65 or older in 2030.

The aging of the U.S. population in the next 20 years is being propelled by one of the most powerful demographic forces in the United States in the last century: the "baby boom" cohort, born between 1946 and 1964. This group of 76 million children grabbed media attention as it moved toward adulthood—changing school systems, colleges, and the workplace. And, this same group of people will change the profile and expectations of old age in the United States over the next 30 years as it moves past age 65. The potential effects of the baby boom on the systems of old-age assistance already are being evaluated. This cohort's consumption patterns, demand for leisure, and use of health care, for example, will leave an indelible mark on U.S. society in the 21st century. Understanding their characteristics as they near older ages will help us anticipate baby-boomers' future needs and their effects on the population.

Until the last 50 years, most gains in life expectancy came as the result of improved child mortality. The survival of larger proportions of infants and children to adulthood radically increased average life expectancy in the United States and many other countries over the past century. Now, gains are coming at the end of life as greater proportions of 65-year-olds are living until age 85, and more 85-year-olds are living into their 90s. These changes raise a multitude of questions: How will these years of added life be spent? Will increased longevity lead to a greater role for the elderly in our society? What are the limits of life expectancy?

Increasing life expectancy, especially accompanied by low fertility, changes the structure of families. Families are becoming more "vertical," with fewer members in each generation, but more generations alive at any one time. Historically, families have played a prominent role in the lives of elderly people. Is this likely to change?

As much as any stage of the life course, old age is a time of growth, diversity, and change. Elderly Americans are among the wealthiest and among the poorest in our nation. They come from a variety of racial and ethnic backgrounds. Some are employed full-time, while others require full-time care. While general health has improved, many elderly suffer from poor health.

The older population in the 21st century will come to later life with different experiences than did older Americans in the last century—more women will have been divorced, more will have worked in the labor force, more will be childless. How will these experiences shape their later years?

The answers to these questions are complex. In some cases, we are confident in our predictions of the future. But for many aspects of life for the elderly, we are entering new territory. This report explores the characteristics of the current older population and speculates how older Americans may differ in the future. It also looks at the impact of aging on the U.S. society and economy.

Increasing Numbers

The United States has seen its elderly population—defined as those age 65 or older—grow more than tenfold during the 20th century. There were just over 3 million Americans age 65 or older in 1900, and nearly 35 million in 2000.

At the dawn of the 20th century, three demographic trends—high fertility, declining infant and child mortality, and high rates of international immigration—were acting in concert in the United States and were keeping the population young. The age distribution of the U.S. population was heavily skewed toward younger ages in 1900, as illustrated by the broad base of the population age-sex pyramid for that year in Figure 1. The pyramid, which shows the proportion of each age and sex group in the population, also reveals that the elderly made up a tiny share of the U.S. population in 1900. Only 4 percent of Americans were age 65 of older, while more than one-half (54 percent) were under age 25.

But adult health improved and fertility fell during the first half of the century. The inflow of international immigrants slowed considerably after 1920. These trends caused an aging of the U.S. population, but they were interrupted after World War II by the baby boom. In the post-war years, Americans were marrying and starting families at younger ages and in greater percentages than they had during the Great Depression. The surge in births between 1946 and 1964 resulted from a decline in childlessness (more women had at least one child) combined with larger family sizes (more women had three or more children). The sustained increase in birth rates during their 19-year period fueled a rapid increase in the child population. By 1970, these

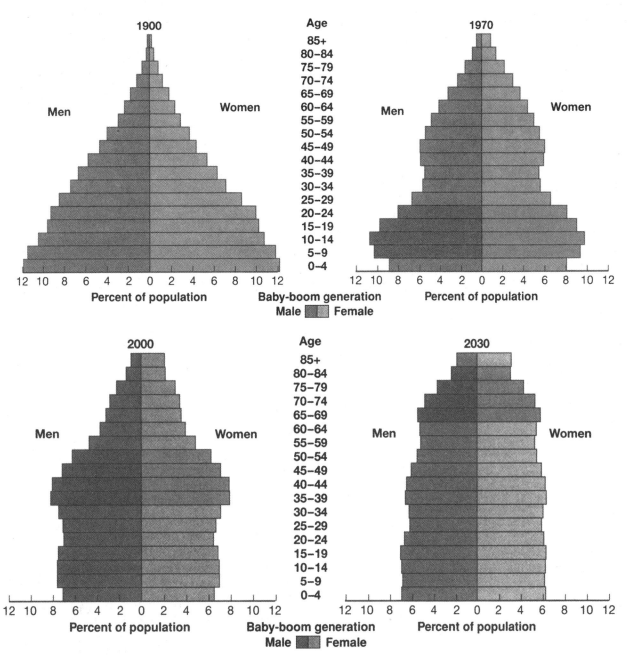

Figure 1 U.S. Population by Age and Sex, 1900, 1970, 2000, and 2030.

Sources: U.S. Census Bureau Publications: *Historical Statistics of the United States: Colonial Times to 1970* (1975); *Census 2000 Summary File* (SFI) (http://factfinder.census.gov, accessed Sept. 5, 2001); and "Population Projections of the United States by Age, Sex, Race, Hispanic Origin, and Nativity: 1999 to 2100" (www.census.gov/population/projections/nation/summary/np-t4-a.txt, accessed Sept. 25, 2001).

Note. U.S. population in 1900 does not include Alaska or Hawaii. The baby-boom generation includes persons born between 1946 and 1964.

baby boomers had moved into their teen and young adult years, creating a bulge in that year's age-sex pyramid shown in Figure 1.

The baby boom was followed by a precipitous decline in fertility: the "baby bust." Young American women reaching adulthood in the late 1960s and 1970s were slower to marry and start families than their older counterparts, and they had fewer children when they did start families. U.S. fertility sank to an all-time low. The average age of the population started to climb as the large baby boom generation moved into adulthood, and was replaced by the much smaller baby-bust cohort. By 2000, the baby-boom bulge had moved up to the middle adult ages. The population's age structure at younger and older ages became more evenly distributed as fluctuations in fertility diminished and survival at the oldest ages increased. By 2030, the large baby-boom cohorts will be age 65 and older, and U.S. Census Bureau

projections show that the American population will be relatively evenly distributed across age groups, as Figure 1 shows.

The radical shift in the U.S. population age structure over the last 100 years provides only one part of the story of the U.S. elderly population. Another remarkable aspect is the rapid growth in the number of elderly, and the increasing numbers of Americans at the oldest ages, above ages 85 or 90. The most rapid growth in the 65-or-older age group occurred between the 1920s and the 1950s (see Table 1). During each of these decades, the older population increased by at least 34 percent, reaching 16.6 million in 1960. The percentage increase slowed after 1960, and between 1990 and 2000, the population age 65 or older increased by just 12 percent. Since the growth of the older population largely reflects past patterns of fertility, and U.S. fertility rates plummeted in the 1930s,

Table 1 U.S. Total Population and Population Age 65 or Older, 1900–2060

Year	Population (in thousands)		Percent 65+	Percent Increase from Preceding Decade	
	Total	Age 65+		Total	Age 65+
Actual					
1900	75,995	3,080	4.1		
1910	91,972	3,950	4.3	21.0	28.2
1920	105,711	4,933	4.7	14.9	24.9
1930	122,755	6,634	5.4	16.1	34.5
1940	131,669	9,019	6.8	7.2	36.0
1950	150,697	12,270	8.1	14.5	36.0
1960	179,323	16,560	9.2	19.0	35.0
1970	203,212	20,066	9.9	13.4	21.2
1980	226,546	25,549	11.3	11.5	27.3
1990	248,710	31,242	12.6	9.8	22.3
2000	281,422	34,992	12.4	13.2	12.0
Projections					
2020	324,927	53,733	16.5	8.4	35.3
2040	377,350	77,177	20.5	7.5	9.8
2060	432,011	89,840	20.8	7.0	9.6

Sources: U.S. Census Bureau publications: *Historical Statistics of the United States: Colonial Times to 1970* (1975); *1980 Census of Population: General Population Characteristics* (PC80-1-B1); *1990 Census of Populations: General Population Characteristics* (1990-CP1); *Census 2000 Demographic Profile,* (www.census.gov/ Press-Release/www/2001/tables/dp_us_2000.xls, accessed Sept. 19, 2001); and *Population Projections of the United States by Age, Sex, Race, Hispanic Origin, and Nativity: 1999 to 2100* (www.census.gov/population/projections/nation/summary/np-t4-a.txt, accessed Sept. 25, 2001).

Note. Data from 1900 to 1950 exclude Alaska and Hawaii. All data refer to the resident U.S. population.

the first decade of the 21st century will also see relatively slow growth of the elderly population. Fewer people will be turning 65 and entering the ranks of "the elderly." Not until the first of the baby-boom generation reaches age 65 between 2010 and 2020 will we see the same rates of increase as those experienced in the mid-20th century.

In the 1940s and 1950s, the rapid growth at the top of the pyramid was matched by growth in the younger ages—the total U.S. population was growing rapidly, and the general profile was still fairly young. That was not the case in the second half of the 20th century, as the share of the population age 65 or older increased to around 12 percent. The elderly share will increase much faster in the first half of the 21st century. This growth in the percentage age 65 or older constitutes population aging.

Many policymakers and health care providers are more concerned about the sheer size of the aging baby-boom generation than the baby boom's share of the total population. The oldest members of this group will reach age 65 in 2011, and by 2029, the youngest baby boomers will have reached age 65. This large group will continue to move into old age at a time of slow growth among younger age groups. The Census Bureau projects that 54 million Americans will be age 65 or older in 2020; by 2060, the number is projected to approach 90 million. The size of this group, and the general aging of the population, are important in planning for the future. Older Americans increasingly are healthy and active and able to take on new roles. At the same time, increasing numbers of older people will need assistance with housing, health care, and other services.

The Oldest-Old

The older population is also aging as more people are surviving into their 80s and 90s. In the 2000 Census, nearly one-half of Americans age 65 or older were above age 74, compared with less than one-third in 1950; one in eight were age 85 or older in 2000, compared with one in 20 in 1950 (see Figure 2).

Percent of 65+ population

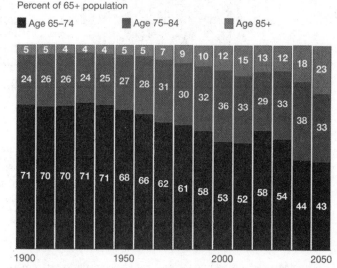

Figure 2 Age Distribution of Older Americans, 1900–2000, and Projection to 2050.

Sources: U.S. Census Bureau publications: *Historical Statistics of the United States: Colonial Times to 1970* (1975); *1980 Census of Population: General Population Characteristics* (PC80-1-B1); *1990 Census of Populations: General Population Characteristics* (1990-CP1); *Census 2000 Demographic Profile,* (www.census .gov/2001/tables/dp_us_2000.xls, accessed Sept. 19, 2001); and "Projections of the Resident Population by Age, Sex, Race, Hispanic Origin, 1990 to 2100" (www .census. gov/population/www/projections/natdet-D1A.html, accessed July 6, 2001).

As the baby boomers enter their late 60s and early 70s around 2020, the U.S. elderly population will be younger: The percentage ages 65 to 74 will rise to 58 percent, as shown in Figure 2. By 2040, however, just 44 percent will be 65 to 74, and 56 percent of all elderly will be age 75 or older.

Those age 85 or older, the "oldest-old," are the fastest growing segment of the elderly population. While those 85 or older made up only about 1.5 percent of the total U.S. population in 2000, they constituted about 12 percent of all elderly. More than 4 million people in the United States were 85 or older in the 2000 Census, and by 2050, a projected 19 million will be age 85 or older. These oldest-old will make up nearly 5 percent of the total population, and more than 20 percent of all elderly Americans. This group is of special interest to planners because those 85 or older are more likely to require health services.

Gender Gap

Women outnumber men at every age among the elderly. In 2000, there were an estimated three women for every two men age 65 or older, and the sex ratio is even more skewed among the oldest-old.

The preponderance of women among the elderly reflects the higher death rates for men than women at every age. There are approximately 105 male babies born for every 100 female babies, but higher male death rates cause the sex ratio to decline as age increases, and around age 35, females outnumber males in the United States. At age 85 and older, the ratio is 41 men per 100 women.[1]

Changes in the leading causes and average ages of death affect a population's sex ratio. In 1900, the average sex ratio for the U.S. total population was 104 men for every 100 women. But during the early 1900s, improvements in health care during and after pregnancy lowered maternal mortality, and a greater proportion of women survived to older ages. Adult male mortality improved much more slowly; death rates for adult men plateaued during the 1960s.

In recent years, however, male mortality improved faster than female mortality, primarily because of a marked decline in deaths from heart disease. The gender gap at the older ages has narrowed, and it is expected to narrow further. The U.S. Census Bureau projects the sex ratio for those age 65 or older to rise to 79 men for every 100 women by 2050. A sex ratio of 62 is anticipated for those age 85 or older.

Most elderly women today will outlive their spouses and face the challenges of later life alone: Older women who are widowed or divorced are less likely than older men to remarry. Older women are more likely than older men to be poor, to live alone, to enter nursing homes, and to depend on people other than their spouses for care. Many of the difficulties of growing older are compounded by past discrimination that disadvantaged women in the workplace and now threatens their economic security.

As the sex differential in mortality diminishes, these differences may lessen, but changes in marriage and work patterns, family structures, and fertility may mean that a greater proportion of older women will not have children or a living spouse. High divorce rates and declining rates of marriage, for instance, mean that many older women will not have spousal benefits available to them through pensions or Social Security.

Ethnic Diversity

The U.S. elderly population is becoming more racially and ethnically diverse, although not as rapidly as is the total U.S. population. In 2000, about 84 percent of the elderly population were non-Hispanic white, compared with 69 percent of the total U.S. population. By 2050, the proportion of elderly who are non-Hispanic white is projected to drop to 64 percent as the growing minority populations move into old age (see Figure 3). Although Hispanics made up only about 5 percent of the elderly population in 2000, 16 percent of the elderly population of 2050 is likely to be Hispanic. Similarly, blacks accounted for 8 percent of the elderly population in 2000, but are expected to make up 12 percent of elderly Americans in 2050.

Percent of population age 65+

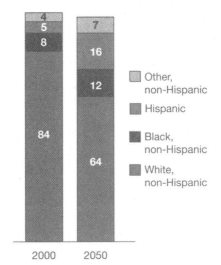

Figure 3 Elderly Americans by Race and Ethnicity, 2000 and 2050.

Sources: U.S. Census Bureau, *Census 2000 Demographic Profile* (2001); and U.S. Census Bureau, "Projections of the Resident Population by Age, Sex, Race and Hispanic Origin, 1999–2100" (www.census.gov/population/www/projections/natdet-D1A.html, accessed Sept. 19, 2001).

Note. The 2000 figures refer to residents who identified with one race. About 2% of Americans identified with more than one race in the 2000 census.

The major racial and ethnic groups are aging at different rates, depending upon fertility, mortality, and immigration among these groups. Immigration has a growing influence on the age structure of racial and ethnic minority groups. Although most immigrants tend to be in their young adult ages, when people are most likely and willing to assume the risks of moving to a new country, U.S. immigration policy also favors the entry of parents and other family members of these young immigrants. The number of immigrants age 65 or older is rapidly increasing as more foreign-born elderly move to the United States from Latin America, Asia, or Africa to join their children.[2] These older immigrants, plus the aging of immigrants who entered as young adults, are altering the ethnic makeup of elderly Americans.

Notes

1. U.S. Census Bureau, *Population Projections of the United States by Age, Sex, Race, Hispanic Origin, and Nativity: 1999 to 2100* (2000), accessed online at: www.census.gov/population/projections/nation/summary/np-t3-a.txt, on Sept. 19, 2001.

2. Janet M. Wilmoth, Gordon F. DeJong, and Christine L. Himes, "Immigrant and Non-Immigrant Living Arrangements in Later Life," *International Journal of Sociology and Social Policy* 17 (1997): 57–82.

Critical Thinking

1. What factors contribute to the increasing life expectancy of the American people?

2. What challenges do aging Americans face?

3. Are older Americans healthier than ever before?

America's Old Getting Older

90-Somethings Triple in Number since 1980

The rolls of America's oldest old are surging: Nearly 2 million now are 90 or over, nearly triple their numbers of just three decades ago.

It's not all good news. They're more likely than the merely elderly to live in poverty and to have disabilities, creating a new challenge to already strained retiree income and health care programs.

First-ever census data on the 90-plus population highlight America's ever-increasing life spans, which are redefining what it means to be old.

Demographers attribute the increases mostly to better nutrition and advances in medical care. Still, the longer life spans present additional risks for disabilities and chronic conditions such as arthritis, diabetes and Alzheimer's disease.

Richard Suzman, director of behavioral and social research at the National Institute on Aging, which commissioned the report, said personal savings for retirement can sometimes be a problem if people don't anticipate a longer life or one with some form of disability.

An Associated Press-LifeGoesStrong.com poll in June found that more than one in four adults expect to live to at least 90, including nearly half of those currently 65 or older. A majority of adults also said they expected people in their generation to live longer than those in their parents' generation, with about 46 percent saying they expected a better quality of life in later years as well.

"A key issue for this population will be whether disability rates can be reduced," Suzman said. "We've seen to some extent that disabilities can be reduced with lifestyle improvements, diet and exercise. But it becomes more important to find ways to delay, prevent or treat conditions such as Alzheimer's disease."

According to the report, the share of people 90–94 who report having some kind of impairment such as inability to do errands, visit a doctor's office, climb stairs or bathe is 13 percentage points higher than those 85–89—82 percent versus 69 percent.

Among those 95 and older, the disability rate climbs to 91 percent.

Census figures show that smaller states had the highest shares of their older Americans who were at least 90.

North Dakota led the list, with about 7 percent of its 65-plus population over 90. It was followed by Connecticut, Iowa and South Dakota.

In absolute numbers, California, Florida and Texas led the nation in the 90-plus population, each with more than 130,000.

Traditionally, the Census Bureau has followed established norms in breaking down age groups, such as under-18 to signify children or 65-plus to indicate seniors.

Since the mid-1980s, the bureau often has released data on the 85-plus population, describing them as the "oldest old"—a term coined by Suzman.

But some of those norms, at least culturally, may be shifting. Young people 18–29 more than ever are delaying their transition to work in the poor job market by pursuing advanced degrees or moving in with Mom and Dad. Older Americans,

---

As America ages . . .

- The oldest of the old are projected to increase from 1.9 million to 8.7 million by midcentury—making up 2 percent of the total U.S. population and one in 10 older Americans.
- A century ago, fewer than 100,000 people reached 90.
- Among the 90-plus population, women outnumber men by a ratio of nearly 3 to 1.
- Broken down by race and ethnicity, non-Hispanic whites made up the vast majority of the 90-plus population, at 88.1 percent. That's compared to 7.6 percent who were black, 4 percent Hispanic, 2.2 percent Asian.
- Most people who were 90 or older lived in households alone, about 37.3 percent. Some 37.1 percent lived in households with family or others, about 23 percent in nursing homes.

who are living longer and staying healthier than prior generations, are now more likely to work past 65.

On Thursday, the Census Bureau said it was putting out its study of the 90-plus age group at NIA's request in recognition of longer life expectancies, which are just over 78 for babies now being born.

By the time a person reaches 65, Americans are generally expected to live close to 20 years longer, up from 12 years in 1930. At age 90, their expectancy is another five years.

Critical Thinking

1. Do older Americans expect to live longer than their parents did?

2. Do older Americans expect to have a better quality of life than their parents did in their later years?

3. What are the key health issues that the 85 and older population are confronted with?

Living Longer: Diet and Exercise

Diet

In the search for the fountain of youth, researchers keep coming back to one fact: what you eat has a tremendous impact not only on your health but on your longevity. Here's why every bite you take counts.

DONNA JACKSON NAKAZAWA

It's hard to get through your first cup of morning coffee without reading a headline about food. Eat blueberries! Inhale kale! Such antioxidant-rich foods will clear your arteries and help prevent the buildup of Alzheimer's plaque in your brain. Add in a cup of green tea in the morning and swish down an ounce or two of dark chocolate with a glass of red wine in the evening and you will be nicely tanked up on healthy fuel for the day.

Or will you? Almost every day, it seems, new studies emerge on the antiaging properties of various foods. One day, soy is good; the next, we find out soy's health benefits may have been oversold. To add to the confusion, this year *The Journal of the American Medical Association (JAMA)* published a study that found caloric restriction—eating about 25 percent less than normal—could extend your life.

So which headlines should we believe? And why should we believe them? The answers lie in research that shows exactly how various foods work at the cellular level. In particular, antioxidant-rich fruits and vegetables are emerging as powerful medicine in the fight against cellular aging.

Here's how it works. In the normal process of metabolism, cells produce unstable oxygen molecules—called free radicals—that damage cells. Worse still, the older we get, the more free radicals we produce. Recent studies suggest that the havoc free radicals wreak "plays a central role in virtually every age-related disease, including cardiovascular diseases such as stroke and atherosclerosis, Parkinson's disease, Alzheimer's, and type 2 diabetes," says Mark Mattson, Ph.D., chief of the Laboratory of Neurosciences at the National Institute on Aging at the National Institutes of Health.

It sounds pretty grim, but in this battle there are, thankfully, superheroes. Enter the vibrant world of antioxidants—substances that bind with free radicals and inhibit them from damaging cells. They are abundant in the most colorful fruits and vegetables, including spinach, broccoli, spirulina (blue-green algae), red apples, cranberries, blueberries, cherries, and grapes, as well as in chocolate and red wine. When you hear doctors say that eating five helpings of fruits and vegetables a day is good for you, antioxidants are the main reason. In the past five years an impressive body of research has emerged showing how antioxidants may protect the body and brain against the ravages of aging.

Paula Bickford, Ph.D., a researcher at the University of South Florida Center of Excellence for Aging and Brain Repair, is particularly interested in the role of antioxidants in brain health. The brain is a good place to study the benefits of antioxidants, says Bickford, because it has one of the highest percentages of fats of any organ in the body, and it is in our fats that free radicals inflict much of their damage. As we age, "communications between neurons become damaged, kind of like what happened to the Tin Man in *The Wizard of Oz*," she explains. "Oxidative damage caused the Tin Man to grow rusty—until Dorothy came along and oiled him." Similarly, antioxidants help to "regrease the lines of communication" in the cells in our brain, says Bickford.

To measure how the communication between cells was affected when groups of rats ate different diets, Bickford and her colleagues placed electrodes in the brains of 20-month-old rats—the equivalent of 60-year-old humans. She then fed one group of rats a diet supplemented with spirulina, another with apples, and a third with cucumbers, which lack the antioxidant qualities of spirulina and apples. Bickford and her colleagues were surprised by the robustness with which "both the spirulina and apple groups demonstrated improved neuron function in the brain, a suppression of inflammatory substances in the brain, and a decrease in oxidative damage." By contrast, there was no improvement in rats fed a diet containing cucumbers. Bickford, who calls the findings "dramatic," reproduced her results in another study, in which rats fed a spinach-rich diet had a reversal in the loss of learning ability that occurs with age.

Most recently, Bickford examined whether eating a diet high in antioxidant-rich spinach and blueberries makes a difference in lab animals suffering from stroke and Parkinson's. "We've seen very positive effects with both of these diseases, as well," she says. "We believe that antioxidants can help people either to delay the onset or to slow the progression of a range of diseases that we tend to get as we age."

Tempting though it may be now to go out and gorge on antioxidant-rich dark chocolate, resist the urge. The hottest discovery in the search to find the fountain of youth through the foods we eat is to—gulp!—eat a lot less of them. A 2006 article in *JAMA* caused a stir by announcing that in both men and women, caloric restriction—as spartan as 890 calories a day—resulted in a decrease in fasting insulin levels and body temperature, two biomarkers of longevity. Why? Because restricting calories also helps to eliminate those nefarious free radicals. Mattson explains: "When you overeat and more energy comes into the cells than you burn off by being active, you are going to have more excess free radicals roaming around." Still, he advises, don't panic over the idea of having to subsist on 890 calories a day. Mattson, who calls such a diet "starvation," believes we can all gain the benefits of healthy eating with a lot less pain.

Richard Miller, M.D., Ph.D., professor of pathology and geriatric medicine at the University of Michigan, agrees. He has spent the last 20 years studying the ways in which dietary and genetic changes can slow the aging process. The research has shown that mice, rats, and monkeys that have undergone severe caloric restriction demonstrate all kinds of mental and physical benefits such as better mental function, less joint disease, and even fewer cases of cataracts. But it's unrealistic to try to replicate that in humans. "To copy what's happening in the lab, a man weighing 200 pounds would have to decrease his caloric intake by 40 percent for life, which would put him at about 120 pounds," Miller explains. "That's just not tenable."

Instead, Mattson and Miller advocate a more moderate approach. According to the Centers for Disease Control and Prevention, the average man in the United States consumes about 2,475 calories a day. That's roughly 500 more, on average, than he really needs. Likewise, the average American woman consumes 1,833 calories, yet probably needs only about 1,600. One way to ratchet down your caloric consumption would be to follow this simple equation: men should aim for about 500 calories at both breakfast and lunch, while women should strive for about 300 at each meal. Both sexes can then shoot for 1,000 calories at dinner.

Bickford, who prefers to think of caloric restriction as caloric selection, underscores the importance of getting as much of your caloric intake as you can not only from antioxidant-rich fruits and vegetables but also from nuts and flaxseed, which are loaded with vitamin E and omega-3 and omega-6 fatty acids. In fact, Bickford takes a page out of her own lab studies and starts

© Corbis/Royalty Free

her day with an antioxidant smoothie. You can try it at home by blending together one cup of frozen blueberries with half a tablespoon of spirulina (available in any health food store), half a cup of nonfat plain yogurt, one teaspoon of ground flaxseed, one tablespoon of almond butter or a half-handful of almonds, and a dash of soy milk. Consider what's in that blender as a gas tank full of high-antioxidant fuel for the day.

Of course, one can't help but ask: what's the fun of living to 102 if you're subsisting on spirulina shakes? Not to worry. If you splurge on a stack of pancakes with eggs, bacon, and sausage—packing in 2,000 calories before 10 A.M.—you can always take heart in new data about to emerge from Mattson's lab, which show that periodic fasting—skipping a meal here and there—can also help to eliminate free radicals quite beautifully. "From an evolutionary standpoint we just aren't used to constant access to food," he explains. "Our bodies are used to going days without eating anything. Yet all of a sudden, we are taking in calories all day long."

In other words, we have gone from thousands of years of intermittently restricting our calories and eating a high-antioxidant diet to, in the past century, constantly eating a low-antioxidant diet. And that means more free radicals and more disease. So indulge in the pancakes or the cheese steak, but not both. Then skip a couple of meals and make your next one an all-out antioxidant feast. It may be counter to the don't-skip-meals philosophy our mothers all taught us; yet as it turns out, Mother Nature just might know better.

DONNA JACKSON NAKAZAWA is a health writer whose next book, a medical mystery about what's behind rising rates of autoimmune disease, will be published by Touchstone/Simon & Schuster in 2007.

Exercise

Regular physical activity has been shown to reduce your risk of heart attack, stroke, Alzheimer's, and some cancers. Now we're finding it also may add years to your life. That's powerful medicine indeed.

SUSAN CRANDELL

There are no guarantees in life and even fewer in death. But if you wish to prolong the former and delay the latter, scientists can now pretty much promise that regular exercise will help. "So many of what we thought were symptoms of aging are actually symptoms of disuse," says Pamela Peeke, M.D., a University of Maryland researcher and author of *Body for Life for Women* (Rodale, 2005). "This is a monster statement." It means that your health is not just a throw of the genetic dice but a factor that is largely under your control. "Our bodies are built for obsolescence after 50," Peeke says. "Up to 50 you can get away with not exercising; after that, you start paying the price."

The most dramatic declines due to aging are in muscle strength. "Unless you do resistance exercise—strength training with weights or elastic bands—you lose six pounds of muscle a decade," says Wayne Westcott, Ph.D., the highly respected fitness research director at the South Shore YMCA in Quincy, Massachusetts. That change in body composition not only saps our strength; it also lowers our metabolism and exposes us to greater risk of age-related disease. In fact, the loss of muscle (and accompanying increase in body fat) puts extra strain on the heart, alters sugar metabolism (increasing the risk for diabetes), and can tip the balance of healthy lipids in the blood, leading to heart attack and stroke.

Building muscle is much easier than you might think. Strength training just 20 minutes a day, two or three times a week, for 10 to 12 weeks can rebuild three pounds of muscle and increase your metabolism by 7 percent. Do you really need a boost in metabolism? Yes, if you want to feel more energetic, more alert, more vital and alive. Plus, the added muscle has a halo effect on many systems of the body, reducing blood pressure, improving your ability to use glucose from the blood by 25 percent, increasing bone mass by 1 to 3 percent, and improving gastrointestinal efficiency by 55 percent. "It's like going from a four-cylinder engine to a six," Westcott says.

If that's not enough to get your attention, consider this: a regular exercise program (30 minutes of physical activity at least three days a week) can reduce your risk of dying in the next eight years by 40 percent, improve brain function, cut your risk of Alzheimer's disease by up to 60 percent, and blunt the symptoms of depression. This is powerful medicine, given that 80 percent of the population over 65 suffers from at least one

chronic condition, and half have two or more, according to a report from the Census Bureau and the National Institute on Aging.

What is it about physical activity that makes it such a panacea? As scientists learn more about how the aging process works, they're finding that exercise—both aerobic exercise and strength training—has a tremendous impact on every cell in the body, reducing inflammation, increasing blood flow, and even reversing the natural declines in oxygen efficiency and muscle mass that come with aging.

Westcott points to a study his organization conducted at a nursing home in Orange City, Florida. Nineteen men and women with an average age of 89, most of whom used wheelchairs, did just ten minutes of strength training a week. "After 14 weeks almost everybody was out of their wheelchairs," Westcott says. "One woman moved back into independent living." The results were published in *Mature Fitness*.

Another inspiring study, published last spring in the *Journal of the American College of Cardiology,* reported that people in their 60s and 70s who walked or jogged, biked, and stretched for 90 minutes three times a week for six months increased their exercise efficiency—their ability to exercise harder without expending more energy—by a whopping 30 percent. But here's the shocker: a comparison group of people in their 20s and 30s showed an efficiency increase of just 2 percent. The results caught even study author Wayne C. Levy, M.D., an associate professor of cardiology at the University of Washington in Seattle, by surprise. "I hadn't anticipated that the older people would improve more than the group in their 20s and 30s," he says.

The explanation, Levy believes, may involve improvement in the function of the mitochondria—spherical or rod-shaped structures in our cells that take glucose, protein, and fat from the food we eat and turn them into energy. In fact, scientists believe that most of the dramatic benefits we get from exercise can be traced to this improvement in the mitochondria. "Mitochondrial function naturally declines with age," explains Kevin Short, Ph.D., who studies mitochondria and exercise at the Mayo Clinic in Rochester, Minnesota. But exercise, he found, can reverse that decline.

When Short and his colleagues put 65 healthy nonexercisers ranging in age from 21 to 87 on a bicycle training program three days a week, they found that everyone's maximum aerobic capacity had increased by about 10 percent after four months. When they studied thigh-muscle samples, they found out why: the mitochondria were pumping out more adenosine triphosphate (ATP), the fuel muscles use to move.

Now, if mightier mitochondria aren't enough to get you on your exercise bike each morning, this might be: it appears physical activity may also combat oxidative damage (see "Browning apples: oxidation at work"). "During exercise there's a tremendous burst of oxidative agents that are injurious to tissue," says Abraham Aviv, M.D., director of the Center of Human Development and Aging at the University of Medicine and Dentistry of New Jersey.

The theory is that although you take in more oxygen while exercising, regular exercise slows your resting heart rate, thereby decreasing the amount of oxygen you need overall and reducing the rate at which you create harmful free radicals.

Finally, to all these substantial benefits of exercise add one more: Professor Tim Spector, director of the Twins UK registry at St. Thomas' Hospital in London, is conducting experiments to determine whether exercise slows down the rate at which our telomeres shrink. (Telomeres are DNA sequences, located on the ends of chromosomes, that shorten as we age—see "Telomeres: your body's biological clock"). Although the results have not yet been published, preliminary findings suggest that in exercising and sedentary twin pairs, the twin who exercises has much longer telomeres "even when you adjust for differences in weight and smoking," says Spector.

In short, the evidence is clear: daily physical activity can transform your life. And it's never too late to start. "I started strength-training my father when he was 82," recalls Westcott. "He's six feet tall, but he was emaciated by the stress of my mother's death and weighed only 124 pounds. In a year and a half, he added 24 pounds of muscle. At 97, he's stronger than people half his age."

Critical Thinking

1. How do antioxidants affect the free radicals in the human body?
2. What effect do free radicals have on the cells in the human brain?
3. How do antioxidants affect the onset of diseases that people get as they age?
4. What are the health effects of a 30-minute exercise program at least three days a week?

SUSAN CRANDELL is the author of *Thinking About Tomorrow: Reinventing Yourself at Midlife.*

How to Live 100 Years

ALICE PARK

A century of life was once a rare thing, but that is changing. Science is slowly unraveling the secrets of the centenarians.

Don't write that down! Put your pencil away!" Agnes Buckley is trying in vain to head off an entertaining story her sisters are telling me about how she used to sneak out of the house as a teenager. (She favored boys with motorcycles.) When their father hid her shoes to keep her at home, Agnes simply bypassed the front door and leaped out the window.

"Everyone is going to think I was a troublemaker," she laments.

Don't worry, Agnes. You may have had some fun as a teen, but there's a lifetime of evidence to prove you've grown into respectability. A lifetime, that is, that already includes a full decade and a half more than the 80 or so years that a girl born in the U.S. today can expect to live. Agnes was born in 1913—the year that Grand Central Terminal opened in New York City and the U.S. Postal Service began delivering packages as well as letters—which makes her 96 years old. Two of her 11 brothers and sisters are nonagenarians too. The other surviving members of the clan are pushing 80 or well beyond it. And, as Agnes points out, "none of us have canes."

In fact, the entire Hurlburt family is a model of long-lived, healthful vigor, which makes it a perfect candidate for the Long Life Family Study (LLFS), an investigation into the factors that help certain families produce members who live into their 80s, 90s and even 100s. The study—sponsored by the National Institute on Aging, part of the National Institutes of Health—includes investigators from four U.S. research centers and one Danish one. The idea, says Dr. Thomas Perls, the principal investigator at the Boston University Medical Center location, is to figure out which genetic, environmental and behavioral factors contribute to longevity.

"When it comes to rare genetic variations that contribute to longevity, family [analysis] is particularly powerful," he says. "But just because something occurs in a family doesn't mean it is necessarily genetic. There are lots of behaviors and traditions that happen in families that play a role in longer life expectancies. We want to use these families to ferret out what these factors are."

There's no denying that longer life expectancy is swelling the number of seniors—people over age 65—in our population.

But it's the fastest-growing subset of that superannuated group that proves the most interesting for researchers—those over age 85, in particular the centenarians born in the late 1800s, who have lived through the 1918 flu pandemic, the Great Depression and both world wars; have witnessed women's suffrage and the moon landings; and are still here, keeping up with world events during the Administration of the nation's first African-American President.

In the most recent Census, health officials predicted that by 2050, more than 800,000 Americans would be pushing into their second century of life. After the numbers from the 2010 Census are tabulated, some experts believe that figure will grow. By all accounts, these new centenarians are far from the frail, ailing, housebound people you might expect. In contrast, the majority of them are mentally alert and relatively free of disability and remain active members of their communities. They may simply represent a new model of aging, one that health experts are hoping more of us can emulate, both to make our lives fuller and to ease the inevitable health care burden that our longer-lived population will impose in coming decades.

Centenarians draw on some reserve that allows them to bounce back from health problems and remain relatively hale until their final days.

Most people today fall prey to chronic diseases that strike in mid to late life—conditions such as cancer, heart disease, stroke and dementia—and end up nursing disabilities stemming from these illnesses for the remainder of their lives. Centenarians, on the other hand, appear to be remarkably resilient when it comes to shrugging off such ailments; they seem to draw on some reserve that allows them to bounce back from health problems and remain relatively hale until their final days.

Dozens of studies have investigated such individuals, with the goal of picking out the secrets to their salubrious seniority. Those analyses, however, have generally followed two separate if parallel tracks. The traditional approach has been to study the lifestyle and behavioral components of vigorous aging—the good habits, such as a healthy diet, regular physical activity and mental exercises that might keep the elderly vibrant through their golden years. The New England Centenarian Study, which includes 850 people entering their 100s, for example, has identified several behavioral and personality traits that seem to be critical to longevity, including not smoking, being extroverted and easygoing and staying lean.

Separately, biologists and geneticists have pursued the secret to longevity on a cellular or molecular level, first in animals and more recently in people. The goal is to identify genes associated with slowing normal aging and avoiding the chronic illnesses that accompany it.

But with advances in genomic technology that allow scientists to scan thousands of genes from a single sample at a time and then link them to specific functions in the body, researchers on aging can finally begin to knit together their two strands of inquiry. The result is an intricate tapestry that is starting to reveal exactly how we can best push the limits of life span. These findings in turn could eventually lead to drugs or other compounds that mimic such natural mechanisms, stretching lives a bit longer by keeping the genome in good repair, for example, or by boosting the body's defenses against free radicals. If we can't stay chronologically young, the scientists reason, we can at least live and feel as if we are.

"We are going through a revolution," says David Sinclair, a professor of pathology at Harvard Medical School, who has studied aging in animals and co-founded Sirtris, a biotech company developing antiaging compounds. "I think we might have our first handle on the molecules that can improve health." Even if we are not endowed with the genes that can ease us into our 100s, most of us can certainly learn something from families like the Hurlburts, who apparently are.

Of Yeast and Men

Until relatively recently, the best clues about the factors involved in growing old came not from healthily aging humans but from other, decidedly less interesting species. Take, for instance, yeast. These organisms provided the first hints about how much of aging was due to genes and innate biology and how much was the product of other variables. It was yeast and, later, flies and rodents that provided the first findings about caloric restriction, the intriguing hypothesis that a drastically reduced intake of calories can extend life span.

While there is no firm evidence that the same phenomenon occurs in humans, researchers like Leonard Guarente at the Massachusetts Institute of Technology found yeast genes that appear to cause a food-restricted metabolism to use energy more efficiently, burning through caloric inventory at just the right rate to maintain life-sustaining processes while keeping something around for future use. Sinclair calls these survival genes. When they're activated, he says, they stabilize DNA and, in the yeast's case, extended survival 30% beyond what is normal. So far, Sinclair and others have identified a dozen similar genes in people. What they are hoping to do is find a way to turn these pathways on without forcing the rest of the body to hunker down in survival mode.

But while genes are certainly an important component of aging, they may not be the most relevant factor, if only because

we don't have much control over them. The good news is that according to animal studies, only about 30% of aging is genetically based, which means that the majority of other variables are in our hands. Not only can getting such factors under control help slow the aging process before it starts, it can also help those who are already in their golden years improve their fitness and strength. Recent studies have shown, for example, that when seniors from ages 65 to 75 exercise with resistance weights, they can improve their scores on cognitive tests of memory and decision-making. Other research, in Germany, found that regular physical activity lowers the risk of developing cognitive impairment in people over age 55.

Only about 30% of aging for most people is genetically based, which means that the other variables are in our hands.

The 70%–30% split between environment and genes, however, doesn't apply to everybody. For lucky oldsters like those who qualify for the LLFS study, the reverse seems to be true. Perls has found that in centenarians, it's principally genes that are the secret to extra years. That's not surprising, since these people represent the extreme limit of our species' life expectancy.

But the centenarians' happy accident of birth may benefit the rest of us too, if Perls and his colleagues are successful in their work. Their first goal is to draw a complete map of their subjects' genomes, to figure out what makes their mortality clocks tick so slowly and for so long. "We think centenarians are going to be really powerful when it comes to genetic variations or combinations that are important to living to really old age," says Perls.

The challenge for researchers is to identify those genes that contribute not just to longevity but to healthy longevity in particular. Based on its unique collection of genetic data from the New England Centenarian Study, Perls' team is close to identifying such a suite of genes. From the evidence gathered so far, it appears that for the most part, people who live to 100 and beyond do not necessarily avoid the chronic diseases of aging that normally claim the rest of us after midlife. About 40% of centenarians have experienced one of these illnesses in their lifetimes, but they seem to push through them without long-term problems or complications. And when they do get sick, according to a study Perls conducted in 1996, they are less likely to log time in the intensive-care unit (ICU) and often require less-expensive care per admission—at least compared with the cardiac surgery, chemotherapy and other ICU procedures that many of their younger elderly counterparts need.

Like other elderly people, centenarians get sick, but they log less time in intensive care and require less-expensive treatment.

Even as the LLFS investigators look for the full sweep of genes behind such resilience, other researchers are focusing on individual areas of the body—particularly the brain. Dr. Bruce Yankner at Harvard Medical School is studying what distinguishes brains that make it to 100 with limited cognitive decline from those that succumb to the ravages of Alzheimer's disease or other forms of dementia before age 85. Yankner zeroed in on genes in the frontal cortex—which is involved in higher learning, planning and goal setting—of people ages 24 to 106. That's a big chronological span, and it netted a big genetic haul: the research identified no fewer than 440 genes that start to slow down after age 40. Using that set as a starting point, Yankner's group is trying to determine just what those genes do to affect individual aging processes.

The virtue of such an approach is that it gives you a look at the entire developmental trajectory of the key genes throughout the adult life span. The disadvantage is that it lacks specificity: you can't ever know which 24-to-80-year-olds will actually make it to 90 and beyond, so you can't be certain from looking at their brains which genes are really at work in extreme old age and which eventually deteriorate. For that reason, Yankner's team—like the LLFS investigators—is also studying the brains of a separate group of people who have already achieved extreme old age. Coming at the data from two different directions could better pinpoint the genes that are truly in play and lead to a reasonable library of targets for deeper research.

Newly discovered genes regulate the connections between brain cells—and it's healthy connections that keep neurons alive.

"It's a work in progress, but we believe that the expression of genes in the brain and how they are regulated is at least an indicator of how well someone is aging," Yankner says. "It may play a causal role as well."

Indeed, a causal role is precisely what the early results suggest. The key function of the collection of brain genes Yankner has identified is to regulate the connections between neurons—vitally important, since it's healthy connections that keep neurons alive. Among the first ones to go when brain cells start dying are those involved in learning and memory. This may help explain why even the sharpest oldsters are prone to so-called senior moments, a tendency to forget newly learned information or repeat stories or questions, sometimes over and over again. Other genes in the collection have more-precise repair duties, fixing small nicks and mistakes in DNA. Without such maintenance work, normal genetic activities are slowly compromised.

Yet despite his excitement over his genetic findings, Yankner too is adamant that DNA is not destiny. Just as you can keep your body fit with good lifestyle habits and by avoiding pollutants, toxins and carcinogens, you may be able to keep your genes healthier. Environmentally triggered alterations in genes—known as epigenetic changes—can affect when a gene

is activated, how robustly it is turned on and how it interacts with neighboring genes. Free radicals provide a very good case study of how epigenetic processes play out.

As the brain ages, it weathers a constant onslaught from these destructive oxygen ions. The body is able to patch over tiny dings and cuts in the genome, but over time, the genetic fixers can no longer keep up, and the function of the gene is compromised. The balance between wear and repair may be the key to a healthily aging brain. By scanning the genomes of centenarians, Yankner hopes to isolate the genes—and the biological processes attached to them—that help them stay ahead of the damage. Those might then be harnessed to give noncentenarians the same edge.

The first step to longer life spans is to get back some of what we lose by living our overfed, overstressed, underactive lifestyles.

That work might also begin to explain the growing body of evidence behind the use-it-or-lose-it hypothesis, which suggests that people can improve their odds of remaining mentally alert by keeping their minds engaged. Learning a new language, picking up a hobby and maintaining a rich network of social connections are all ways to keep brain neurons firing. Yankner and others hope to isolate which brain circuits seem to be most active in this process.

A Different Kind of Youth

If everyone could begin to mimic what the centenarians do naturally, we'd all benefit—as the Hurlburts vividly illustrate. Agnes was mentally nimble enough as she aged that she learned to drive when she was 63, and she only recently gave up her license ("I was a very fast driver, but they never caught me," she confesses); Walter, 84, is an accomplished painter; Muriel, 89, writes poetry and sews quilts; James, 91, is also a poet; Peter, 80, taught himself to play the piano and ice-skate after midlife; Millie, 93, burns through half a dozen books every few weeks ("I like exciting books with a lot of action," she says); Helen, 88, sews intricate dolls, complete with period costumes; and Peggy, the baby at 79, loves to cook and read. Even when they're watching *Jeopardy!*, says Peter's granddaughter Nicole, they're calling out the answers—in the form of a question, of course.

If studies are going to determine how adopting such behaviors can influence and strengthen genes, they're going to need a lot of volunteers, and the LLFS, like the New England study, is ready. So far, the trial includes 840 families like the Hurlburts, with 4,800 siblings who were at least 79 when they enrolled in 2006—and many of their children. All of the participants signed on knowing they'd be sitting still for in-depth interviews, recounting family histories and providing blood and DNA samples. And all have happily done their part. "I am interested to see if their influence can carry over to our generation," says

Janet Kinnally, 61, who joined the study along with her mother Helen. "I hope the research leads to things that are helpful for generations to come."

None of this means that centenarian studies will produce a youth pill for the rest of us anytime soon—or ever, despite all the overblown claims made by hawkers of antiaging compounds such as human growth hormone or resveratrol, an ingredient found in red wine. The goal, at least at first, will be merely to give us back some of what we lose by living a modern—which is to say, overfed, overstressed and underactive—lifestyle. "One misconception of aging research is that we are looking to prevent aging," says Sinclair. "What we are hoping to do is to come up with something that will give us a lifestyle that now only centenarians enjoy."

That's an idea that certainly appeals to the Hurlburts' three dozen children, who like to believe that their parents' genes give them a leg up but aren't taking any chances. "Our lifestyles are more stressful than theirs were," says Maureen Miraglia, 62, one of Agnes' daughters. "But I am trying to change to be more like my mother. Most of my friends are talking about retiring, but I look at my mother, and I'm looking forward to my next decade and trying to figure out what I want to do." As studies of the longest-lived among us continue to reveal more secrets to living well into old age, we can hope that's a happy dilemma that more of us will have.

Critical Thinking

1. What are the behavioral and personality traits that seem to be critical to longevity?

2. What are the biologists and geneticists trying to do to identify to explain the aging process?

3. What are the scientists hoping to find by focusing on long life family studies?

Will You Live to Be 100?

THOMAS PERLS, MD AND MARGERY HUTTER SILVER, EdD

After completing a study of 150 centenarians, Harvard Medical School researchers Thomas Perls, M.D., and Margery Hutter Silver, Ed.D., developed a quiz to help you calculate your estimated life expectancy.

Longevity Quiz

Score

1. Do you smoke or chew tobacco, or are you around a lot of secondhand smoke? Yes (−20) No (0)

2. Do you cook your fish, poultry, or meat until it is charred? Yes (−2) No (0)

3. Do you avoid butter, cream, pastries, and other saturated fats as well as fried foods (e.g., French Fries)? Yes (+3) No (−7)

4. Do you minimize meat in your diet, preferably making a point to eat plenty of fruits, vegetables, and bran instead? Yes (+5) No (−4)

5. Do you consume more than two drinks of beer, wine, and/or liquor a day? (A standard drink is one 12-ounce bottle of beer, one wine cooler, one five-ounce glass of wine, or one and a half ounces of 80-proof distilled spirits.) Yes (−10) No (0)

6. Do you drink beer, wine, and/or liquor in moderate amounts (one or two drinks/day)? Yes (+3) No (0)

7. Do air pollution warnings occur where you live? Yes (−4) No (+1)

8. **a.** Do you drink more than 16 ounces of coffee a day? Yes (−3) No (0) **b.** Do you drink tea daily? Yes (+3) No (0)

9. Do you take an aspirin a day? Yes (+4) No (0)

10. Do you floss your teeth every day? Yes (+2) No (−4)

11. Do you have a bowel movement less than once every two days? Yes (−4) No (0)

12. Have you had a stroke or heart attack? Yes (−10) No (0)

13. Do you try to get a sun tan? Yes (−4) No (+3)

14. Are you more than 20 pounds overweight? Yes (−10) No (0)

15. Do you live near enough to other family members (other than your spouse and dependent children) that you can and want to drop by spontaneously? Yes (+5) No (−4)

16. Which statement is applicable to you? **a.** "Stress eats away at me. I can't seem to shake it off." Yes (−7) **b.** "I can shed stress." This might be by praying, exercising, meditating, finding humor in everyday life, or other means. Yes (+7)

17. Did both of your parents either die before age 75 of nonaccidental causes or require daily assistance by the time they reached age 75? Yes (−10) No (0) Don't know (0)

18. Did more than one of the following relatives live to at least age 90 in excellent health: parents, aunts/uncles, grandparents? Yes (+24) No (0) Don't know (0)

19. **a.** Are you a couch potato (do no regular aerobic or resistance exercise)? Yes (−7) **b.** Do you exercise at least three times a week? Yes (+7)

20. Do you take vitamin E (400–800 IU) and selenium (100–200 mcg) every day? Yes (+5) No (−3)

Score

STEP 1: Add the negative and positive scores together. Example: -45 *plus* $+30 = -15$. Divide the preceding score by 5 (-15 divided by $5 = -3$).

STEP 2: Add the negative or positive number to age 84 if you are a man or age 88 if you are a woman (example: $-3 + 88 = 85$) to get your estimated life span.

The Science behind the Quiz

Question 1 Cigarette smoke contains toxins that directly damage DNA, causing cancer and other diseases and accelerating aging.

Question 2 Charring food changes its proteins and amino acids into heterocyclic amines, which are potent mutagens that can alter your DNA.

Questions 3, 4 A high-fat diet, and especially a high-fat, high-protein diet, may increase your risk of cancer of the breast, uterus, prostate, colon, pancreas, and kidney. A diet rich in fruits and vegetables may lower the risk of heart disease and cancer.

Questions 5, 6 Excessive alcohol consumption can damage the liver and other organs, leading to accelerated aging and increased susceptibility to disease. Moderate consumption may lower the risk of heart disease.

Question 7 Certain air pollutants may cause cancer; many also contain oxidants that accelerate aging.

Question 8 Too much coffee predisposes the stomach to ulcers and chronic inflammation, which in turn raise the risk of heart disease. High coffee consumption may also indicate and exacerbate stress. Tea, on the other hand, is noted for its significant antioxidant content.

Question 9 Taking 81 milligrams of aspirin a day (the amount in one baby aspirin) has been shown to decrease the risk of heart disease, possibly because of its anticlotting effects.

Question 10 Research now shows that chronic gum disease can lead to the release of bacteria into the bloodstream, contributing to heart disease.

Question 11 Scientists believe that having at least one bowel movement every 20 hours decreases the incidence of colon cancer.

Question 12 A previous history of stroke and heart attack makes you more susceptible to future attacks.

Question 13 The ultraviolet rays in sunlight directly damage DNA, causing wrinkles and increasing the risk of skin cancer.

Question 14 Being obese increases the risk of various cancers, heart disease, and diabetes. The more overweight you are, the higher your risk of disease and death.

Questions 15, 16 People who do not belong to cohesive families have fewer coping resources and therefore have increased levels of social and psychological stress. Stress is associated with heart disease and some cancers.

Questions 17, 18 Studies show that genetics plays a significant role in the ability to reach extreme old age.

Question 19 Exercise leads to more efficient energy production in the cells and overall, less oxygen radical formation. Oxygen (or free) radicals are highly reactive molecules or atoms that damage cells and DNA, ultimately leading to aging.

Question 20 Vitamin E is a powerful antioxidant and has been shown to retard the progression of Alzheimer's, heart disease, and stroke. Selenium may prevent some types of cancer.

Critical Thinking

1. What stomach problems can be the result of too much coffee consumption?
2. What are the advantages in terms of one's health to being a member of a stable family?
3. What are the health problems associated with smoking?

Adapted from *Living to 100: Lessons in Living to Your Maximum Potential at Any Age* (Basic Books, 1999) by **Thomas Perls, MD**, and **Margery Hutter Silver, EdD**, with **John F. Lauerman**.

Long Live . . . Us

In never-say-die America, life expectancy is longer than ever.

Mark Bennett

Six members of the Class of '74 sit around a restaurant table.

They sip red wine and munch on a trail-mix-style bowl filled with fish oil, flaxseed oil and DHEA gel tabs. A joke about a classmate's spring break photo with her great-grandson's frat brothers on Facebook sparks hysterical laughter. As the chuckles subside, they check their iPhone clocks, realize the abs-crunch marathon fundraiser for the Macrobiotic Diet Consortium starts in an hour, and get busy planning their 85th reunion.

A retro "Dancing with the Stars" theme wins unanimous approval. One guy tweets his mother-in-law about next week's library tax protest, the class president picks up the tab, and they scatter out the door.

Sure, the ages of the folks in that futuristic dinner party would be around 103, but in never-say-die America, life expectancy is longer than ever, according to a report issued this month by the U.S. Centers for Disease Control and Prevention.

A baby born in 2009 will live an average of 78 years and two months. If that kid is a girl, she will likely linger on Earth for 80.6 years, compared to 75.7 for a boy. Back in 1930, a man's life expectancy was 58 and a woman's 62.

The CDC won't say why Americans live longer until the second half of its life expectancy report is released later this year, but the agency has a pretty good guess. Improved medical treatment, vaccinations and anti-smoking campaigns have helped drop the death rate to a record low as deaths from strokes, Alzheimer's, diabetes, heart disease and cancer decreased during the past 12 months.

Plus, our ancestors had no idea that red wine contained antioxidants and resveratol that protect blood vessels and reduce "bad" cholesterol. Or that DHEA supposedly repairs damage to cells in our bodies. Or that fish oil and flaxseed oil fight free radicals, which are cell-damaging molecules, not 1960s fugitives.

So, with almonds stashed in our shirt pockets instead of Marlboros, we've nearly tacked an extra decade onto our lives since 1970, when life expectancy in the U.S. was 70.8 years.

"It does go up every year, little by little," CDC statistician Ken Kochanek said by telephone from Washington, D.C., last week.

Seemingly, this age-defying trend could extend and create bizarre cultural dynamics, not unlike the aforementioned class reunion committee meeting. In Britain, for example, government researchers estimate that by 2014—just a little more than two years from now—the number of Brits ages 65 and older will surpass that of the under-16 population. Think of the implications—there are more people sitting around the UK who look like Keith Richards than fresh-faced kids. Actually, the Stones guitarist (now 67) would be considered a mere pup, if a BBC report is true. That story quoted a *Science* magazine analysis that concluded there is no natural limit to human life. The greeting card companies may be printing a new "Happy 200th" line someday.

Mel Brooks' 2,000-year-old man comes to mind. When asked if he knew Joan of Arc, Mel's character responded, "Know her? I went with her, dummy."

Reality continues to apply, though. Humans are managing to live longer, but not indefinitely. Though 36,000 fewer Americans died in 2009 than the year before, a total of 2.4 million still passed on in '09. The leading causes were, in order, heart disease, malignant neoplasms, chronic lower respiratory diseases, cerebrovascular diseases, accidents, Alzheimer's, diabetes, flu and pneumonia and nephritis. "In general, you have the same problems that have existed for a long time," said Kochanek.

Men show up in those statistics sooner than women, apparently because we do dumb stuff more often, such as smoking and exceeding the speed limit. "Men take more risks, and that affects life expectancy," Kochanek said. Both genders eat less wisely, too, even if we're popping those Omega-3 pills. Americans in the sixtysomething age range are, on average, 10 pounds heavier than folks of a similar vintage a decade earlier, according to FDA statistics cited by *U.S. News & World Report*.

The impact of poor choices in our lifetimes can be tabulated. For those dying to know how much time they've got, Northwestern Mutual Life Insurance Co. provides an online calculator. Just punch in your age, height, weight, then answer 11 other questions about your lifestyle, family history and habits and—voila!—your final number appears. If you want something handy enough to stick onto the front of the fridge, the

U.S. Census Bureau offers a less detailed chart subtitled "Average Number of Years of Life Remaining."

Of course, those are national figures. Averages. They vary by location. According to a nationwide study by the Robert Wood Johnson Foundation of the University of Wisconsin Population Health Institute, Vigo County's mortality rate ranks 69th out of 92 counties in Indiana, which isn't good. The mortality rate is a measure of premature death—the years of potential life lost prior to age 75.

Why do Vigo Countians die so young?

Well, in terms of health behaviors (smoking, binge drinking, car crashes, diet and exercise, STDs and teen birth rates), Vigo County rates an abysmal 80th out of 92 counties. (Apparently, very few of the wine-drinking, fish-oil-eating, fitness-crazed baby boomers described earlier call Vigo County home.) When calculating mortality rates, health behaviors account for nearly one-third of the influencing factors, along with clinical care, socioeconomics and physical environment, the Population Health Institute study said.

Given those real numbers, the secret of long life may not be such a secret after all. Author and psychologist Howard Friedman's new book, *The Longevity Project*, explores the topic. In a *Time* magazine interview this month, he explained that "conscientiousness" was a primary enhancer of life expectancy.

"The most intriguing reason why conscientious people live longer is that having a conscientious personality leads you into healthier situations and relationships," Friedman told *Time*. "In other words, conscientious people find their way to happier marriages, better friendships and healthier work situations. They help create healthy, long-life pathways for themselves. This is a new way of thinking about health."

That should give Keith Richards something to consider every time the Stones play "Time Is On My Side."

Critical Thinking

1. Why is the life expectancy of men lower than the life expectancy of women?
2. What were the leading causes of death in the United States in 2009?
3. How has the weight of persons over 60 changed in the last ten years?
4. Why does Howard Friedman believe that conscientious people live longer?

MARK BENNETT can be reached at (812) 231–4377 or mark.bennett@tribstar.com.

UNIT 2

The Quality of Later Life

Unit Selections

Learning Outcomes

After reading this Unit, you will be able to:

- Name the foods a person can eat that would reduce the risk of developing Alzheimer's disease.

- Identify the chronic health problems that are often associated with dementia.

- Explain why life is happier for people in their older years.

- Explain why older people have fewer rows and come up with better solutions to conflict.

- Compare the percentage of the current baby-boomer population that are obese with that of persons who are younger and older.

- Cite how much more Medicare pays for an obese senior than one who is at a healthy weight.

- List the six popular myths about longevity that the authors question.

- List the qualifications the authors introduce to the myths to improve their accuracy.

Student Website

www.mhhe.com/cls

Internet References

Aging with Dignity
    www.agingwithdignity.org
The Gerontological Society of America
    www.geron.org
The National Council on the Aging
    www.ncoa.org

Although it is true that one ages from the moment of conception to the moment of death, children are usually considered to be "growing and developing," but adults are often thought of as "aging." Having accepted this assumption, most biologists concerned with the problems of aging focus their attention on what happens to individuals after they reach maturity. Moreover, most of the biological and medical research dealing with the aging process focuses on the later part of the mature adult's life cycle. A commonly used definition of *senescence* is "the changes that occur generally in the postreproductive period and that result in decreased survival capacity on the part of the individual organism" (B. L. Shrehler, *Time, Cells and Aging,* New York: Academic Press, 1977).

As a person ages, physiological changes take place. The skin loses its elasticity, becomes more pigmented, and bruises more easily. Joints stiffen, and the bone structure becomes less firm. Muscles lose their strength. The respiratory system becomes less efficient. The individual's metabolism changes, resulting in different dietary demands. Bowel and bladder movements are more difficult to regulate. Visual acuity diminishes, hearing declines, and the entire system is less able to resist environmental stresses and strains.

Increases in life expectancy have resulted largely from decreased mortality rates among younger people rather than from increased longevity after age 65. In 1900, the average life expectancy at birth was 47.3 years; in 2000, it was 76.9 years. Thus, in the last century, the average life expectancy rose by 29.6 years. However, those who now live to the age of 65 do not have an appreciably different life expectancy than did their 1900 cohorts. In 1900, 65-year-olds could expect to live approximately 11.9 years longer, and in 2000, they could expect to live approximately 17.9 years longer, an increase of six years.

Although more people survive to age 65 today, the chances of being afflicted by one of the major killers of older persons is still about as great for this generation as it was for its grandparents. Medical science has had considerable success in controlling the acute diseases of the young—such as measles, chicken pox, and scarlet fever—but it has not been as successful in controlling the chronic conditions of old age, such as heart disease, cancer, and emphysema. Organ transplants, increased knowledge of the immune system, and undiscovered medical technologies will probably increase the life expectancy for the 65-and-over population, resulting in longer life for the next generation. Although people 65 years of age today are living only slightly longer than 65-year-olds did in 1900, the quality of their later years has greatly improved. Economically, Social Security and a multitude of private retirement programs have given most older persons a more secure retirement. Physically, many people remain active, mobile, and independent throughout their retirement years. Socially, most older persons are married, involved in community activities, and leading productive lives. Although they may experience some chronic ailments, most people 65 or older are able to live in their own homes, direct their own lives, and involve themselves in activities they enjoy.

© McGraw-Hill Companies

The articles in this section examine health, psychological, social, and spiritual factors that affect the quality of aging. All of us face the process of aging, and by putting a strong emphasis on health—both mental and physical—a long, satisfying life is much more attainable. In "Age-Proof Your Brain," Beth Howard notes the 10 steps a person could take to reduce the risk of developing dementia or Alzheimer's disease. The article "The U-bend of Life" identifies reasons why older people are happier than young and middle-aged people. The article "Poll: Obesity hits more boomers in U.S." notes that current baby boomers who are approaching retirement age are more obese than those of similar age were in previous generations. Because of their weight problems, boomers are more likely to be at risk for cancer, heart trouble, and diabetes.

Finally, in "The Myths of Living Longer," Howard Friedman and Leslie Martin point out six popular beliefs about living longer and attempt to determine their accuracy.

Age-Proof Your Brain

10 Easy Ways to Stay Sharp Forever

BETH HOWARD

Alzheimer's isn't inevitable. Many experts now believe you can prevent or at least delay dementia—even if you have a genetic predisposition. Reducing Alzheimer's risk factors like obesity, diabetes, smoking and low physical activity by just 25 percent could prevent up to half a million cases of the disease in the United States, according to a recent analysis from the University of California, San Francisco.

"The goal is to stave it off long enough so that you can live life without ever suffering from symptoms," says Gary Small, M.D., director of the UCLA Longevity Center and coauthor of *The Alzheimer's Prevention Program: Keep Your Brain Healthy for the Rest of Your Life.* Read on for new ways to boost your brain.

1 Get Moving

"If you do only one thing to keep your brain young, exercise," says Art Kramer, Ph.D., professor of psychology and neuroscience at the University of Illinois. Higher exercise levels can reduce dementia risk by 30 to 40 percent compared with low activity levels, and physically active people tend to maintain better cognition and memory than inactive people. "They also have substantially lower rates of different forms of dementia, including Alzheimer's disease," Kramer says.

Working out helps your hippocampus, the region of the brain involved in memory formation. As you age, your hippocampus shrinks, leading to memory loss. Exercise can reverse this process, research suggests. Physical activity can also trigger the growth of new nerve cells and promote nerve growth.

How you work up a sweat is up to you, but most experts recommend 150 minutes a week of moderate activity. Even a little bit can help: "In our research as little as 15 minutes of regular exercise three times per week helped maintain the brain," says Eric B. Larson, M.D., executive director of Group Health Research Institute in Seattle.

2 Pump Some Iron

Older women who participated in a yearlong weight-training program at the University of British Columbia at Vancouver did 13 percent better on tests of cognitive function than a group of women who did balance and toning exercises. "Resistance training may increase the levels of growth factors in the brain such as IGF1, which nourish and protect nerve cells," says Teresa Liu-Ambrose, Ph.D., head of the university's Aging, Mobility, and Cognitive Neuroscience Laboratory.

3 Seek Out New Skills

Learning is like Rogaine for your brain: It spurs the growth of new brain cells. "When you challenge the brain, you increase the number of brain cells and the number of connections between those cells," says Keith L. Black, M.D., chair of neurosurgery at Cedars-Sinai Medical Center in Los Angeles. "But it's not enough to do the things you routinely do—like the daily crossword. You have to learn new things, like sudoku or a new form of bridge."

UCLA researchers using MRI scans found that middle-aged and older adults with little Internet experience could trigger brain centers that control decision-making and complex reasoning after a week of surfing the net. "Engaging the mind can help older brains maintain healthy functioning," says Cynthia R. Green, Ph.D., author of *30 Days to Total Brain Health.*

4 Say *"Omm"*

Chronic stress floods your brain with cortisol, which leads to impaired memory. To better understand if easing tension changes your brain, Harvard researchers studied men and women trained in a technique called mindfulness-based stress reduction (MBSR). This form of meditation—which involves focusing one's attention on sensations, feelings and state of mind—has been shown to reduce harmful stress hormones. After eight weeks, researchers took MRI scans of participants' brains. The density of gray matter in the hippocampus increased significantly in the MBSR group, compared with a control group.

5 Eat Like a Greek

A heart-friendly Mediterranean diet—fish, vegetables, fruit, nuts and beans—reduced Alzheimer's risk by 34 to 48 percent in studies conducted by Columbia University.

"We know that omega-3 fatty acids in fish are very important for maintaining heart health," says Keith Black of Cedars-Sinai. "We suspect these fats may be equally important for maintaining a healthy brain." Data from several large studies suggest that seniors who eat the most fruits and vegetables, especially the leafy-green variety, may experience a slower rate of cognitive decline and a lower risk for dementia than meat lovers.

And it may not matter if you get your produce from a bottle instead of a bin. A study from Vanderbilt University found that people who downed three or more servings of fruit or vegetable juice a week had a 76 percent lower risk for developing Alzheimer's disease than those who drank less than a serving weekly.

6 Spice It Up

Your brain enjoys spices as much as your taste buds do. Herbs and spices like black pepper, cinnamon, oregano, basil, parsley, ginger and vanilla are high in antioxidants, which may help build brainpower. Scientists are particularly intrigued by curcumin, the active ingredient in turmeric, common in Indian curries. "Indians have lower incidence of Alzheimer's, and one theory is it's the curcumin," says Black. "It bonds to amyloid plaques that accumulate in the brains of people with the disease." Animal research shows curcumin reduces amyloid plaques and lowers inflammation levels. A study in humans also found those who ate curried foods frequently had higher scores on standard cognition tests.

7 Find Your Purpose

Discovering your mission in life can help you stay sharp, according to a Rush University Medical Center study of more than 950 older adults. Participants who approached life with clear intentions and goals at the start of the study were less likely to develop Alzheimer's disease over the following seven years, researchers found.

8 Get a (Social) Life

Who needs friends? You do! Having multiple social networks helps lower dementia risk, a 15-year study of older people from Sweden's Karolinska Institute shows. A rich social life may protect against dementia by providing emotional and mental stimulation, says Laura Fratiglioni, M.D., Ph.D., director of the institute's Aging Research Center. Other studies yield similar conclusions: Subjects in a University of Michigan study did better on tests of short-term memory after just 10 minutes of conversation with another person.

9 Reduce Your Risks

Chronic health conditions like diabetes, obesity and hypertension are often associated with dementia. Diabetes, for example, roughly doubles the risk for Alzheimer's and other forms of dementia. Controlling these risk factors can slow the tide.

"We've estimated that in people with mild cognitive impairment—an intermediate state between normal cognitive aging and dementia—good control of diabetes can delay the onset of dementia by several years," says Fratiglioni. That means following doctor's orders regarding diet and exercise and taking prescribed medications on schedule.

10 Check Vitamin Deficiencies

Older adults don't always get all the nutrients they need from foods, due to declines in digestive acids or because their medications interfere with absorption. That vitamin deficit—particularly vitamin B_{12}—can also affect brain vitality, research from Rush University Medical Center shows. Older adults at risk of vitamin B_{12} deficiencies had smaller brains and scored lowest on tests measuring thinking, reasoning and memory, researchers found.

Critical Thinking

1. What food that a person consumes seems to reduce the risk of Alzheimer's disease?

2. What is the advantage of an active social life for reducing the person's chances of developing dementia?

3. How does learning new skills reduce the risk of dementia?

The U-bend of Life

Why, Beyond Middle Age, People Get Happier as They Get Older

THE ECONOMIST

Ask people how they feel about getting older, and they will probably reply in the same vein as Maurice Chevalier: "Old age isn't so bad when you consider the alternative." Stiffening joints, weakening muscles, fading eyesight and the clouding of memory, coupled with the modern world's careless contempt for the old, seem a fearful prospect—better than death, perhaps, but not much. Yet mankind is wrong to dread ageing. Life is not a long slow decline from sunlit uplands towards the valley of death. It is, rather, a U-bend.

When people start out on adult life, they are, on average, pretty cheerful. Things go downhill from youth to middle age until they reach a nadir commonly known as the mid-life crisis. So far, so familiar. The surprising part happens after that. Although as people move towards old age they lose things they treasure—vitality, mental sharpness and looks—they also gain what people spend their lives pursuing: happiness.

This curious finding has emerged from a new branch of economics that seeks a more satisfactory measure than money of human well-being. Conventional economics uses money as a proxy for utility—the dismal way in which the discipline talks about happiness. But some economists, unconvinced that there is a direct relationship between money and well-being, have decided to go to the nub of the matter and measure happiness itself.

These ideas have penetrated the policy arena, starting in Bhutan, where the concept of Gross National Happiness shapes the planning process. All new policies have to have a GNH assessment, similar to the environmental-impact assessment common in other countries. In 2008 France's president, Nicolas Sarkozy, asked two Nobel-prize-winning

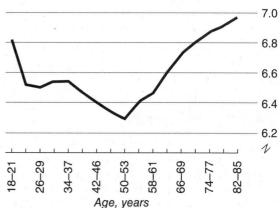

The U-bend
Self-reported well-being, on a scale of 1–10

Age, years

Source: PNAS Paper: "A snapshot of the age distribution of Psychological well-being in the United States" by Arthur Stone

economists, Amartya Sen and Joseph Stiglitz, to come up with a broader measure of national contentedness than GDP. Then last month, in a touchy-feely gesture not typical of Britain, David Cameron announced that the British government would start collecting figures on well-being.

There are already a lot of data on the subject collected by, for instance, America's General Social Survey, Eurobarometer and Gallup. Surveys ask two main sorts of question. One concerns people's assessment of their lives, and the other how they feel at any particular time. The first goes along the lines of: thinking about your life as a whole, how do you feel? The second is something like: yesterday, did you feel happy/contented/angry/anxious? The first sort of question is said to measure global well-being, and the second hedonic or emotional well-being. They do not always elicit the same response: having children, for instance, tends to make people feel better about their life as a whole, but also increases the chance that they felt angry or anxious yesterday.

Statisticians trawl through the vast quantities of data these surveys produce rather as miners panning for gold. They are trying to find the answer to the perennial question: what makes people happy?

Four main factors, it seems: gender, personality, external circumstances and age. Women, by and large, are slightly happier than men. But they are also more susceptible to depression: a fifth to a quarter of women experience depression at some point in their lives, compared with around a tenth of men. Which suggests either that women are more likely to experience more extreme emotions, or that a few women are more miserable than men, while most are more cheerful.

Two personality traits shine through the complexity of economists' regression analyses: neuroticism and extroversion. Neurotic people—those who are prone to guilt, anger and anxiety—tend to be unhappy. This is more than a tautological observation about people's mood when asked about their feelings by pollsters or economists. Studies following people over many years have shown that neuroticism is a stable personality trait and a good predictor of levels of happiness. Neurotic people are not just prone to negative feelings: they also tend to have low emotional intelligence, which makes them bad at forming or managing relationships, and that in turn makes them unhappy.

Whereas neuroticism tends to make for gloomy types, extroversion does the opposite. Those who like working in teams and who relish parties tend to be happier than those who shut their office doors in the daytime and hole up at home in the evenings. This personality trait may help explain some cross-cultural differences: a study comparing similar groups of British, Chinese and Japanese people found that the British were, on average, both more extrovert and happier than the Chinese and Japanese.

Then there is the role of circumstance. All sorts of things in people's lives, such as relationships, education, income and health, shape the way they feel. Being married gives people a considerable uplift, but not as big as the gloom that springs from being unemployed. In America, being black used to be associated with lower levels of happiness—though the most recent figures suggest that being black or Hispanic is nowadays associated with greater happiness. People with children in the house are less happy than those without. More educated people are happier, but that effect disappears once income is controlled for. Education, in other words, seems to make people happy because it makes them richer. And richer people are happier than poor ones—though just how much is a source of argument.

The View from Winter

Lastly, there is age. Ask a bunch of 30-year-olds and another of 70-year-olds (as Peter Ubel, of the Sanford School of Public Policy at Duke University, did with two colleagues, Heather Lacey and Dylan Smith, in 2006) which group they think is likely to be happier, and both lots point to the 30-year-olds. Ask them to rate their own well-being, and the 70-year-olds are the happier bunch. The academics quoted lyrics written by Pete Townshend of The Who when he was 20: "Things they do look awful cold / Hope I die before I get old." They pointed out that Mr Townshend, having passed his 60th birthday, was writing a blog that glowed with good humour.

Mr Townshend may have thought of himself as a youthful radical, but this view is ancient and conventional. The "seven ages of man"—the dominant image of the life-course in the 16th and 17th centuries—was almost invariably conceived as a rise in stature and contentedness to middle age, followed by a sharp decline towards the grave. Inverting the rise and fall is a recent idea. "A few of us noticed the U-bend in the early 1990s," says Andrew Oswald, professor of economics at Warwick Business School. "We ran a conference about it, but nobody came."

Since then, interest in the U-bend has been growing. Its effect on happiness is significant—about half as much, from the nadir of middle age to the elderly peak, as that of unemployment. It appears all over the world. David Blanchflower, professor of economics at Dartmouth College, and Mr Oswald looked at the figures for 72 countries. The nadir varies among countries—Ukrainians, at the top of the range, are at their most miserable at 62, and Swiss, at the bottom, at 35—but in the great majority of countries people are at their unhappiest in their 40s and early 50s. The global average is 46.

The U-bend shows up in studies not just of global well-being but also of hedonic or emotional well-being. One paper, published this year by Arthur Stone, Joseph Schwartz and Joan Broderick of Stony Brook University, and Angus Deaton of Princeton, breaks well-being down into positive and negative feelings and looks at how the experience of those emotions varies through life. Enjoyment and happiness dip in middle age, then pick up; stress rises during the early 20s, then falls sharply; worry peaks in middle age, and falls sharply thereafter; anger declines throughout life; sadness rises slightly in middle age, and falls thereafter.

Turn the question upside down, and the pattern still appears. When the British Labour Force Survey asks people whether they are depressed, the U-bend becomes an arc, peaking at 46.

Happier, No Matter What

There is always a possibility that variations are the result not of changes during the life-course, but of differences between cohorts. A 70-year-old European may feel different to a 30-year-old not because he is older, but because he grew up during the second world war and was thus formed by different experiences. But the accumulation of data undermines the idea of a cohort effect. Americans and Zimbabweans have not been formed by similar experiences, yet the U-bend appears in both their countries. And if a cohort effect were responsible, the U-bend would not show up consistently in 40 years' worth of data.

Another possible explanation is that unhappy people die early. It is hard to establish whether that is true or not; but, given that death in middle age is fairly rare, it would explain only a little of the phenomenon. Perhaps the U-bend is merely an expression of the effect of external circumstances. After all, common factors affect people at different stages of the life-cycle. People in their 40s, for instance, often have teenage children. Could the misery of the middle-aged be the consequence of sharing space with angry adolescents? And older people tend to be richer. Could their relative contentment be the result of their piles of cash?

The answer, it turns out, is no: control for cash, employment status and children, and the U-bend is still there. So the growing happiness that follows middle-aged misery must be the result not of external circumstances but of internal changes.

People, studies show, behave differently at different ages. Older people have fewer rows and come up with better solutions to conflict. They are better at controlling their emotions, better at accepting misfortune and less prone to anger. In one study, for instance, subjects were asked to listen to recordings of people supposedly saying disparaging things about them. Older and younger people were similarly saddened, but older people less angry and less inclined to pass judgment, taking the view, as one put it, that "you can't please all the people all the time."

There are various theories as to why this might be so. Laura Carstensen, professor of psychology at Stanford University, talks of "the uniquely human ability to recognise our own mortality and monitor our own time horizons." Because the old know they are closer to death, she argues, they grow better at living for the present. They come to focus on things that matter now—such as feelings—and less on long-term goals. "When young people look at older people, they think how terrifying it must be to be nearing the end of your life. But older people know

what matters most." For instance, she says, "young people will go to cocktail parties because they might meet somebody who will be useful to them in the future, even though nobody I know actually likes going to cocktail parties."

Death of Ambition, Birth of Acceptance

There are other possible explanations. Maybe the sight of contemporaries keeling over infuses survivors with a determination to make the most of their remaining years. Maybe people come to accept their strengths and weaknesses, give up hoping to become chief executive or have a picture shown in the Royal Academy, and learn to be satisfied as assistant branch manager, with their watercolour on display at the church fete. "Being an old maid", says one of the characters in a story by Edna Ferber, an (unmarried) American novelist, was "like death by drowning—a really delightful sensation when you ceased struggling." Perhaps acceptance of ageing itself is a source of relief. "How pleasant is the day," observed William James, an American philosopher, "when we give up striving to be young—or slender."

Whatever the causes of the U-bend, it has consequences beyond the emotional. Happiness doesn't just make people happy—it also makes them healthier. John Weinman, professor of psychiatry at King's College London, monitored the stress levels of a group of volunteers and then inflicted small wounds on them. The wounds of the least stressed healed twice as fast as those of the most stressed. At Carnegie Mellon University in Pittsburgh, Sheldon Cohen infected people with cold and flu viruses. He found that happier types were less likely to catch the virus, and showed fewer symptoms of illness when they did. So although old people tend to be less healthy than younger ones, their cheerfulness may help counteract their crumbliness.

Happier people are more productive, too. Mr Oswald and two colleagues, Eugenio Proto and Daniel Sgroi, cheered up a bunch of volunteers by showing them a funny film, then set them mental tests and compared their performance to groups that had seen a neutral film, or no film at all. The ones who had seen the funny film performed 12% better. This leads to two conclusions. First, if you are going to volunteer for a study, choose the economists' experiment rather than the psychologists' or psychiatrists'. Second, the cheerfulness of the old should help counteract their loss of productivity through declining cognitive skills—a point worth remembering as the world works out how to deal with an ageing workforce.

The ageing of the rich world is normally seen as a burden on the economy and a problem to be solved. The U-bend argues for a more positive view of the matter. The greyer the world gets, the brighter it becomes—a prospect which should be especially encouraging to *Economist* readers (average age 47).

Critical Thinking

1. How did the stress level in people affect how they responded to wounds and health problems?

2. Why are older people believed to be better at living for the present?

3. What are the human emotions that rise or dip in the middle years?

Poll: Obesity Hits More Boomers in U.S.

Baby boomers say their biggest health fear is cancer. Given their waistlines, heart disease and diabetes should be atop that list, too.

Boomers are more obese than other generations, a new poll finds, setting them up for unhealthy senior years.

And for all the talk of "60 is the new 50" and active aging, even those who aren't obese need to do more to stay fit, according to the Associated Press-LifeGoesStrong.com poll.

Most baby boomers say they get some aerobic exercise, the kind that revs up your heart rate, at least once a week. But most adults are supposed to get 2½ hours a week of moderate-intensity aerobic activity–things like a brisk walk, a dance class, pushing a lawn mower. Only about a quarter of boomers polled report working up a sweat four or five times a week, what the average person needs to reach that goal.

Worse, 37 percent never do any of the strength training so crucial to fighting the muscle loss that comes with aging.

Walking is their most frequent form of exercise. The good news: Walk enough and the benefits add up.

"I have more energy, and my knees don't hurt anymore," says Maggie Sanders, 61, of Abbeville, S.C. She has lost 15 pounds by walking four miles, three times a week, over the past few months, and eating better.

More boomers need to heed that feel-good benefit. Based on calculation of body mass index from self-reported height and weight, roughly a third of the baby boomers polled are obese, compared with about a quarter of both older and younger responders. Only half of the obese boomers say they are are regularly exercising.

An additional 36 percent of boomers are overweight, though not obese.

The nation has been bracing for a surge in Medicare costs as the 77 million baby boomers, the post-war generation born from 1946 to 1964, begin turning 65. Obesity—with its extra risk of heart disease, diabetes, high blood pressure and arthritis—will further fuel those bills.

"They're going to be expensive if they don't get their act together," says Jeff Levi of the nonprofit Trust for America's Health. He points to a study that found Medicare pays 34 percent more on an obese senior than one who's a healthy weight.

About 60 percent of boomers polled say they're dieting to lose weight, and slightly more are eating more fruits and vegetables or cutting cholesterol and salt.

But it takes physical activity, not just dieting, to shed pounds. That's especially important as people start to age and dieting alone could cost them precious muscle in addition to fat, says Jack Rejeski of Wake Forest University, a specialist in exercise and aging.

Whether you're overweight or just the right size, physical activity can help stave off the mobility problems that too often sneak up on the sedentary as they age. Muscles gradually become flabbier until people can find themselves on the verge of disability and loss of independence, like a canoe that floats peacefully until it gets too near a waterfall to pull back, Rejeski says.

He led a study that found a modest weight loss plus walking 2½ hours a week helped people 60 and older significantly improve their mobility. Even those who didn't walk that much got some benefit. Try walking 10 minutes at a time two or three times a day, he suggests, and don't wait to start.

"I don't think there's any question the earlier you get started, the better," says Rejeski, who at 63 has given up running in favor of walking, and gets in 30 miles a week. "If you allow your mobility to decline, you pay for it in terms of the quality of your own life."

When it comes to diseases, nearly half of boomers polled worry most about cancer. The second-leading killer, cancer does become more common with aging.

"It's the unknown nature, that it can come up without warning," says Harry Forsha, 64, of Clearwater, Fla., and Mill Spring, N.C.

Heart disease is the nation's No. 1 killer, but it's third in line on the boomers' worry list. Memory loss is a bigger concern.

In fact, more than half of boomers polled say they regularly do mental exercises such as crossword puzzles.

After Harding retires, he plans to take classes to keep mentally active. For now, he's doing the physical exercise that's important for brain health, too. He also takes fish oil, a type of fatty acid that some studies suggest might help prevent mental decline.

Sanders, the South Carolina woman, says it was hard to make fitness a priority in her younger years.

"When you're younger, you just don't see how important it is," says Sanders, whose weight began creeping up when breast cancer in her 40s sapped her energy. Now, "I just know that my lifestyle had to change."

Critical Thinking

1. Why is dieting alone not the most efficient way to lose weight?

2. What is the most efficient way to stave off mobility problems in later life?

3. What is the biggest health problem on the worry list of the baby boomers?

The Myths of Living Longer

At the end of an exhaustive study, it was discovered that many of the mantras you hear (Eat your vegetables! Get married! Relax!) are good for you in lots of ways but don't ensure a longer life.

Howard S. Friedman, PhD and Leslie R. Martin, PhD

In 1921, two precocious children named Patricia and John were pulled out of their San Francisco classrooms by Lewis Terman, a Stanford University psychologist who was interested in discovering the sources of intellectual leadership.

Eighty years later, both Patricia and John were still alive and in good health—at age 91. What was their secret? As health scientists, we've spent the past 20 years following up with all of Terman's 1,500 subjects—whose lives were tracked for eight decades as they grew up and had kids and grandkids—to discover why some of them thrived well into old age while others did not.

We looked at not only how long each participant lived, but also how they died. We studied a range of other factors—from schools to jobs to personality type—to see which traits predicted longevity. Turns out that some of the things you think you know about longevity simply aren't true.

Myth #1: Marriage Guarantees a Longer Life

That's not necessarily true. Scientific studies show it's not married people who live longer but married men. The bulk of the evidence shows little, if any, advantage for married women. With men, the key risk appears to be divorce, which can disrupt vital ties to family members and friends for years to come. In the Terman study, steadily married men were likely to live to age 70 and beyond, but fewer than a third of the divorced men reached old age. Divorce not only harms men directly but also sets in motion other unhealthy behaviors. Steadily married women in the Terman study lived somewhat longer than women who divorced and then remarried. But women who divorced and never remarried did just fine—in fact, they usually lived long lives.

Myth #2: Taking It Easy Adds Years to Your Life

Relaxation and an early retirement do not ensure long-lasting health.

Terman study subjects with the most career success were the least likely to die young. In fact, on average, the most successful men lived five years longer than the least successful. Ambition, perseverance, impulse control, and high motivation contributed to a resilient work life, and that led to more years overall. Usually, increased responsibility brings more challenges and a heavier workload, but this paradoxically correlates with long-term health.

Findings were especially dramatic among the oldest participants. Continually productive men and women lived much longer than their more laid-back comrades. A sustained work life mattered a great deal more than even their sense of happiness. So think carefully before retiring. Giving up an interesting, demanding job to live in a golf community away from your friends could actually increase the risk to your health.

Myth #3: You Can Worry Yourself to Death

Actually, the opposite is true: Terman's study clearly revealed that the best predictor of longevity in children was conscientiousness—being prudent, well organized, even somewhat obsessive. The same was true later in life. Adults who were thrifty, persistent, detail-oriented, and responsible lived the longest. Patricia, for example, "planned her work in detail" and had "definite purposes." (And dependable doesn't have to mean dull: Many of the most conscientious Terman subjects led exciting lives.)

One of the most obvious explanations is that conscientious people do more to protect their health—for example, wearing seat belts or following doctors' orders—and engage in fewer risky activities, like smoking, drinking to excess, abusing drugs, or driving too fast. They are not necessarily risk-averse, but they tend to be sensible in evaluating how far to push the envelope. Having this trait leads people into happier marriages, better friendships, and healthier work situations. That's right: Conscientious people create long-life pathways for themselves. And you aren't locked into—or out of—this trait. One Terman subject who lived to an old age scored very low in conscientiousness as a youngster. As an adult, he found a job he liked and had a very solid marriage. He became conscientious—and reaped the rewards.

Myth #4: More Degrees Mean More Years

Not so fast. We got some big surprises when we studied the effect of education on life span. During the era when Terman participants were children, it was common for parents to enroll their kids in school early and let them skip grades. But we found that when children entered first grade at age 5, not age 6, they often did not live as long. No single thing explained the higher risk, but because relating to classmates is so important, an early start may have launched some kids down erratic paths.

As for higher education, we found that level of schooling by itself was not a very important predictor of longevity. The-better-educated did tend to be healthier and live a little longer—but much more relevant than how many years of advanced formal education a person received were productivity and persistence in the face of challenges.

Myth #5: Friendly, Outgoing People Thrive

This widely held assumption is flawed. Americans tend to view extroversion as desirable—we worry if our children are shy. But our research indicates that sociable children did not, for the most part, live any longer than their more introverted classmates.

John is a good example: A shy child who tried to avoid playing in large groups, he preferred chess and checkers to tag or charades. He later became a physicist and was healthy into his 90s.

Why doesn't sociability necessarily set one on a path to long life? After all, outgoing children grow up to have better social relations, and that's normally a sign of good health, right? In the study, children like John tended to move into stable jobs, have long-lasting marriages, and work in a responsible manner.

Highly sociable people, in contrast, may be leaders in their businesses because of their enthusiasm and charm—but they're also more likely to go along with social pressures to drink or smoke. A "people person" may often join in the dangers of the moment—and that affects longevity.

Similarly, we often hear that optimism is the secret to a healthy life. But the data suggest that cheerful, optimistic children were actually less likely to live to an old age than their more staid, sober counterparts. Cheerfulness was comparable to high blood pressure and high cholesterol as a risk factor for early death. Happiness and good health often go hand in hand—but that doesn't mean happiness is the direct cause of good health. We found that it is usually some other set of characteristics that makes someone both happier and healthier. And optimism has a serious downside: No-worry folks may underestimate or ignore real threats and thereby fail to take precautions or follow medical advice.

Myth #6: Jocks Outlive Nerds

Regular physical exercise is good for your heart, no question. But if you're athletic when young, then gradually become—and stay—sedentary in your middle years, you lose any longevity benefit. Being active in middle age is the key. And exercise doesn't have to be intense, like running long distances every day, to be effective. John, the shy scientist, loved to ski. Linda, another Terman subject who lived a long life, made time for dancing, tennis, and gardening. The important thing is to find activities that suit you and stick with them over the long haul.

Critical Thinking

1. How does marriage affect longevity of men in comparison to women?
2. How was being retired, as compared to continuing to work and being productive, likely to affect longevity?
3. What personal characteristics did the authors believe lead to happier marriages, better friendships, and healthier work situations?
4. What are the critical factors about exercise and activity that cause them to increase a person's longevity?

As seen in *Parade*, February 20, 2011; reprinted from *The Longevity Project: Surprising Discoveries for Health and Long Life from the Landmark Eight-Decade Study* by Howard S. Friedman and Leslie R. Martin (Hudson Street Press, 2011). Copyright © 2011 by Howard S. Friedman and Leslie R. Martin. Reprinted by permission of Hudson Street Press, a member of Penguin Group (USA) Inc.

UNIT 3

Societal Attitudes toward Old Age

Unit Selections

Learning Outcomes

After reading this Unit, you will be able to:

- Explain why younger adults often avoid spending time around older persons.

- Describe how the media stereotypes the image of older persons.

- Discuss the different decisions that were made by the lower courts and the Supreme Court in the Jack Gross age discrimination in employment case.

- Explain how the Supreme Court's ruling in the Jack Gross case that age had to be the exclusive factor in the business decision rather than just a motivating factor for age discrimination to have occurred made it more difficult for demoted older workers to win their cases in court.

- Explain why older adults are inclined to be less confrontational in dealing with others with whom they interact.

- Explain why older adults report better interpersonal relationships than younger age groups do.

- Describe the advantages and disadvantages that one's attitude on aging can have on his or her behavior.

- Cite the advantages of feeling younger for older persons.

Student Website

www.mhhe.com/cls

Internet References

Adult Development and Aging: Division 20 of the American Psychological Association
   www.iog.wayne.edu/APADIV20/APADIV20.HTM
American Society on Aging
   www.asaging.org/index.cfm
Canadian Psychological Association
   www.cpa.ca

There is a wide range of beliefs regarding the social position and status of the aged in U.S. society today. Some people believe that the best way to understand the problems of the elderly is to regard them as a minority group faced with difficulties similar to those of other minority groups. Discrimination against older people, like racial discrimination, is believed to be based on a bias against visible physical traits. Because the aging process is viewed negatively, it is natural that the elderly try to appear and act younger. Some spend a tremendous amount of money trying to make themselves look and feel younger.

The theory that old people are a weak minority group is questionable because too many circumstances prove otherwise. The U.S. Congress, for example, favors its senior members and delegates power to them by bestowing considerable prestige on them. The leadership roles in most religious organizations are held by older persons. Many older Americans are in good health, have comfortable incomes, and are treated with respect by friends and associates.

Perhaps the most realistic way to view people who are aged is as a status group, like other status groups in society. Every society has some method of "age grading" by which it groups together individuals of roughly similar age. ("Preteens" and "senior citizens" are some of the age-grade labels in U.S society.) Because it is a labeling process, age grading causes members of the age group to be perceived by themselves as well as other's in terms of the connotations of the label. Unfortunately, the tag "old age" often has negative connotations in U.S. society. The readings included in this section illustrate the wide range of stereotypical attitudes toward older Americans. Many of society's typical assumptions about the limitations of old age have been refuted. A major force behind this reassessment of the elderly is that so many people are living longer and healthier lives, and in consequence, playing more of a role in all aspects of our society. Older people can remain productive members of society for many more years than has been traditionally assumed.

Such standard stereotypes of the elderly as frail, senile, childish, and sexually inactive are topics discussed in this section. Mary Pipher, in "Society Fears the Aging Process," contends that young people often avoid interacting with older persons because it reminds them that someday they too will get old and die. She further argues that the media most often portray a negative and stereotypical view of the elderly.

© Realistic Reflections

Jack Gross writes in "We Need to Fight Age Bias" about his demotion from his job to a lower position because of his age and sued the company for age discrimination. The court decisions through the Supreme Court are presented. In "Friendships, Family Relationships Get Better with Age Thanks to Forgiveness, Stereotypes," Amy Patterson Neubert points out why older people view their interpersonal relationships in more positive terms. In "How Old Do You Feel Inside?" Alexia Elejalde-Ruiz observes the advantages that a positive self-perception has for men and women in later life.

Society Fears the Aging Process

Americans fear the processes of aging and dying, Mary Pipher contends in the following viewpoint. She claims that younger and healthier adults often avoid spending time around the aging because they want to avoid the issues of mortality and loss of independence. In addition, she contends that negative views of the aging process are portrayed in the media and expressed through the use of pejorative words to describe the elderly. Pipher is a psychologist and author of several books, including *Another Country: Navigating the Emotional Terrain of Our Elders,* the book from which this viewpoint was excerpted.

MARY PIPHER

We segregate the old for many reasons—prejudice, ignorance, a lack of good alternatives, and a youth-worshiping culture without guidelines on how to care for the old. The old are different from us, and that makes us nervous. Xenophobia means fear of people from another country. In America we are xenophobic toward our old people.

How Greeting Cards Reflect Culture

An anthropologist could learn about us by examining our greeting cards. As with all aspects of popular culture, greeting cards both mirror and shape our realities. Cards reflect what we feel about people in different roles, and they also teach us what to feel. I visited my favorite local drugstore and took a look.

There are really two sets of cards that relate to aging. One is the grandparent/grandchild set that is all about connection. Even a very dim-witted anthropologist would sense the love and respect that exist between these two generations in our culture. Young children's cards to their grandparents say, "I wish I could hop on your lap," or, "You're so much fun." Grandparents' cards to children are filled with pride and love.

There is another section of cards on birthdays. These compare human aging to wine aging, or point out compensations. "With age comes wisdom, of course that doesn't make up for what you lose." We joke the most about that which makes us anxious. "Have you picked out your bench at the mall yet?" There are jokes about hearing loss, incontinence, and losing sexual abilities and interest. There are cards on saggy behinds, gray hair, and wrinkles, and cards about preferring chocolate or sleep to sex. "You know you're getting old when someone asks if you're getting enough and you think about sleep."

Fears of Aging and Dying

Poking fun at aging isn't all bad. It's better to laugh than to cry, especially at what cannot be prevented. However, these jokes reflect our fears about aging in a youth-oriented culture. We younger, healthier people sometimes avoid the old to avoid our own fears of aging. If we aren't around dying people, we don't have to think about dying.

We baby boomers have been a futureless generation, raised in the eternal present of TV and advertising. We have allowed ourselves to be persuaded by ads that teach that if we take good care of ourselves, we will stay healthy. Sick people, hospitals, and funerals destroy our illusions of invulnerability. They force us to think of the future.

Carolyn Heilbrun said, "It is only past the meridian of fifty that one can believe that the universal sentence of death applies to oneself." Before that time, if we are healthy, we are likely to be in deep denial about death, to feel as if we have plenty of time, that we have an endless vista ahead. But in hospitals and at funerals, we remember that we all will die in the last act. And we don't necessarily appreciate being reminded.

When I first visited rest homes, I had to force myself to stay. What made me most upset was the thought of myself in a place like that. I didn't want to go there, literally or figuratively. Recently I sat in an eye doctor's office surrounded by old people with white canes. Being in this room gave me intimations of mortality. I thought of Bob Dylan's line: "It's not dark yet, but it's getting there."

We know the old-old will die soon. The more we care and the more involved we are with the old, the more pain we feel at their suffering. Death is easier to bear in the abstract, far away and clinical. It's much harder to watch someone we love fade before our eyes. It's hard to visit an uncle in a rest home and realize he no longer knows who we are or even who he is. It's hard to see a grandmother in pain or drugged up on morphine. Sometimes it's so hard that we stay away from the people who need us the most.

Our culture reinforces our individual fears. To call something old is to insult, as in *old hat* or *old ideas.* To call something young is to compliment, as in *young thinking* or *young acting.* It's considered rude even to ask an old person's age. When we meet an adult we haven't seen in a long time, we compliment her by saying, "You haven't aged at all." The taboos against acknowledging age tell us that aging is shameful.

Many of the people I interviewed were uncomfortable talking about age and were unhappy to be labeled old. They said, "I don't feel old." What they meant was, "I don't act and feel like the person who the stereotypes suggest I am." Also, they were trying to avoid being put in a socially undesirable class. In this country, it is unpleasant to be called old, just as it is unpleasant to be called fat or poor. The old naturally try to avoid being identified with an unappreciated group. . . .

The Elderly Are Treated Poorly

Nothing in our culture guides us in a positive way toward the old. Our media, music, and advertising industries all glorify the young. Stereotypes suggest that older people keep younger people from fun, work, and excitement. They take time (valuable time) and patience (in very short supply in the 1990s). We are very body-oriented, and old bodies fail. We are appearance-oriented, and youthful attractiveness fades. We are not taught that old spirits often shimmer with beauty.

Language is a problem. Old people are referred to in pejorative terms, such as *biddy, codger,* or *geezer,* or with cutesy words, such as *oldster, chronologically challenged,* or *senior citizen.* People describe themselves as "eighty years young." Even *retirement* is an ugly word that implies passivity, uselessness, and withdrawal from the social and working world. Many of the old are offended by ageist stereotypes and jokes. Some internalize these beliefs and feel badly about themselves. They stay with their own kind in order to avoid the harsh appraisals of the young.

Some people do not have good manners with the old. I've seen the elderly bossed around, treated like children or simpletons, and simply ignored. Once in a cafe, I heard a woman order her mother to take a pill and saw the mother wince in embarrassment. My mother-in-law says she sees young people but they don't see her. Her age makes her invisible.

In our culture the old are held to an odd standard. They are admired for not being a bother, for being chronically cheerful. They are expected to be interested in others, bland in their opinions, optimistic, and emotionally generous. But the young certainly don't hold themselves to these standards.

Accidents that old drivers have are blamed on age. After a ninety-year-old friend had his first car accident, he was terrified that he would lose his license. "If I were young, this accident would be perceived as just one of those things," he pointed out. "But because I am old, it will be attributed to my age." Now, of course, some old people are bad drivers. But so are some young people. To say "He did that because he's old" is often as narrow as to say, "He did that because he's black" or "Japanese." Young people burn countertops with hot pans, forget appointments, and write overdrafts on their checking accounts. But when the old do these same things, they experience double jeopardy. Their mistakes are not viewed as accidents but rather as loss of functioning. Such mistakes have implications for their freedom.

Media Stereotypes

As in so many other areas, the media hurts rather than helps with our social misunderstandings. George Gerbner reported on the curious absence of media images of people older than sixty-five. Every once in a while a romantic movie plot might involve an older man, but almost never an older woman. In general, the old have been cast as silly, stubborn, and eccentric. He also found that on children's programs, older women bear a disproportionate burden of negative characteristics. In our culture, the old get lumped together into a few stereotyped images: the sweet old lady, the lecherous old man, or the irascible but softhearted grandfather. Almost no ads and billboards feature the old. Every now and then an ad will show a grandparent figure, but then the grandparent is invariably youthful and healthy.

In *Fountain of Age,* Betty Friedan noted that the old are portrayed as sexless, demented, incontinent, toothless, and childish. Old women are portrayed as sentimental, naive, and silly gossips, and as troublemakers. A common movie plot is the portrayal of the old trying to be young—showing them on motorbikes, talking hip or dirty, or liking rock and roll. Of course there are exceptions, such as *Nobody's Fool, On Golden Pond, Mr. and Mrs. Bridge, Driving Miss Daisy, Mrs. Brown,* and *Twilight.* But we need more movies in which old people are portrayed in all their diversity and complexity.

The media is only part of much larger cultural problems. We aren't organized to accommodate this developmental stage. For example, being old-old costs a lot of money. Assisted-living housing, medical care, and all the other services the old need are expensive. And yet, most old people can't earn money. It's true that some of our elders are wealthy, but many live on small incomes. Visiting the old, I heard tragic stories involving money. I met Arlene, who, while dying of cancer, had to fear losing her house because of high property taxes. I met Shirley, who lived on noodles and white rice so that she could buy food for her cat and small gifts for her grandchildren. I met people who had to choose between pills and food or heat.

The American Obsession with Independence

Another thing that makes old age a difficult stage to navigate is our American belief that adults need no one. We think of independence as the ideal state for adults. We associate independence with heroes and cultural icons such as the Marlboro man and the Virginia Slims woman, and we associate dependence with toxic families, enmeshment, and weakness. To our post-modern, educated ears, a psychologically healthy but dependent adult sounds oxymoronic.

We all learn when we are very young to make our own personal declarations of independence. In our culture, *adult* means "self-sufficient." Autonomy is our highest virtue. We want relationships that have no strings attached instead of understanding, as one lady told me, "Honey, life ain't nothing but strings."

These American ideas about independence hurt families with teens. Just when children most need guidance from parents, they turn away from them and toward peers and media. They are socialized to believe that to be an adult, they must break away from parents. Our ideas about independence also hurt families with aging relatives. As people move from the young-old stage into the old-old stage, they need more help. Yet in our culture we provide almost no graceful ways for adults to ask for help. We make it almost impossible to be dependent yet dignified, respected, and in control.

As people age, they may need help with everything from their finances to their driving. They may need help getting out of bed, feeding themselves, and bathing. Many would rather pay strangers, do without help, or even die than be dependent on those they love. They don't want to be a burden, the greatest of American crimes. The old-old often feel ashamed of what is a natural stage of the life cycle. In fact, the greatest challenge for many elders is learning to accept vulnerability and to ask for help.

If we view life as a time line, we realize that all of us are sometimes more and sometimes less dependent on others. At certain stages we are caretakers, and at other stages we are cared for. Neither stage is superior to the other. Neither implies pathology or weakness. Both are just the results of life having seasons and circumstances. In fact, good mental health is not a matter of being dependent or independent, but of being able to accept the stage one is in with grace and dignity. It's an awareness of being, over the course of one's lifetime, continually interdependent.

Rethinking Dependency

In our culture the old fear their deaths will go badly, slowly, and painfully, and will cost lots of money. Nobody wants to die alone, yet nobody wants to put their families through too much stress. Families are uneasy as they negotiate this rocky terrain. The trick for the younger members is to help without feeling trapped and overwhelmed. The trick for older members is to accept help while preserving dignity and control. Caregivers can say, "You have nurtured us, why wouldn't we want to nurture you?" The old must learn to say, "I am grateful for your help and I am still a person worthy of respect."

As our times and circumstances change, we need new language. We need the elderly to become elders. We need a word for the neediness of the old-old, a word with less negative connotations than *dependency,* a word that connotes wisdom, connection, and dignity. *Dependency* could become mutuality or

interdependency. We can say to the old: "You need us now, but we needed you and we will need our children. We need each other."

However, the issues are much larger than simply which words to use or social skills to employ. We need to completely rethink our ideas about caring for the elderly. Like the Lakota, we need to see it as an honor and an opportunity to learn. It is our chance to repay our parents for the love they gave us, and it is our last chance to become grown-ups. We help them to help ourselves.

We need to make the old understand that they can be helped without being infantilized, that the help comes from respect and gratitude rather than from pity or a sense of obligation. In our society of disposables and planned obsolescence, the old are phased out. Usually they fade away graciously. They want to be kind and strong, and, in America, they learn that to do so means they should ask little of others and not bother young people.

Perhaps we need to help them redefine kindness and courage. For the old, to be kind ought to mean welcoming younger relatives' help, and to be brave ought to mean accepting the dependency that old-old age will bring. We can reassure the old that by showing their children how to cope, they will teach them and their children how well this last stage can be managed. This information is not peripheral but rather something everyone will need to know.

Further Readings

Henry J. Aaron and Robert D. Reischauer. *Countdown to Reform: The Great Social Security Debate.* New York: Century Foundation Press, 2001.

Claude Amarnick. *Don't Put Me in a Nursing Home.* Deerfield Beach, FL: Garrett, 1996.

Dean Baker and Mark Weisbrot. *Social Security: The Phony Crisis.* Chicago: University of Chicago Press, 1999.

Margret M. Baltes. *The Many Faces of Dependency in Old Age.* Cambridge, England: Cambridge University Press, 1996.

Sam Beard. *Restoring Hope in America: The Social Security Solution.* San Francisco: Institute for Contemporary Studies, 1996.

Robert H. Binstock, Leighton E. Cluff, and Otto von Mering, eds. *The Future of Long-Term Care: Social and Policy Issues.* Baltimore: Johns Hopkins University Press, 1996.

Robert H. Binstock and Linda K. George, eds. *Handbook of Aging and the Social Sciences.* San Diego: Academic Press, 1996.

Jimmy Carter. *The Virtues of Aging.* New York: Ballantine, 1998.

Marshall N. Carter and William G. Shipman. *Promises to Keep: Saving Social Security's Dream.* Washington, DC: Regnery, 1996.

Martin Cetron and Owen Davies. *Cheating Death: The Promise and the Future Impact of Trying to Live Forever.* New York: St. Martin's Press, 1998.

William C. Cockerham. *This Aging Society.* Upper Saddle River, NJ: Prentice-Hall, 1997.

Peter A. Diamond, David C. Lindeman, and Howard Young, eds. *Social Security: What Role for the Future?* Washington, DC: National Academy of Social Insurance, 1996.

Ursula Adler Falk and Gerhard Falk. *Ageism, the Aged and Aging in America: On Being Old in an Alienated Society.* Springfield, IL: Charles C. Thomas, 1997.

Peter J. Ferrara and Michael Tanner. *A New Deal for Social Security.* Washington, DC: Cato Institute, 1998.

Arthur D. Fisk and Wendy A. Rogers, eds. *Handbook of Human Factors and the Older Adult.* San Diego: Academic Press, 1997.

Muriel R. Gillick. *Lifelines: Living Longer: Growing Frail, Taking Heart.* New York: W. W. Norton, 2000.

Margaret Morganroth Gullette. *Declining to Decline: Cultural Combat and the Politics of the Midlife.* Charlottesville: University Press of Virginia, 1997.

Charles B. Inlander and Michael A. Donio. *Medicare Made Easy.* Allentown, PA: People's Medical Society, 1999.

Donald H. Kausler and Barry C. Kausler. *The Graying of America: An Encyclopedia of Aging, Health, Mind, and Behavior.* Urbana: University of Illinois Press, 2001.

Eric R. Kingson and James H. Schulz, eds. *Social Security in the Twenty-First Century.* New York: Oxford University Press, 1997.

Thelma J. Lofquist. *Frail Elders and the Wounded Caregiver.* Portland, OR: Binford and Mort, 2001.

Joseph L. Matthews. *Social Security, Medicare, and Pensions.* Berkeley, CA: Nolo, 1999.

E. J. Myers. *Let's Get Rid of Social Security: How Americans Can Take Charge of Their Own Future.* Amherst, NY: Prometheus Books, 1996.

Evelyn M. O'Reilly. *Decoding the Cultural Stereotypes About Aging: New Perspectives on Aging Talk and Aging Issues.* New York: Garland, 1997.

S. Jay Olshansky and Bruce A. Carnes. *The Quest for Immortality: Science at the Frontiers of Aging.* New York: W. W. Norton, 2001.

Fred C. Pampel. *Aging, Social Inequality, and Public Policy.* Thousand Oaks, CA: Pine Forge Press, 1998.

Peter G. Peterson. *Gray Dawn: How the Coming Age Wave Will Transform America—And the World.* New York: Times Books, 1999.

Peter G. Peterson. *Will America Grow Up Before It Grows Old?: How the Coming Social Security Crisis Threatens You, Your Family, and Your Country.* New York: Random House, 1996.

John W. Rowe and Robert L. Kahn. *Successful Aging.* New York: Pantheon Books, 1998.

Sylvester J. Schieber and John B. Shoven. *The Real Deal: The History and Future of Social Security.* New Haven, CT: Yale University Press, 1999.

Ken Skala. *American Guidance for Seniors—And Their Caregivers.* Falls Church, VA: K. Skala, 1996.

Max J. Skidmore. *Social Security and Its Enemies: The Case for America's Most Efficient Insurance Program.* Boulder, CO: Westview Press, 1999.

Richard D. Thau and Jay S. Heflin, eds. *Generations Apart: Xers vs. Boomers vs. the Elderly.* Amherst, NY: Prometheus Books, 1997.

Dale Van Atta. *Trust Betrayed: Inside the AARP.* Washington, DC: Regnery, 1998.

James W. Walters, ed. *Choosing Who's to Live: Ethics and Aging.* Urbana: University of Illinois Press, 1996.

David A. Wise, ed. *Facing the Age Wave.* Stanford, CA: Hoover Institutional Press, Stanford University, 1997.

Periodicals

W. Andrew Achenbaum. "Perceptions of Aging in America," *National Forum,* Spring 1998. Available from the Honor Society of Phi Kappa Phi, Box 16000, Louisiana State University, Baton Rouge, LA 70893.

America. "Keep an Eye on the Third Age," May 16, 1998.

Robert Butler. "The Longevity Revolution," *UNESCO Courier,* January 1999.

Issues and Controversies on File. "Age Discrimination," May 21, 1999. Available from Facts on File News Services, 11 Penn Plaza, New York, NY 10001-2006.

Margot Jefferys. "A New Way of Seeing Old Age Is Needed," *World Health,* September/October 1996.

Ann Monroe. "Getting Rid of the Gray: Will Age Discrimination Be the Downfall of Downsizing?" *Mother Jones,* July/August 1996.

Bernadette Puijalon and Jacqueline Trincaz. "Sage or Spoilsport?" *UNESCO Courier,* January 1999.

Jody Robinson. "The Baby Boomers' Final Revolt," *Wall Street Journal,* July 31, 1998.

Dan Seligman. "The Case for Age Discrimination," *Forbes,* December 13, 1999.

Ruth Simon. "Too Damn Old," *Money,* July 1996.

John C. Weicher. "Life in a Gray America," *American Outlook,* Fall 1998. Available from 5395 Emerson Way, Indianapolis, IN 46226.

Ron Winslow. "The Age of Man," *Wall Street Journal,* October 18, 1999.

Critical Thinking

1. Why is it that many older persons do not want to be labeled "old"?

2. Why is it that television most often casts young people as the leading characters in their shows?

3. Why is being independent and self-sufficient in American society problematic for older persons?

We Need to Fight Age Bias

Congress should act where the courts failed.

JACK GROSS

I never, never imagined when I was demoted seven years ago and then filed an age discrimination suit that I would end up in the U.S. Supreme Court, that I would testify before five congressional committees, or that my name would become associated with the future of age discrimination laws in our country. I do believe, however, that it happened for a reason.

This all began in January 2003. When my employer, Farm Bureau Financial Group (FBL) in Iowa, merged with the Kansas Farm Bureau, the company apparently wanted to purge claims employees who were over age 50. All the Kansas claims employees over 50 with a certain number of years of employment were offered a buyout, which most accepted. In Iowa, virtually every claims supervisor over 50 was demoted.

Being 54, I was included in that sweep, despite 13 consecutive years of top performance reviews. The company claimed this was not discrimination but simply a reorganization. In 2005, a federal jury spent a week hearing testimony and seeing the evidence. The jurors agreed with me, and determined that age was a motivating factor in my demotion. Since then, the case has taken on a life of its own, including an appeal to the 8th Circuit Court and a U.S. Supreme Court hearing and decision.

Since the Age Discrimination in Employment Act was passed in 1967, courts had ruled consistently that the law protected individuals if their age was a factor in any employment decision. But in my case, the Supreme Court unexpectedly changed course and ruled that age had to be the exclusive reason for my demotion, even though that wasn't the question before them. They simply hijacked my case and used it as a vehicle to water down the workplace discrimination laws passed by Congress.

This new and much higher standard of proof is clearly inconsistent with the intent of the ADEA and four decades of precedent, and will affect millions of workers. A new trial was ordered and is scheduled for November, nearly eight years after my demotion.

I did not pursue this case just for myself. From my observation, discrimination victims are usually the most vulnerable among us, those who simply cannot fight back. Thanks to my attorneys, who believed in me, my case, and now our cause, I was able to take a stand against my unjust and unlawful treatment. Many of my friends are also farm or small-town "kids" who feel like they are the forgotten minority. Many have been forcibly retired or laid off. Some have been looking for work for months, only to find doors closed when they reveal the year they graduated. Others are working as janitors despite good careers and college degrees. They all know that age discrimination is very real and pervasive.

We now look to Congress to pass the Protecting Older Workers Against Discrimination Act (H.R. 3721), to provide the same protection for older people as protection given to people of color, women or people of different faiths.

While this ordeal has been stressful, observing all levels of our judicial and congressional processes "up close and personal" has been a real education. My faith in our judicial system was shattered by the Supreme Court's errant 5–4 decision. I believe Congress, as representatives of we, the people, will rectify it. You can help by contacting your own senators and representatives to encourage their support.

I am sincerely grateful for the assistance of people and groups truly dedicated to ending workplace discrimination of any kind in our great nation.

Critical Thinking

1. How did the Supreme Court's decision in the Jack Gross age discrimination case change the rules that determined if the employers had violated the Age Discrimination in Employment Act of 1967?
2. What bill now before Congress would give older workers the same protection as are given to people of color, women, or people of different faiths?
3. Does Jack Gross believe that the U.S. Congress will pass the new Protecting Older Workers Against Discrimination Act (H.R. 3721) which would re-establish the previous rules for judging age discrimination in employment which were established in 1967?

JACK GROSS was aided by AARP in the U.S. Supreme Court's precedent-setting age discrimination case.

Friendships, Family Relationships Get Better with Age Thanks to Forgiveness, Stereotypes

AMY PATTERSON NEUBERT

Part of what makes those relationships so golden during the golden years is that people of all ages are more likely to forgive and respect one's elders, according to research from Purdue University.

"Older adults report better marriages, more supportive friendships and less conflict with children and siblings," said Karen Fingerman, the Berner-Hanley Professor in Gerontology, Developmental and Family Studies. "While physical and cognitive abilities decline with age, relationships improve. So what is so special about old age? We found that the perception of limited time, willingness to forgive, aging stereotypes and attitudes of respect all play a part. But it's more than just about how younger people treat an older person, it's about how people interact."

Fingerman and Susan T. Charles, an associate professor of psychology and social behavior at the University of California in Irvine, published their research in this month's *Current Directions in Psychological Science.*

This article is based on their earlier work, including research showing that older adults are less confrontational than younger adults when they are upset. The article also builds on studies published in 2009 in the *Journal of Gerontology: Psychological Sciences* and in 2008 in the journal *Psychology and Aging.*

One study compared young adults, ages 22–35, and older adults, ages 65–77, by asking the participants to respond to several stories about personal interactions. The study participants heard stories about how an adult committed a social transgression, such as rudeness towards a waitress or ignoring property boundaries. Half the subjects read the story with the offending character portrayed as an older adult and the other half read the same story, but the offending character was portrayed as a younger adult. When the offending character was elderly, participants of all ages indicated that the person who was offended would avoid conflict and not react, but the opposite was found if the offending character was younger. When participants read a story in which a young adult committed a social faux pas, they thought other characters should confront that person and tell them they were upset.

These assumptions play out in daily interactions that Fingerman compares to a dance.

"Each person is acting and reacting in response to his or her partner, and, in this case, each partner is anticipating the next person's move, and that determination is often based on age," she said. "People vary their behavior with social partners depending on their age. When there is a negative interaction, younger people are generally more aggressive and confrontational than older people are. But younger people often are more accommodating to older people when there is a negative interaction."

For example, an older adult may be more cordial because of the assumption that a younger person may be confrontational. At the same time, the younger adult may conform to age stereotypes that indicate they should be more patient with an older person or they may hold stereotypes that older adults cannot change and do not attempt to change this person.

"Also, with age, people get better at regulating their emotions when something upsets them," Fingerman said. "The other advantage is that older people often have more opportunity to select who they want to associate with because they are retired and do not go to work."

Other reasons for better treatment of older adults reflect care, concern and cherishing the moment. No matter the age, people are going to be more pleasant if they perceive that there is little time left in a relationship, Fingerman said. That applies not just to people who are elderly, but even young people who may not see each other because of life changes such as moving out of state or serving in the military. When time is limited, people want to make the most of their remaining interactions and enjoy the other person rather than spending time fighting.

"We've also seen this in studies when adult daughters don't want to confront their elderly mothers or discuss negative things with them because they feel there is little time left with them," Fingerman said.

Fingerman plans to study how the "need to respect one's elders" plays a role in other cultures. Her work is supported by the Department of Child Development and Family Studies.

Critical Thinking

1. Are younger people generally more or less aggressive in dealing with the negative reactions of other people with whom they interact?

2. In general do older persons' relationships with others improve or decline with age?

3. How does the perception that there is little time left in a relationship affect the quality of the interaction between people?

How Old Do You Feel Inside?

The Key to Staying Healthy and Living Longer Is Deciding You're Not Old and Decrepit

Alexia Elejalde-Ruiz

Those of us lucky enough to grow old must contend with the miserable stereotypes of what it's like: the frailty, the forgetfulness, the early bird specials.

But in aging, as in many things, attitude can make all the difference. Research has shown that how people feel inside, and their expectations of their capabilities, can have a greater impact on health, happiness and even longevity than the date on their birth certificates.

In her seminal "counterclockwise" study, in 1979, Harvard University psychologist Ellen Langer brought men in their 70s and 80s to a weeklong retreat that was retrofitted, from the music to the newspapers, to look and feel like 1959. One group of men was told to reminisce about the era. The other group was told to let themselves be who they were 20 years earlier.

By the end of experiment, both groups of men, who upon entering had been highly reliant on relatives to do things for them, were functioning independently, actively completing chores, and showed significant improvements in hearing, memory, strength and intelligence tests. The group told to behave like they were 20 years younger also showed better dexterity, flexibility and looked younger, according to outside observers who judged photos of the participants taken before and after the retreat.

Expectation, not biology, leads many elderly people to set physical limits on themselves, Langer concluded; they assume they'll fall apart, so they let it happen.

"What we want to do is not get older people to think of themselves as young, but to change their mindsets about what it means to be older," Langer said. And being older doesn't have to equal decay.

Take memory. Thirty-year-olds forget lots of things, but they don't blame dementia. Older people jump to the conclusion that memory failures are part of their inevitable decline, when in fact it could be that their values change about what's meaningful enough to remember, Langer said.

Rather than declare failure when they aren't as nimble on the tennis court or spry on the stairs as they used to be, older people should recognize that anything is still possible; they just may have to try a few different strategies, Langer says.

Internalizing negative stereotypes about aging can have dire health consequences, even among the young, some studies suggest.

Men and women over 50 with more positive self-perceptions of aging lived 7.6 years longer than those with negative perceptions, according to a 2002 study led by Yale University epidemiology and psychology professor Becca Levy. Young, healthy people under 50 who held negative attitudes toward the elderly were more likely to experience a cardiovascular disorder over the next four decades than their peers who had more positive view of the elderly, a 2006 study by Levy found.

Pessimism about elderly decline, the researchers suggest, becomes a self-fulfilling prophecy.

Other studies that look at age identity—also known as subjective, or felt, age—have found that feeling younger than you really are is linked to better health, life satisfaction and cognitive abilities.

It's not clear what comes first: If identifying as younger makes you vital and sharp, or if people who feel vital and sharp associate that with feeling younger, said Markus Schafer, assistant professor of sociology at the University of Toronto, who last year published a study on age identity while a graduate student at Purdue University.

His study, in which people on average felt 12 years younger than their actual age, found subjective age was more important than chronological age in predicting performance on memorization and other mental tasks 10 years later. The cognitive benefits of feeling young were slightly more pronounced among women, he said, perhaps because of greater pressure on women to maintain youthfulness.

Regardless of what causes the correlation, he said, there's benefit to staying engaged.

"Learning new things, reading in a new area, at least trying to become connected with new technologies and platforms: Those are ways people can feel connected with the ebb and flow of the world," Schafer said.

The concept of "feeling younger" can be misleading: People usually mean that they feel healthier than they expected to feel at a particular age, not that they're denying their age or yearning for youth, said Laura Carstensen, founding director of the Stanford Center on Longevity. When asked in studies how old they'd like to be, most people say they wish to be 10 years younger—70-year-olds want to be 60, 60-year-olds wish to be 50—because they'd be healthier. No one wants to be 20, she said.

More important than reversing the clock is to be optimistic about it, she said. And aging does have its upsides.

Emotional satisfaction and stability tend to improve as people get older, despite sad events like losing friends or social status, Carstensen said. Because time seems short, elderly people focus on what matters most to them, such as personal relationships, rather than flailing about in the uncertain what-ifs of youth, she said. It's not a happy-go-lucky happiness, but a deeper sense of gratitude.

"The misery myth is one of the most pernicious myths, because when you think the future is really bleak if you don't plan," Carstensen said. "When you think, 'I'm going to be the coolest 80-year-old and will start a line of clothing for old people,' there is so much possibility."

7.6 years: How much longer men and women over 50 with more positive self-perceptions of aging lived compared to those with negative perceptions, according to one study.

Critical Thinking

1. In terms of performance on mental tasks, which was the more important: the individual's subjective age or chronological age?

2. When asked how old they would like to be, how do most older people respond?

3. How is the person's stability and emotional satisfaction affected by getting older?

UNIT 4

Problems and Potentials of Aging

Unit Selections

Learning Outcomes

After reading this Unit, you will be able to:

- Cite the risk factors that are most likely to cause a person to have a heart attack.

- List the six steps a person could take to appreciably reduce the chance of ever having a heart attack.

- Describe the mistakes that were identified as causing serious health problems for patients in hospitals throughout the country.

- Explain how 100 Michigan hospital intensive care units managed to reduce patient infections by two-thirds.

- Describe how the baby boomers' views of aging differ from those of younger adults.

- Cite what factors baby boomers consider to be the most undesirable aspects of getting older.

- Discuss the advantages that both European and U.S. studies found for persons age 50 and older who started and maintained a regular exercise program.

- Compare the advantage of a moderate exercise program over a light exercise program in terms of the death rates of the participants.

Student Website

www.mhhe.com/cls

Internet References

AARP Health Information
www.aarp.org/bulletin
Alzheimer's Association
www.alz.org
A.P.T.A. Section on Geriatrics
http://geriatricspt.org
Caregiver's Handbook
www.acsu.buffalo.edu/~drstall/hndbk0.html
Caregiver Survival Resources
www.caregiver.com
International Food Information Council
www.ifi c.org
University of California at Irvine: Institute for Brain Aging and Dementia
www.alz.uci.edu

Viewed as part of the life cycle, aging might be considered a period of decline, poor health, increasing dependence, social isolation, and—ultimately—death. It often means retirement, decreased income, chronic health problems, and death of a spouse. In contrast, the first 50 years of life are seen as a period of growth and development.

For a young child, life centers around the home and then the neighborhood. Later, the community and state become a part of the young person's environment. Finally, as an adult, the person is prepared to consider national and international issues—wars, alliances, changing economic cycles, and world problems. During the later years, however, life space narrows. Retirement may distance the individual from national and international concerns, although he or she may remain actively involved in community affairs. Later, even community involvement may decrease, and the person may begin to stay close to home and the neighborhood. For some, the final years of life may once again focus on the confines of home, be it an apartment or a nursing home.

Many older Americans try to remain masters of their own destinies for as long as possible. They fear dependence and try to avoid it. Many are successful at maintaining independence and the right to make their own decisions. Others are less successful and must depend on their families for care and to make critical decisions. However, some older people are able to overcome the difficulties of aging and to lead comfortable and enjoyable lives.

In "Never Have a Heart Attack," Gina Kolata points out the factors that are most likely to cause a person to have a heart attack and the steps that an individual could take to significantly

© Realistic Reflections

reduce his or her chance of having a heart attack. In "The Worst Place to Be If You're Sick," Katharine Greider notes the number of persons who die in hospitals each year from preventable hospital mistakes. The Associated Press article "Poll: Upbeat Baby Boomers Say They're not Old Yet" examines the current generation of baby boomers to determine their view of aging, when old age starts, and how they view their future retirement years. The *Harvard Men's Health Watch* article "Never Too Late: Exercise Helps Late Starters" points out how a regular exercise program even after age 50 helps to improve the health and longevity of older persons.

Never Have a Heart Attack

Reduce your risk to almost zero by following these six proven steps.

GINA KOLATA

TAKE A GUESS:

Which of the following people is likely to suffer a heart attack?

- Chris Conway, 54, is thin, eats a healthy diet, takes a baby aspirin every day, and exercises regularly.
- Howard Wainer, 66, has diabetes. Until recently, his blood pressure and blood sugar were too high.
- Naomi Atrubin, 79, has already had two heart attacks.

So who's at risk? Surprise—it's all three of them.

Wainer and Atrubin have obvious risk factors, but Conway has to contend with family history—his father had a heart attack in his mid-40s, and died of one at 66. All these people, however, share a common concern about their health: about 1.1 million Americans will suffer a heart attack this year, and some 500,000 will not survive it.

Despite the risks, most people don't understand what causes a heart attack. The common view is that it's simply a plumbing problem—cholesterol builds up, clogging arteries like sludge in a pipe. When an artery supplying blood to the heart becomes completely obstructed, portions of the heart, deprived of oxygen, die. The result is a heart attack, right?

Not quite, say heart experts. Heart disease involves the gradual buildup of plaque. And plaque is like a pus-filled pimple that grows within the walls of arteries. If one of those lesions pops open, a blood clot forms over the spot to seal it and the clot blocks the artery. Other things can stop your heart, but *that's* what causes a heart attack.

The bigger issue is how to stop it from happening. There's no way to predict where an artery-blocking clot will originate, so prying open a section of an artery with a stent will not necessarily prevent a heart attack. Stents

relieve chest pain, but people who have no symptoms—such as Howard Wainer—are better off adhering to tried-and-true measures to slow plaque growth and prevent the lesions from bursting. Those measures, says Peter Libby, M.D., chief of cardiovascular medicine at Brigham and Women's Hospital in Boston, "are things no one wants to hear: keep your weight down, make physical activity a part of your life, stop smoking if you smoke." And, of course, keep your blood pressure and cholesterol under control, taking medications if necessary.

About 1.1 million of us will have a heart attack this year.

Few people are following that advice. Twenty-five percent of Americans over age 50 have at least two risk factors, such as high blood pressure or cholesterol levels, or an elevated blood-sugar level. Only 10 percent of Americans have every risk factor under control.

"In the majority of cases when someone has a heart attack, at least two or three risk factors might have been avoided," says Valentin Fuster, M.D., a cardiologist at Mount Sinai School of Medicine in New York City.

In the majority of cases when someone has a heart attack, most risk factors might have been avoided.

In fact, a 50-year-old man with none of the risk factors has only a 5 percent chance over the next 45 years of ever having a heart attack, according to Daniel Levy,

M.D., director of the Framingham Heart Study, a federal study of heart disease in Framingham, Massachusetts. But if that man has even one risk factor, such as high cholesterol, his chance of having a heart attack soars to 50 percent. For a woman with no risk factors, the chance of having a heart attack is 8 percent; with just one risk factor, it goes to 38 percent. (Assess your own ten-year risk at hp2010.nhlbihin.net/atpiii/calculator.asp.)

By focusing on a few key risk factors, most people can significantly reduce their odds of ever having a heart attack. "There's a lot we can do," says Libby.

Keep Your Cholesterol in Check

Excess cholesterol gets stuck in artery walls. The walls become inflamed with white blood cells of the immune system, and those cells release chemicals that cause plaque. The normal level of so-called bad cholesterol, or LDL cholesterol, is 60 to 130. But if you are at high risk of a heart attack—because you have diabetes, for example—your level should be below 100 and, ideally, no higher than 70. Diet and weight loss are the preferred way to control your cholesterol, say heart-disease experts. If that doesn't work, statins—a class of cholesterol-lowering drugs—can reduce your LDL enough to help prevent heart attacks. Two decades of large and rigorous studies have shown that statins are safe for almost everyone.

Exercise Regularly

For optimal heart health, heart researchers recommend 30 minutes of moderate exercise—such as brisk walking—most days of the week. Exercise can help you control your weight, and it can also help you avoid diabetes if your blood sugar is inching up.

Lower Your Blood Pressure

High blood pressure can damage artery walls, causing them to become stiff and narrow. Ideally your blood pressure should be below 120/80. If you can get it that low with diet and exercise, great; if not, medications may do the job. Studies have shown that blood-pressure medications can reduce heart attack risk by 27 percent.

Control Your Weight

Obesity increases the likelihood that your cholesterol, blood pressure, and blood sugar will be too high; losing weight can often bring these numbers down. Being even slightly overweight also boosts your risk of heart attack, particularly if you tend to gain weight around your middle.

Stop Smoking

Smokers are two to three times more likely to die from heart disease than nonsmokers, says the American Heart Association. In addition to raising blood pressure and lowering HDL (good) cholesterol, smoking injures blood vessels, boosting your risk of having a heart attack. Even if you've been smoking for years, kicking the habit will help your heart. Studies have found that within one year of quitting, your heart attack risk is cut almost in half; within 15 years, it's like that of a nonsmoker.

Control Your Blood Sugar

High blood sugar can promote the growth of plaque. To be safe, your blood sugar level, tested after fasting, should be from 70 to 130 milligrams per deciliter of blood. Your doctor can order this test as part of a physical exam.

"I witness the cholesterol story time and time again," says Elliott Antman, M.D., director of the cardiac-care unit at Brigham and Women's Hospital. "People come to me for a second opinion after having a heart attack and I ask them, 'Have you ever been told what your cholesterol levels were?' The person will say, 'Yes, I was told they were normal.' That's not good enough anymore," if you've already had a heart attack. If you can get your LDL cholesterol level below 70, he says, you are unlikely to have another heart attack.

An LDL of less than 70 is also a good goal for people who have never had a heart attack, says Daniel Rader, M.D., head of preventive cardiovascular medicine at the University of Pennsylvania. Rader offers extra tests, including one for the blood protein CRP; if this protein is elevated, it indicates an increased heart-disease risk. Rader also offers heart scans to assess the extent of plaque in a person's arteries. If the tests reveal additional risk, he will suggest drugs to drive an LDL level down to 70. With an LDL level that low, Rader says, "your lifetime risk of heart disease will be reduced dramatically." It may not reach zero, he says, but it will be a lot lower.

Naomi Atrubin is counting on it. Her LDL cholesterol level, with medication, is currently 69; she's taking another drug to control her blood pressure, and she exercises. "I feel good," she says, though she's knows what's at stake: that only an aggressive approach on all fronts will help her avoid a third—and potentially fatal—heart attack.

Critical Thinking

1. What is the chance that a 50-year-old man who has none of the risk factors for a heart attack having a heart attack in the next 45 years?

2. If a 50-year-old man has one risk factor for a heart attack, such as high cholesterol, what are his chances of having a heart attack in the next 45 years?

3. What do doctors recommend as the safest level of a person's LDL or bad cholesterol in order to avoid a heart attack?

4. List the risk factors that are identified as problems that can lead to a heart attack.

GINA KOLATA is a science writer for *The New York Times*.

Reprinted from *AARP The Magazine*, January/February 2010, pp. 22–23. Copyright © 2010 by Gina Kolata. Reprinted by permission of Gina Kolata and AARP.

The Worst Place to Be If You're Sick

KATHARINE GREIDER

**Hospital errors cause 100,000 deaths yearly.
These are preventable deaths.
What's wrong, and can it be made right?**

American hospitals are capable of great medical feats, but they also are plagued by daily errors that cost lives. No one knows that better than Ilene Corina. In the 1990's, she saw a medical team rescue her fragile premature newborn, but she also endured the death of another son—a healthy 3-year-old—when, she says, doctors failed to attend to complications from a routine tonsillectomy.

When a family member dies because of a hospital's mistake, "what do we care about the excellence in the system?" says Corina, 51, of Long Island, N.Y., founder and president of a patient safety advocacy group. "We have to voice our anger about the problems we see in the health care system."

Corina had already joined the patient safety movement when, in 1999, the Institute of Medicine's now-famous report, *To Err Is Human,* burst into public consciousness with its startling announcement: Each year as many as 100,000 Americans die in hospitals from preventable medical mistakes.

Today, more than a decade into the fight against medical errors, there's little reason to believe the risks have declined substantially for the 37 million people hospitalized each year. In fact, recent studies suggest a problem that's bigger and more complex than many had imagined. A report released in January on Medicare patients found that hospital staff did not report a whopping 86 percent of harms done to patients. If most errors that harm patients aren't even reported, they can never be tracked or corrected, the Health and Human Services Department report pointed out.

The number of patients who die each year from hospital errors is equal to 4 jumbo jets crashing each week.

This latest study built on an earlier HHS study of Medicare patients that found one in seven suffered serious or long-term injuries, or died, as a result of hospital care. Researchers said about 44 percent of the problems were preventable.

In another key study published last spring in the journal *Health Affairs,* researchers examined patient charts at three of America's leading hospitals and found that an astounding one in three admissions included some type of harm to the patient.

Mistakes run the gamut. The surgeon nicks a healthy blood vessel; a nurse mistakenly administers a toxic dose of medicine; the staff fails to adequately disinfect a room, and a patient contracts a dangerous "superbug."

The number of patients who die each year from preventable hospital errors is equal to four full jumbo jets crashing each week. If airline tragedies of that magnitude were occurring with such frequency, no one would tolerate the loss.

One study of Medicare patients found that 1 in 7 died or were harmed by their hospital care.

"At its deepest level, what we're now having trouble with is the enormous complexity of medicine," says Atul Gawande, a surgeon, Harvard associate professor and author who promotes the use of medical checklists to save lives. "We now have 13,600 diagnoses, 6,000 drugs, 4,000 medical and surgical procedures," he says. And yet "we have not paid attention to the nuts and bolts of what's required to manage complexity." Experts like Gawande say one reason medical errors continue at such high rates is that hospitals have only recently begun to copy aviation's decades-long effort to create safety procedures that take into account human fallibility—often using only simple checklists.

There has been some progress, to be sure. Around the country, safety innovators have introduced promising ways to minimize slipups—from using checklists to reporting hospital infection rates on state websites. Last spring the Obama administration announced it would spend $1 billion to fund safety measures by hospitals, with the ambitious goal of reducing preventable patient injuries by 40 percent by the end of next year.

Still, the question of how close hospitals can ever come to being error-free is controversial. It seems fair to expect them to reduce the number of times—as many as 40 per week—that U.S. surgeons operate on the wrong person or body part. But what about other procedures?

Patient safety advocates have been able to raise the bar on hospitals in some key areas, showing that they *can* prevent harm to even the most vulnerable patients. A case in point: bloodstream infections that result from inserting a tube into a large vein near the heart to deliver medication. For years, these infections, which resulted in some 30,000 deaths annually, were viewed as largely unavoidable.

But then, in a program launched in 2004, more than 100 Michigan intensive care units managed to reduce these infections by two-thirds—and save some 1,500 lives in just 18 months—using a short checklist of practices for handling the catheters, and a culture change aimed at getting all staff on board. Hospitals around the country then took up the challenger, and the results were impressive.

The trouble is, there are plenty of other problems that may not be susceptible to an approach that tests a simple process that can then be used nationwide. A recent program looking at lapses that could lead to surgery on the wrong section of the patient found that errors can creep in just about anywhere, from scheduling to the marking of the surgical site. A couple of hospitals, for example, were using pens those ink washed off during surgical prep, making the marks useless. Flaws in this process vary from one hospital or surgery center to another, says Mark Chassin, M.D., president of the Joint Commission, the major accrediting organization for hospitals.

1,500 lives were saved in 18 months when Michigan ICUs began using a checklist of practices for handling catheters.

Other, apparently straight-forward problems—like health care workers not washing their hands—have proved surprisingly stubborn. Only about half of hospital workers follow hand washing guidelines, despite excellent staff training and ubiquitous hand sanitizer dispensers at many hospitals, says Robert Wachter, M.D., a patient safety expert at the University of California, San Francisco. He points out an airline pilot would be disciplined or fired for ignoring safety rules. But while penalizing careless individuals remains controversial—and largely untried—in health care, activities have made hospitals more accountable.

Public reporting of hospital performance, more or less unheard of a decade ago, has been an important strategy. Twenty-nine states now require public reporting of hospital infection rates, and 28 require some information on medical errors. The HHS website has now added a key catheter infection rate, along with other results.

There are hundreds of ways to measure safety performance, from death rates after heart surgery to whether doctors gave the right antibiotic. What to report has been a major debate. Infection rates, initially resisted by hospitals, are now generally regarded as some of the most reliable data available to the public, since in most cases reports are made through a standard system developed by the U.S. Centers of Disease Control and Prevention.

Money may be another motivator for hospitals. In 2008 Medicare took the small step of restricting payments to hospitals for extra costs associated with 10 hospital-acquired conditions. This year it will begin giving extra money to hospitals that score the highest on a set of standards linked to better results for patients.

Naturally, many patients want to compare the safety records of their local hospitals before checking in. But that's still tough to do. "There are no existing data that can allow you to be confident you've picked the safest, highest-quality place to get care," says Chassin, who helped prepare the seminal *To Err is Human* report "One reason is that safety and quality varies even within health systems. Just because they're great in one area doesn't mean that they're great in another."

Protect Yourself from Hospital Errors

Advocates agree that patients can minimize their risks by keeping a close eyes on their care. Hospitals are busy places with lots of moving parts. "You cannot assume that people in the hospital have a really clear idea of who you are or why you're there," says Jean Rexford, director of the Connecticut Center for Patient Safety. Here are some tips on how to protect yourself:

- Bring an advocate—a friend or family member—especially for check-in and discharge. Many hospitals have a patient advocate or staff person you can consult. Or you can hire your own advocate, but be aware that the profession lacks licensing requirements, so get referrals and check credentials.
- Bring a notebook. Write down all your medications, why you take them and who prescribed them.Include phone numbers of key personal and medical contacts (and don't forget your cellphone and charger). In the hospltal, when questions arise, write them down.
- Bring a big bottle of hand sanitizer. Put it by your bed to remind you and the staff to keep hands clean.

For More:

- Hospitalcompare.hhs.gov
- Agency for Healthcare Research and Quality, ahrq.gov
- Consumers Union, consumerreports.org
- Connecticut Center for Patient Safety ("5 Things to Know"), ctcps.org

Critical Thinking

1. Twenty-nine states now require what kind of public reporting on medical problems?

2. What financial measures has Medicare taken to hospitals to force them to comply with safer procedures and results?

3. Why is there no data available that allows the patients to be sure they are choosing the best hospital?

Poll: Upbeat Baby Boomers Say They're Not Old Yet

Baby boomers say wrinkles aren't so bad and they're not that worried about dying. Just don't call them "old."

The generation that once powered a youth movement isn't ready to symbolize the aging of America, even as its first members are becoming eligible for Medicare. A new poll finds three-quarters of all baby boomers still consider themselves middle-aged or younger, and that includes most of the boomers who are ages 57–65.

Younger adults call 60 the start of old age, but baby boomers are pushing that number back, according to the Associated Press-LifeGoesStrong.com poll. The median age they cite is 70. And a quarter of boomers insist you're not old until you're 80.

"In my 20s, I would have thought the 60s were bad, but they're not so bad at all," says 64-year-old Lynn Brown, a retired legal assistant and grandmother of 11 living near Phoenix in Apache Junction, Ariz.

The 77 million boomers are celebrating their 47th through 65th birthdays this year.

Overall, they're upbeat about their futures. Americans born in the population explosion after World War II are more likely to be excited about the positive aspects of aging, such as retirement, than worried about the negatives, like declining health. A third of those polled feel confident about growing older, almost twice as many as find it frustrating or sad. Sixteen percent report they're happy about aging, about equal to the number who say they're afraid. Most expect to live longer than their parents.

"I still think I've got years to go to do things," says Robert Bechtel, 64, of Virginia Beach, Va. He retired last year after nearly four decades as a retail manager. Now Bechtel has less stress and more time to do what he pleases, including designing a bunk bed for his grandchildren, remodeling a bathroom and teaching Sunday school.

A strong majority of baby boomers are enthusiastic about some perks of aging–watching their children or grandchildren grow up, doing more with friends and family, and getting time for favorite activities. About half say they're highly excited about retirement. Boomers most frequently offered the wisdom accumulated over their lives as the best thing about aging.

"The older you get, the smarter you get," says Glenn Farrand, 62, of Ankeny, Iowa.

But, he adds, "The physical part of it is the pits."

Baby boomers most often brought up failing health or fading physical abilities when asked to name the worst thing about getting older.

Among their top worries: physical ailments that would take away their independence (deeply worrisome to 45 percent), losing their memory (44 percent), and being unable to pay medical bills (43 percent). Many also fret about running out of money (41 percent).

Only 18 percent say they worry about dying. Another 22 percent are "moderately" concerned about it. More than two-thirds expect to live to at least age 76; 1 in 6 expects to make it into the 90s.

About half predict a better quality of life for themselves than their parents experienced as they aged.

"My own parents, by the time they were 65 to 70, were very, very inactive and very much old in their minds," says Brown. So they "sat around the house and didn't go anywhere."

"I have no intentions of sitting around the house," says Brown, whose hobbies include motorcycle rides with her husband. "I'm enjoying being a senior citizen more than my parents did."

But a minority of boomers–about a fourth–worry things will be harder for them than for the previous generation.

"I think we'll have less," said Vicki Mooney, 62, of Dobbs Ferry, N.Y., who fears older people will be pinched by cuts to Social Security and Medicare and rising health care costs. "The main difference in the quality of life is wondering if we will have a safety net."

Baby boomers with higher incomes generally are more optimistic about aging than their poorer peers. Women tend to feel sunnier than men; college graduates are more positive than those without a degree.

A third of baby boomers say their health has declined in the last five years, and that group is more likely to express fear or frustration about aging. Still, most boomers rate themselves in good or even excellent health overall, with less than 1 in 10 doing poorly.

Looking older is seriously bugging just 12 percent of baby boomers. The vast majority say they wouldn't get plastic surgery. That includes Johanna Taisey, 61, of Chandler, Ariz., who says aging is "no problem at all . . . it's just nature."

"Age with dignity," Taisey advises.

Among the 1 in 5 who have had or would consider cosmetic surgery, about half say they might improve their tummy or eyes.

A sagging chin is the next biggest worry–nearly 40 percent would consider getting that fixed.

Only 5 percent of baby boomers say they might use the chemical Botox to temporarily smooth away wrinkles; 17 percent would consider laser treatments to fix varicose veins.

But boomers, especially women, are taking some steps to look younger. A majority of the women–55 percent–regularly dye their hair, and they overwhelmingly say it's to cover gray. Only 5 percent of the men admit using hair color.

A quarter of the women have paid more than $25 for an anti-aging skincare product, such as a lotion or night cream. Just 5 percent of the men say they've bought skincare that expensive.

Almost all baby boomers–90 percent–have tried to eat better. Three-quarters say they're motivated more by a desire to improve their health than their appearance. Most boomers–57 percent–say in the past year they've taken up a regular program of exercise. About the same number do mental exercises, such as crossword puzzles or video games, to stay sharp.

Sixty-four-year-old Loretta Davis of Salem, W.Va., reads and plays games on her computer and takes walks. Diabetes and hypertension keep her focused on her diet these days. "I wish I had been more conscious of what I was eating earlier in life," said Davis, who worked in a grocery store, a factory and an ice cream shop before being disabled by polio in the 1980s.

But Davis says getting older doesn't bother her: "I'm just glad to still be here."

The AP-LifeGoesStrong.com poll was conducted from June 3 to June 12 by Knowledge Networks of Menlo Park, Calif., and involved online interviews with 1,416 adults, including 1,078 baby boomers born between 1946 and 1964. The margin of sampling error for results from the full sample is plus or minus 4.4 percentage points; for the boomers, it is plus or minus 3.3 percentage points.

Knowledge Networks used traditional telephone and mail sampling methods to randomly recruit respondents. People selected who had no Internet access were given it free.

Critical Thinking

1. When considering getting older, what are the things that worry the baby boomers the most?

2. What did boomers consider to be the best thing about aging?

3. How do most of the boomers rate their overall health at their current age in life?

Never Too Late: Exercise Helps Late Starters

HARVARD MEN'S HEALTH WATCH

The Industrial Revolution changed America forever, and the Information Era has changed it still further. More than ever before, men are working with their brains instead of their backs. It's great progress, but it does have unintended consequences, including global economic competition and unprecedented levels of stress. Another consequence is diminished physical activity. Now that most men don't need to exercise to earn their keep, many view exercise as kids' stuff, the fun and games that fill childhood—or used to in the days before video games and flat-screen TVs.

America has become a nation of spectators. That deprives men of the exercise that improves cholesterol levels, lowers blood sugar, burns away body fat, strengthens muscles and bones, improves mood and sleep, and protects against diabetes, dementia, certain cancers, and especially heart attacks and strokes.

Men who stay physically active throughout life reap these benefits and more. But what about men who slide into sloth once they're too old for school sports? Can a late start make up for years of sedentary living?

Second chances are rare in this life. But when it comes to exercise, research reinforces earlier studies that tell older men not to act their age.

Starting Late in Sweden

A 35-year study from Sweden provides strong evidence that starting to exercise late in life is better than never starting at all—much better, in fact.

The subjects were 2,205 male residents of the municipality of Uppsala. All the men were between the ages of 49 and 51 when they volunteered for the study between 1970 and 1973. During the course of the investigation, the men were evaluated five times, at ages 50, 60, 70, 77, and 82. At each evaluation, the men submitted detailed information about their exercise, smoking, and drinking habits, and the researchers measured body height and weight, blood sugar and cholesterol levels, and blood pressure.

The researchers divided the men into three groups based on their exercise levels. At age 50, most of the men rated their own health as good, and there was little difference in body mass index, blood pressure, or cholesterol between the low-, moderate-, and high-exercise groups, but smoking was less prevalent in high- versus low-level exercisers (47 percent vs. 61 percent). Over the next 35 years, though, major differences in health emerged. Most importantly, men who were highly physically active at age 50 were 32 percent less likely to die during the study than those who were least active; moderately active men enjoyed a smaller, but still respectable, 13 percent lower death rate than the least active gents.

The protective effect of regular exercise comes as no surprise. But the long-term nature of the Swedish study allowed the scientists to follow men who were sedentary at age 50 but who increased their exercise level between ages 50 and 60. For the first five years, the major result was disappointment, since these men continued to die at the same high rate as men who remained inactive. But over the next five years, the benefit kicked in; by 10 years of follow-up, the men who adopted exercise in middle age enjoyed the same low mortality rate as men who began before age 50. All in all, men who adopted exercise after 50 had a 49 percent lower death rate than the men who remained inactive, a benefit even greater than the 40 percent risk reduction experienced by men who quit smoking after age 50. And the protective effect of exercise remained significant even after the scientists adjusted their results for the impact of smoking, drinking, obesity, diabetes, cholesterol, blood pressure, and socioeconomic status.

Men looking for an excuse to stay on the couch may suspect a catch, wondering if they have to become long-distance runners to benefit from taking up exercise in midlife. Quite the reverse. According to the Swedish

Turning Back the Clock

Ponce de Leon learned it the hard way: There is no fountain of youth. But an interesting study tells us that exercise can make arteries act younger.

As people age, their arteries tend to constrict (narrow), reducing the tissue's supply of oxygen-rich blood. To find out if exercise can improve age-related vascular function, scientists compared 13 healthy men with an average age of 27 and 15 healthy men with an average age of 62. As expected, the older gents' arteries were more prone to constrict and less apt to dilate (widen). But for the next three months, eight of the older men began an exercise program, averaging nearly five hours a week of moderate aerobic training. At the end of that time, the arterial function tests were repeated, and the men who began to exercise in their 60s scored younger.

The great 17th-century physician Thomas Sydenham said, "A man is as old as his arteries." Twenty-first-century research suggests older men can use their legs to turn back the hands of their arterial clock.

study, men were classified as moderate exercisers if they simply took frequent walks or often went cycling for pleasure. And high-level exercise involved a minimum of just three hours of serious gardening or recreational sports a week. And in case you're tempted to cook up another excuse, you'll soon see that this important study does not stand alone.

Late Bloomers in Britain

Between 1978 and 1980, scientists evaluated 7,735 men from 24 British towns. In 1992, researchers were able to re-evaluate 5,934 of the men, who then had an average age of 63 years. The scientists tracked these men for an additional four years, comparing their risk of illness and death to their amount of physical activity.

At each evaluation, the researchers collected information about recreational and occupational exercise, smoking, drinking, social class, obesity, and health status, but they did not measure cholesterol, blood pressure, or blood sugar levels.

As in the Swedish study, the British research revealed a strong link between exercise and survival. Even light exercise was protective, reducing the rate of death by 39 percent; moderate exercise was even better, cutting the mortality rate by 50 percent. Most importantly, exercise was beneficial for men who were sedentary in 1978–80 but who began exercising sometime during the next 12 to

14 years; men who began to exercise later in life enjoyed a 45 percent lower mortality rate than men who remained sedentary throughout. And the benefits of late-life exercise were evident in men who already had heart disease by the time they became active as well as in men who were still healthy when they began to exercise.

News from Norway

A third European study, this time from Norway, confirms the findings from Sweden and England. Beginning in 1972, researchers evaluated 2,014 healthy men who were 40 to 60 years old. When the study began, each man got a comprehensive medical work-up and an exercise test. The evaluations were repeated between 1980 and 1982, and the scientists continued to keep track of the men through 1994.

As in the other studies, men who were physically fit enjoyed substantial protection from cardiovascular disease and early death; in all, the most fit men had a 55 percent lower mortality rate than the least fit. In addition, men who took up exercise and improved their fitness

Not By Exercise Alone

Men who become physically active later in life enjoy better health and a lower death rate than men who remain sedentary. That's good news for couch potatoes everywhere—but will reforming other health habits in midlife also help?

A study of 15,708 American men and women ages 45 to 64 says the answer is an emphatic yes. At the start of the study, only 1,344 people had all four of these healthy lifestyle habits: eating five or more servings of fruits and vegetables daily, not being obese, not smoking, and exercising regularly. But over the next six years, another 970 people adopted the healthful habits. The late adopters were quickly rewarded with improved health; over the next four years they enjoyed a 35 percent lower risk of cardiovascular events and a 40 percent lower death rate than their peers who failed to reform.

Exercise was one of the newly acquired health habits, but since the benefits of starting to exercise later in life take five years to kick in, exercise itself can't account for these rapid improvements. Better late than never, and better all than one.

It's a simple but powerful message, but it seems to fall on deaf ears. Only 8 percent of Americans between the ages of 40 and 74 have all four of these health habits plus moderate alcohol use—and that percentage has actually declined from a still woeful 15 percent in 1988.

levels between 1972 and 1982 reduced their risk of dying during the study—but men who let their exercise slide lost the protective effect of physical fitness.

American Veterans

The benefits of catch-up exercise are not confined to Europeans. A 2010 study of 5,314 male veterans ages 65 to 92 shows that fitness pays off on both sides of the Atlantic. All the volunteers underwent exercise tolerance testing at VA Medical Centers in Washington, D.C., and Palo Alto, Calif. Researchers followed the men for up to 25.3 years. During that time, the men who were most fit enjoyed a 38 percent lower mortality rate than those who were least fit. But the men who began to exercise during the follow-up period nearly caught up with the men who were in shape at the start of the study; unfit individuals who improved their fitness had a 35 percent lower mortality rate than their peers who remained unfit.

Harvard Men, Too

These four studies that show it's never too late to get fit confirm and extend the findings of an earlier American investigation that focused on middle-aged men. A 1993 report evaluated 10,269 Harvard alumni who were 45 or older when the study began in 1977. Over the next eight years, researchers tracked the effects of lifestyle changes on mortality. Previously sedentary men who began exercising after age 45 clearly benefited, enjoying a 23 percent lower rate of death than their classmates who remained inactive. The maximum benefits were linked to an amount of exercise equivalent to walking for about 45 minutes a day at a pace of about 17 minutes per mile. Not surprisingly, the Harvard study found that other lifestyle changes also helped, even if they did not occur until after age 45; quitting cigarette smoking, maintaining normal blood pressure, and avoiding obesity were all associated with less heart disease and longer life.

Which changes matter most? To find out, researchers evaluated some 36,500 male Harvard graduates and 21,000 male and female graduates of the University of Pennsylvania. All in all, sedentary individuals gained 1.6 years of life expectancy from becoming active later in life, smokers gained 1.8 years from quitting, and those who maintained normal blood pressure gained 1.1 years. Best of all was a combination of changes; sedentary smokers gained 3.7 years from quitting and becoming active.

Never Too Late

From both sides of the Atlantic, the message is clear: exercise is beneficial for all stages of life, and it's never too late to start. But men who start exercising after age 50 also need to exercise caution. Here are some tips:

- Get a check-up to be sure that you're healthy. In addition to checking for diabetes, hypertension, abnormal cholesterol levels, and evidence of cardiovascular disease, your doctor should be sure your joints and muscles don't merit special precautions.
- Pick an activity that's right for you. For many older gents (and for younger guys, too), walking is ideal. Biking and swimming are also excellent sports, and physically active hobbies such as serious gardening fill the bill, too.
- Set a realistic goal. Aim for 30 to 40 minutes of moderate exercise, such as brisk walking, nearly every day. But don't try to morph from couch potato to jock all at once. Instead, start out gradually and build up to your goal slowly but steadily. For example, you may want to begin exercising for 15 minutes three times a week, and then add minutes and days as you improve. And even when you're in top shape, it's always smart to alternate hard workouts with easier ones and to vary your routine.
- For best results, add stretching exercises, which are ideal for warming up before and cooling down after your workout. Remember, too, that strength training will complement aerobic training to build a balanced exercise program; all it takes is two to three sessions a week.
- Once you find yourself enjoying exercise, don't be afraid to extend yourself. Walkers, for example, might try a little jogging, golfers should walk the course, and doubles tennis players could switch to singles (or find younger partners).
- Get practical advice from friends and relatives who enjoy exercise and know the tricks of the trade. Consider professional guidance from a trainer or pro, and don't hesitate to spend a few bucks on good shoes or other gear.
- Make exercise part of a comprehensive health makeover. It's particularly important to avoid tobacco in all its forms and to eat right, control your weight, reduce stress, get enough sleep, and get regular medical care. But just as you've eased your way into exercise, make the other lifestyle changes you need gradually, and don't get down on yourself if you backslide.
- Above all, listen to your body. In most cases, you'll hear sounds of improvement, but if you detect distress signals—particularly chest pain or

pressure, undue fatigue or breathlessness, or an irregular heartbeat or lightheadedness—back off and report it to your physician.

It's never too late to start taking care of yourself, and it's never too early, either. Whether you started early or later, keep going throughout life. And spread the gospel of exercise for health to the younger generations, who have grown distressingly fat and lazy. One of the best ways to lead is by example.

Critical Thinking

1. In the Harvard study of men over 45, what were the lifestyle changes other than exercise that were associated with less heart disease and a longer life?

2. In a study of American veterans age 65 and older, how much did unfit veterans who exercised to improve their fitness lower their mortality rate?

3. How much did men in the British study who began exercises lower their mortality rate?

From *Harvard Men's Health Watch*, March 2011. Copyright © 2011 by Harvard Health Publications Group, Harvard University. Reprinted by permission. www.health.harvard.edu

UNIT 5

Retirement: American Dream or Dilemma?

Unit Selections

Learning Outcomes

After reading this Unit, you will be able to:

- Discuss the advantages to older workers of working beyond the anticipated retirement age.

- Explain how working beyond retirement age causes preretirement savings to grow.

- Explain why waiting until your late 70s or early 80s is the best time to begin buying or cashing in on a monthly annuity.

- Enumerate the advantages of waiting until age 70 rather than age 62 to begin drawing your Social Security.

- Discuss the advantages and disadvantages of beginning to withdraw from the Social Security Program at age 62.

- Describe the conditions that would qualify a person who never worked to receive a Social Security payments.

- Describe the variables that best explain why men and women receive the same retirement benefits.

- Cite the reasons why immigrants most often don't receive retirement programs and benefits from their employers.

- List the six lifestyle choices that older persons may choose from when they arrive at retirement age.

- Discuss the reasons why older persons make different choices about what they prefer to do at retirement age.

Student Website

www.mhhe.com/cls

Internet References

American Association of Retired People
   www.aarp.org

Health and Retirement Study (HRS)
   www.umich.edu/~hrswww

Since 1900, the number of people in America who are 65 years or more of age has been increasing steadily, but a decreasing proportion of that age group remains in the workforce. In 1900, nearly two-thirds of those over the age of 65 worked outside the home. By 1947, this number had declined to about 48 percent, and in 1975, about 22 percent of men age 65 and over were still in the workforce. The long-range trend indicates that fewer and fewer people are employed beyond the age of 65. Some choose to retire at age 65 or earlier; for others, retirement is mandatory. A recent change in the law, however, allows individuals to work as long as they want with no mandatory retirement age.

Gordon Strieb and Clement Schneider (*Retirement in American Society,* 1971) observed that for retirement to become an institutionalized social pattern in any society, certain conditions must be present. A large group of people must live long enough to retire; the economy must be productive enough to support people who are not in the workforce; and there must be pensions or insurance programs to support retirees.

Retirement is a rite of passage. People can consider it either as the culmination of the American Dream or as a serious problem. Those who have ample incomes, interesting things to do, and friends to associate with often find the freedom of time and choice that retirement offers very rewarding. For others, however, retirement brings problems and personal losses. Often, these individuals find their incomes decreased; they miss the status, privilege, and power associated with holding a position in the occupational hierarchy. They may feel socially isolated if they do not find new activities to replace their previous work-related ones. Additionally, they might have to cope with the death of a spouse and/or their own failing health.

Older persons approach retirement with considerable concern about financial and personal problems. Will they have enough retirement income to maintain their current lifestyle? Will their income remain adequate as long as they live? Given their current state of health, how much longer can they continue to work? The next articles deal with changing Social Security regulations and changing labor demands that are encouraging older persons to work beyond the age of 65. In "Live for Today, Save for Tomorrow," Carla Fried notes that the advantage of working beyond retirement age can allow people to save less before retirement; the longer they work, the more their savings will increase. Jane Bryant Quinn in "Do-It-Yourself Financial Freedom" describes 12 easy steps that people need to take throughout their life to ensure an adequate retirement income. In "Top 25 Social Security Questions," Stan Hinden addresses numerous questions and concerns people may have about

© John Lund/Drew Kelly/Blend Images LLC

their qualifications to receive Social Security in their retirement years. In "Paying for Retirement: Sex Differences in Inclusion in Employer-Provided Retirement Plans," Rosemary Wright discusses her investigation into sex differences among baby boomer workers in terms of their likelihood of being covered by an employer-provided retirement plan. And in "Work/Retirement Choices and Lifestyle Patterns of Older Americans," Harold Cox and colleagues write about their findings regarding six different work, retirement, and leisure patterns that older people may consider in choosing which would be most satisfying.

Live for Today, Save for Tomorrow

CARLA A. FRIED

What if working longer meant more fun, not less—and a bigger nest egg, too? You can make it happen if you start planning now.

As a senior financial planner, Christine Fahlund is not in the habit of telling people to stop saving for retirement. You wouldn't expect her employer, T. Rowe Price, to be wild about the idea, either. They are in the business of gathering investors' money into mutual funds and 401(k) plans. (Disclosure: Among those plans is the one for employees of AARP.) But in a new strategy that the company has been promoting this year, not only do Fahlund and T. Rowe Price suggest that you stop saving for retirement once you hit age 60; they encourage you to take the money you were previously putting into your 401(k) or other retirement account and—brace yourself—spend it. On fun stuff. "Your 60s should be a time when you start to enjoy yourself more," Fahlund says. "Take more trips. Spend time with the grandkids. Buy the boat or put in the pool you've been dreaming of."

And here's the kicker: If you follow their advice, you could end up with a higher income in retirement than you might have otherwise.

Is this a joke? Did Fahlund and company just snooze through the Great Recession? It's not, and they didn't. What T. Rowe Price calls "practice retirement" could, in fact, be a realistic option for you. But there's a big catch. Two catches, in fact. You have to have significant savings by the time you hit 60. And you have to commit to working well past your early 60s, because you're going to live off that income while your savings and your Social Security benefits sit untouched, gaining in value.

You may already be postponing your retirement: More than 60 percent of workers say they expect to retire at age 65 or later, according to the most recent survey by the Employee Benefit Research Institute, up from 45 percent in 1991. But few view the prospect with enthusiasm. Working longer is Plan B, a sign that something went wrong in your retirement schedule.

"Practice retirement" operates from a different set of assumptions. Steven Sass, director of the Financial Security Project at the Center for Retirement Research at Boston College, says most people think the point of working longer is to sacrifice and save. That's not it. "The payoff of working longer," says Sass, who coauthored *Working Longer: The Solution to the Retirement Income Challenge,* "is that you can preserve your retirement savings and delay taking Social Security." Medical researchers have long known that staying on the job pays benefits to the mind and body. By protecting your nest egg, enhancing your benefits, and limiting the number of years your stash needs to support you, working longer has a similar effect on your financial health.

And that creates some opportunities, including the one at the heart of Fahlund's suggestion: Put yourself in a position where you can afford to stop saving, or at least slow down, when you reach 60. Then: Live a little. "Get back to looking forward to

Table 1   How Much You Need to Save

Your Retirement Will be More Comfortable if you Work Well into your 60s		
If You Plan to Retire at Age 62		
And your total household income is	$50,000 $75,000 $100,000		
You'll need this much in savings by age 60	$600,000 $975,000 $1.4 million		
If You Plan to Retire at Age 65		
And your total household income is	$50,000 $75,000 $100,000		
You'll need this much in savings by age 60	$450,000 $825,000 $1.1 million		
If You Plan to Retire at Age 70		
And your total household income is	$50,000 $75,000 $100,000		
You'll need this much in savings by age 60	$250,000 $525,000 $700,000		

Notes. T. Rowe Price assumes you will want to replace 75 percent of your income and that you will not make any withdrawals from your retirement account, or initiate your Social Security payout, until you retire. The calculation also assumes a portfolio will earn 7 percent before retirement and 6 percent after.

Source: T. Rowe Price.

your 60s as a time to be enjoyed," she says. "You are delaying retirement, but you don't have to delay enjoyment."

Still sound too good to be true? Here are some answers to your probable concerns:

You'd Need to Save a Fortune to Take "Practice Retirement" at Age 60

Obviously, you can't stop saving at age 60 if you never really started. You need a healthy sum of money in the bank. But the required amount may be less than you're probably thinking.

The table estimates how much you need to squirrel away by age 60 to be able to turn off the savings spigot at that point. What you'll need depends on your current income, as well as the date when you expect to start tapping your savings and collecting Social Security. Bottom line: The longer you keep your hands off the retirement cookie jar, the less you'll need to have saved up by age 60. *Dramatically* less.

For example, a couple with $75,000 in joint household income who want to retire at 62 and have 75 percent of their preretirement income would need $975,000 in savings by age 60. But if they're willing to keep working until age 67, T. Rowe Price estimates they'd need $675,000. Those five extra years on the job cut the amount needed at age 60 by almost one-third. And if the couple don't touch their savings until 70, they need to set aside an even lower amount—$525,000. Hello, mission possible.

One assumption is critical: This model assumes your portfolio will earn 7 percent before you retire and 6 percent in retirement. That might seem too optimistic. To build in a margin of safety, you could assume a 5 percent preretirement return and 4 percent afterward. (By comparison, AARP's financial-planning tool assumes a 6 percent return preretirement, 3.6 percent afterward.) If the more cautious assumption proves accurate, you'd need to work one more year than you anticipated. But even that scenario is probably more affordable than you guessed. That's because the key ingredient in the recipe isn't the rate of return. It's your intention to keep working. "The investment earnings on your contributions at this later stage are less important," says Sass. "The value is that you have a job that supports you and helps you preserve your retirement security by not beginning to draw down your savings. We're talking about a few extra years of working to secure your finances for decades."

Come On—Decades? Working a Few Years More Can't Possibly Make That Much Difference

Most retirement experts say that it does. The Retirement Policy Center at the Urban Institute, for example, estimates that for every year you work past age 62, you increase your eventual retirement income by an average of 9 percent. At that rate, working eight years longer would double your retirement income. Here's why:

- Working longer means your retirement savings need not stretch over so many years. You've probably already heard this longevity riff: A 65-year-old man today has an average life expectancy of 17 years; a woman, 20 years. So you figure, "Okay, if I make it to 65, I will die at 82 or 85."

  But that's not necessarily correct. Your life expectancy isn't a calculation of when you will die; it's the age at which 50 percent of your age group will still be alive. So if you're 65 today, you've got even odds of making it into your mid-80s and beyond. It's even trickier if you're married. There's a better than 60 percent chance that one spouse of a 65-year-old couple today will still be alive at age 90. In other words, if you don't delay retirement—the average American man leaves the workforce at age 64; the average woman, at 62—the chances are good that your nest egg will have to stretch for 30 years.

  That can spread your savings thin. You can see the effect by plugging numbers into AARP's retirement calculator (aarp.org/retirementcalculator). Based on AARP's assumptions, a 60-year-old woman making $75,000 a year who retires at age 62 with a nest egg of $250,000 can sustain an annual income of about $31,000 through age 91. That same nest egg could support a healthier income of nearly $41,000 if she didn't touch her savings and delayed retiring until age 70.

- You give your savings more time to grow. If you work until age 70, your nest egg will be bigger than at 62 because it has eight more years to incubate. As long as you have a respectable amount saved by 60, letting that money grow undisturbed matters more to your financial security than does your adding new cash each year. If you have $250,000 in your 401(k) at age 60, the 7 percent annual rate of return assumed by T. Rowe Price would add $17,500 to your account in the first year alone. That's probably more than you'd contribute to a 401(k) or IRA. Over 10 years that 7 percent rate would lift your savings from $250,000 up to $500,000 by the time you retire, even if you never saved another penny.

- You can delay claiming your Social Security. Individuals can begin receiving benefits as early as age 62. But as the table shows, you'll lock in a higher payout if you hold off. "People's jaws drop when I tell them how much bigger their benefit will be if they wait," says Sass.

  Michael Wilson, a financial planner in Orland, Indiana, notes that the financial crisis makes it crucial to consider delaying. "If your 401(k) tanked, you will be leaning on Social Security even more."

- Finally, you reduce your out-of-pocket health care costs. Not many employers still offer retirement health coverage, so if you retire before 65 you may face stiff private insurance costs until Medicare kicks in. "The longer you can hold on to employer health benefits, the more you'll help preserve your retirement savings," says Richard Johnson of the Urban Institute's Retirement Policy Center.

What It Takes to Keep Working

Even before the Great Recession triggered massive layoffs, older workers often faced unique job disruption. About one-third of workers ages 51 through 55 in 1992 were involuntarily bounced from their jobs by the time they reached their mid to late 60s, according to a 2009 Urban Institute study. One-fourth lost their jobs because of a layoff or business closing; another 12 percent were forced to stop working because of illness.

But the upside to working through your 60s is so strong that it's worth fighting back to stay on the job, if you can. These principles should help.

Move the Goalposts

If you're still harboring thoughts that retiring at 62 is "right," you risk mentally retiring at 60 or so. That makes you easier pickings if the boss decides to cut overhead. Plan to work until at least your late 60s and you will stay more engaged in your work.

Quitting Is not an Option

Don't think you can give full retirement a whirl at age 62 and then just go back to work if your new life doesn't shake out as expected. "Retirement is a bit of a black hole," says *Working Longer* coauthor Sass. "It's habit-forming."

Be a Problem Solver

"Look around and see what holes your employer needs to fill, then offer to step in," says Sass. "The more flexible you are, the more valuable you are."

If You Have to Switch Jobs, Plan on Making Less

Some good news: If you've been at your job for a long time, you're in a better position than colleagues with less tenure. "Older workers are better protected from losing a job, but once they lose that job, they have a much harder time [than younger workers] finding a new job," says Richard Johnson, an Urban Institute retirement-policy expert. And the next job will likely be at a lower salary, so don't hold out for a fatter paycheck. Remember, though, that the main goal is to earn enough to cover your living costs.

Take Care of Yourself

A healthier you increases the odds you'll be able to keep working. It also makes it likelier you'll enjoy your 60s—and beyond.

It's Crazy Not to Save During Your 60s. What if the Market Collapses? What if you Get Sick? What if you Lose Your Job?

Working longer gives you the chance for some immediate gratification in your 60s, but it's not a free ticket to fiscal irresponsibility. Don't stop contributing to your 401(k) if your employer provides a match, for example; instead, dial back your contributions but keep saving enough to qualify for the maximum match. Otherwise you're essentially passing up free money. Don't drag debt into retirement. If you carry credit card balances, pay them off before you get into practice retirement's live-it-up mode. (Then keep them paid off.) Fahlund also recommends making big-ticket purchases while you have the income to cover them. And stay alert to market headwinds. If T. Rowe Price's 7 percent preretirement and 6 percent postretirement return assumptions look dicey after a few years, you may have to adjust by diverting more of your income into savings again, or trimming your expenses, or even delaying retirement by a year or more.

Can you really count on keeping your current job all the way to 70? Even if your employer is willing, your health may have other ideas. If you think that you're hale enough to go the distance, and secure in your position, practice retirement could be a possibility. "You have to take a look at your current job circumstances and ask yourself what is the likelihood you will be with that employer at age 67," Sass says. "If you do change jobs, you will probably lose money."

But don't forget that you can safely earn less than you once did. Since you are no longer diverting 10 or 15 percent of your salary into savings, you can bring home 10 or 15 percent less and still maintain the same quality of life. The aim is simply to resist tapping your savings and Social Security benefits until you are deep in your 60s.

Which brings us to the true benefit of working to a later age: options. One option is to have fun and spend more in a practice retirement. Another is to earn less money and take your foot off the career gas—or do work that's more meaningful to you. As long as you're still earning your living, the choice is yours. And with a Plan B like that, who really misses Plan A?

Social Security: Patience Pays

Your Social Security benefits revolve around your Normal Retirement Age (NRA)—the age at which you are entitled to 100 percent of your benefit. If you were born in 1960 or later, your NRA is 67. If you were born from 1943 to 1954, your NRA is 66, and if you were born from 1955 to 1959 your NRA is somewhere between 66 and 67. If you wait until your NRA or later to claim your benefit, you'll receive much higher monthly payments.

	How much bigger your benefit will be if you defer claiming your benefit until your NRA	Additional annual benefit increase between your NRA and 70	How much bigger your benefit will be if you wait until 70 to start receiving Social Security, compared with taking payouts at 62
If your NRA is 66 . . .	25%	8%	76%
If your NRA is 67 . . .	30%	8%	77%

A new AARP online calculator will give you a personalized snapshot of how waiting can balloon your Social Security benefit. Go to **aarp.org/socialsecuritybenefits**.

Critical Thinking

1. What critical factors should a person consider before deciding to work beyond their anticipated retirement age?

2. If the individual works into their late 60s or early 70s, are they likely to be more or less engaged in their work?

3. In terms of a worker's knowledge and skill in their present job or their flexibility in assuming a new job, what is the biggest advantage in terms of the worker's ability to continue being employed in their later years?

Reprinted from *AARP The Magazine,* December 2011/January 2012, pp. 43–44, 60–61. Copyright © 2012 by Carla A. Fried. Reprinted by permission of American Association for Retired Persons (AARP) and Carla A. Fried. www.aarpmagazine.org 1-888-687-2227

Do-It-Yourself Financial Freedom

Jane Bryant Quinn

Safety nets fray when times get hard. Retirements that once looked secure are hanging by a thread. The message for those in their 50s is clear: Mend the nets while there's still time. Those in their 60s and 70s have fewer options. Still, there are ways of making sure your money lasts for life. **Here's how to do it in 12 easy steps:**

1 Get rid of debt.

Nothing is more destructive of retirement than carrying debt when your paycheck stops. If you're in your early 50s, start debt reduction now. Try to prepay your mortgage, too, so you'll own your home free and clear. If you're retiring now and prepaying would use up too much cash, consider the other extreme: Reduce your payments by taking a new, 30-year mortgage. It's counterintuitive, but it works. Or use your equity to buy a smaller place that will leave you with no house payment or a much smaller one.

Don't fall prey to the slimy promises of commercial debt consolidators. Here are two legitimate and low-cost places to go for help with debt reduction: The National Foundation for Credit Counseling (www.nfcc.org, 1-800-388-2227) and the Association of Independent Consumer Credit Counseling Agencies (www.aiccca.org, 1-800-703-8787).

In the worst case, consider bankruptcy. Never tap retirement accounts to cover unpayable debts. IRAs and 401(k)s are protected in bankruptcy. You'll need those funds for a fresh start.

2 Build a better budget.

When you're thinking about retirement, nothing is more important than knowing how far your income will stretch. What will your expenses be? How much income will you have, including prudent withdrawals from your savings? Get your spending under control sooner rather than later. The longer you kid yourself, the greater your chance of running out of money.

3 Increase your savings.

Save, save, save—even if it means changing your lifestyle or not helping your grandchildren with tuition. The kids have a lifetime to repay their student loans, but you're running out of time. If you arrive at retirement with too little money, you're cooked.

4 Wise up on investments.

Among older people, there's a stampede to safety. Money poured out of stock-owning mutual funds after the panic of 2008-09, and into funds invested in bonds. Many older investors still don't want to take a risk in stocks.

But inflation and taxes will cut the real returns on your bonds and bond funds down to practically nothing. In your 50s and 60s—with 30 or 40 years of retirement ahead—you need to keep some money invested in stocks for long-term growth.

I don't mean individual stocks. For safety reasons, get rid of them—every single share. You have no idea what is going on inside companies, including the one you work for. Even blue chips can be laid low—look what happened to the country's leading banks. Are you holding on to individual stocks to avoid paying tax on capital gains? That tax is probably lower today than it ever will be. Bite the bullet, sell now and diversify.

As a first step, divide your nest egg into three parts:

- Money you'll need within four or five years. Keep it in a bank or a money market fund—any account that is readily accessible when the need arises.
- Money you won't have to touch for 15 years or more. Keep it in well-diversified stock index funds, which track the market as a whole rather than trying to pick individual companies. Low-cost stock index funds are offered by Vanguard and Fidelity Investments. T. Rowe Price has index funds, too, but they cost a little more.
- In-between money. Keep it in bond mutual funds. When interest rates rise (as most people expect to

happen in coming years), the value of bond fund shares will fall. But managers will be snapping up those new, higher-interest bonds, so the income from your fund will rise. When rates fall again, in the next recession, the value of your shares will go back up. If you reinvested your dividends, you'll have more shares working for you, too.

5 Keep your job, if possible.

Or get one, if you've already retired. Every extra year of work improves your Social Security benefit, increases your savings (assuming you save) and reduces the number of years that your nest egg has to last. It might bring you health insurance, too. Public schools, hospitals and government agencies offer benefits. Some private companies—including Costco, Home Depot and Wal-Mart—give benefits even to part-timers (usually with a waiting period).

6 Do whatever you can to keep health insurance.

If your company offers retiree coverage, don't even think of moving to another city or state until you find out if you can take your coverage with you. Most plans won't follow you or will charge you more at a new location.

If you need individual coverage, check with local health insurance agents who can round up plans suitable for you (you can find an agent through the National Association of Health Underwriters). For the lowest premium, pick a policy with a high deductible. You may pay more out of pocket if you become sick, but you're protected from catastrophic, bankruptcy-inducing costs. Once you have signed up, you're in the insurer's PPO network, which gives you discounts of up to 50 percent or so, even on bills you pay yourself.

Health care reform would be helpful for those not yet in Medicare. Any new law is likely to bar rejection for preexisting conditions (at my age, life is a preexisting condition) and provide faster access to generic drugs and subsidies to help cover costs. Those on Medicare will likely see the "doughnut hole"—which requires them to pay some Medicare Part D costs—close over the next few years.

7 Be smart about Social Security.

Draw from your 401(k) or IRA first, and claim Social Security benefits later. If you can wait until 70, your check will be about 76 percent higher than if you had started at 62, and will improve the protection for your spouse as well.

8 Be smart about retirement funds, too.

If you're with a large employer, consider leaving your 401(k) money in your company plan, provided that it offers flexible withdrawal options. Your money will be managed at a much lower cost than you'll find elsewhere, and the funds have been chosen carefully for people in your situation. If you have a traditional pension and take it as a lump sum, don't hand it to a broker or planner who wants to sell you products. Choose index funds yourself or work with a fee-only financial planner (see below).

9 Put off reverse mortgages.

When you turn 62, salespeople come out in force, urging you to strip the equity out of your home to support your spending now. Don't do it. The fees and effective interest rates are high, and the proceeds are low. Save the reverse mortgage option for your late 70s or early 80s, when other money might be running low. AARP has tons of good information at www.aarp.org/money/personal/reverse_mortgages/.

10 Annuities.

When you're retired, there's nothing like receiving a regular check. One way to get it is with an immediate annuity. You take a sum of money and use it to buy an income for life. Your state of health doesn't matter. The fixed payments are based entirely on your age and the type of benefit you want (for cost comparisons, see www.immediateannuities.com). But fixed payments will be whittled away by inflation, so don't buy an annuity too early. Buy in your late 70s or early 80s, when they won't have to last as long.

Stay away from the fancy, tax-deferred annuities that make big promises about future income benefits. They're too complicated to dissect here, so I'll say only that the cost is much higher than you think and the odds are good that they won't perform as you expect. My personal rule is, "if it's complicated, forget it." Deferred annuities with income benefits fit that bill.

11 Work with a financial planner.

Planners are very helpful in working with budgets and projecting how much you can afford to spend when you retire. But work with fee-only planners, who don't sell products and who charge only for their advice. Planners who take commissions on products could steer you wrong (for example, by selling you those awful, complex annuities). Three places to find a fee-only planner near you: GarrettPlanningNetwork.com, the Alliance of Cambridge Advisors (CambridgeAdvisors.com), and the National Association of Personal Financial Advisors (www.napfa.org).

12 Move in with your kids.

The last resort, if all else fails. That should be motivation enough to get moving on your own plan for financial success.

Critical Thinking

1. Why is it unwise to take a reverse mortgage on your house at 62?

2. When retired, what is the advantage of keeping a large share of your money invested in stocks rather than in bonds?

3. Why is it wise, if you retire from a large employer who has your retirement money in a 401K plan, to leave it in the plan rather than drawing it out and reinvesting?

JANE BRYANT QUINN is a financial columnist and the author of *Making the Most of Your Money Now.*

Top 25 Social Security Questions

Confused about when to claim or whether you're eligible for benefits? We have answers.

STAN HINDEN

H ere are the most frequently asked questions about Social Security that AARP has received from you.

1. **I am about to turn 62 and plan to file for Social Security. How do I get started?**
   You should apply three months before you want to start collecting. Sign up online or call 1-800-772-1213. Here are some documents you may have to produce: your Social Security card or a record of the number; your birth certificate; proof of U.S. citizenship or lawful alien status; military discharge papers if you served before 1968; and last year's W-2 tax form or tax return if you're self-employed.

2. **How is my Social Security benefit calculated?**
   Benefits are based on the amount of money you earned during your lifetime—with an emphasis on the 35 years in which you earned the most. Plus, lower-paid workers get a bigger percentage of their preretirement income than higher-paid workers. In 2010, the average monthly benefit for retirees is $1,172.

3. **If I remarry, can I still collect Social Security benefits based on my deceased first husband's record?**
   You can—subject to several rules. In general, you cannot receive survivor benefits if you remarry before age 60 unless that marriage ends, too, whether by annulment, divorce or death of your new husband. If you remarry after age 60 (50 if disabled), you can still collect benefits on your former spouse's record. After you reach 62, you may get retirement benefits on the record of your new spouse if they are higher.

4. **Why won't retirees get a cost-of-living adjustment for 2011? Many of us count on this for food, medicine and other bills.**
   COLAs are based on the consumer price index, which tracks inflation. Because inflation has been flat, according to the CPI, there will be no benefit increase—for the second year in a row. AARP is calling on Congress to provide beneficiaries with financial relief.

5. **I am 56 and receive Social Security disability benefits. At what point will I switch to regular Social Security? Will the monthly amount change?**
   When you reach full retirement age, your disability benefits will automatically convert to retirement benefits. The amount will remain the same.

6. **My friend died at 66. She worked full time and had not applied for benefits. What happens to the money she contributed to Social Security? Can her children claim benefits?**
   The money people contribute goes into a fund from which benefits are paid to eligible workers and their families. These include a widower, a surviving divorced husband, dependent parents, disabled children, and children if they have not aged out.

7. **My husband and I are getting a divorce. He wants the settlement agreement to say I will not get his Social Security benefits. Can he do that?**
   No, he has no control over your future benefits. You can qualify for a divorced spouse's benefits if you were married at least 10 years, are now unmarried, are 62 or older, and if any benefit from your own work record would be less than the divorced spouse's benefit.

8. **Cleaning out my mother's home after her death, we found Social Security checks from the 1980s. Can we cash them?**
   No. The checks are negotiable for only 12 months after issue.

9. **My man and I have lived together for over seven years. If he dies, can I collect his Social Security benefits?**
   If your state recognizes your common-law marriage, then you'll likely be eligible for survivor benefits. But you'll have to provide evidence that includes sworn statements, mortgage or rent receipts, or insurance policies.

10. **Do my Social Security contributions go into a personal retirement account for me and earn interest?**

Although many people think so, the answer is no. Social Security operates under a pay-as-you-go system, which means that today's workers pay for current retirees and other beneficiaries. Workers pay 6.2 percent of their wages up to a cap of $106,800; employers pay the same. The money that younger people contribute will pay for our benefits when we retire.

11. **How much money does the U.S. government owe to the Social Security trust fund, and will it be repaid?**

To prepare for the boomers' retirement, Social Security has collected more in taxes than it pays in benefits. Surplus funds go into the trust fund and are invested in U.S.-guaranteed Treasury bonds. In 2009, the trust fund held $2.5 trillion in bonds and earned 4.9 percent in interest. These bonds are just as real as U.S. Treasury bonds held by mutual funds or foreign banks. Ultimately, it's up to the American people to ensure the government keeps its promise to retirees, just as it would to other investors.

12. **I have a pension from the Army. Will that affect my Social Security benefits?**

It will not. You can get both your Social Security benefits and your military pension. If you served in the military before 1957, you did not pay Social Security taxes, but you will receive special credit for some of that service. Special credits also are available to people who served from 1957 to 1967 and from 1968 to 2001.

13. **I didn't work enough to qualify for Social Security. My husband gets it, but he is ill and may not live much longer. Will I be able to collect benefits?**

Yes, but your benefit will depend on your age and situation: If you are at full retirement age or older, you'll get 100 percent of your deceased husband's benefit. A widow or widower between 60 and full retirement age receives a reduced benefit.

14. **Is it true that some people are collecting Social Security benefits who never paid into the system?**

Social Security is an earned benefit. In order to collect a retirement benefit, a worker must pay into the system for at least 10 years. In some cases, nonworking family members, such as a spouse, may be eligible for benefits based on the worker's record. Tough rules in place assure that only legal residents can collect Social Security benefits.

15. **I filed for Chapter 13 bankruptcy after being laid off. Do Social Security benefits count as income in bankruptcy, or are they protected?**

Your benefits are protected. Social Security is excluded from the calculation of disposable income when setting up a debtor repayment plan.

16. **My husband died recently. Can I choose between my own benefit and that as a widow? Can I collect both?**

Eligibility for a widow's benefit begins at age 60, or 50 if you are disabled. If you are full retirement age, your survivor benefit will be 100 percent of his benefit; if you take it early, the amount will be reduced. You can switch to your own benefit as early as 62. In any event, you can only get one benefit, whichever is higher.

17. **I began drawing Social Security at age 62 in 2006, but I'm still working. Since I'm still paying Social Security taxes, will my benefits increase?**

If your latest work years are among your highest-earning years, the SSA refigures your benefit and pays you any increase due. This is automatic, with new benefits starting in December of the following year.

18. **My wife is 62 and collects Social Security based on her own work record. Can she receive spousal benefits based on my record when I retire in a few years?**

If she is eligible for both benefits, yours and hers, Social Security will pay her own benefits first. If she is due additional benefits, she will get a combination of benefits equaling the higher spouse's benefit.

19. **Why would changes in Social Security be considered as a way to help balance the federal budget?**

Some policymakers say all spending, including Social Security, should be cut. Social Security has not contributed to the deficit. In fact, the trust fund is projected to reach $4.3 trillion by 2023. AARP believes that Social Security benefits should not be targeted to reduce the deficit.

20. **If I retire to a foreign country, can I have my Social Security benefits sent there?**

If you are a U.S. citizen, you may receive your benefits in most foreign countries, usually by check or direct deposit. If you are not a U.S. citizen, the answer is more complicated, with certain rules applying to certain countries. For specifics, see the Social Security publication "Your Payments While You Are Outside the United States."

21. **I started collecting Social Security at 62. I heard that if I changed my mind, I could pay back the amount I'd collected and get a higher payment. Is that possible?**

Yes, but the sum you'd be paying back may be quite large, perhaps prohibitive. You must repay all benefits that you and your family received, plus any money withheld from your checks for Medicare Parts B, C and D; also, any tax withheld. For specifics, you'll need to contact Social Security.

22. **Can I collect Social Security and unemployment compensation at the same time?**

Yes. Unemployment benefits aren't counted as wages under Social Security's annual earnings test, so you'd still receive your benefit. However, the amount of your unemployment benefit could be cut if you receive a pension or other retirement income, including Social Security and railroad retirement benefits. Contact your state unemployment office for information on whether your state applies a reduction.

23. **I am 63 and collecting Social Security. If I work, will my benefit be cut?**

It depends on your income. Between age 62 and the start of the year when you reach full retirement age, $1 in benefits is withheld for every $2 you earn above a limit, which is $14,160 in 2010. In the year you reach full retirement age, $1 is withheld for every $3 above another limit, $37,680 in 2010. In your birthday month, the limits go away—and your benefit will be recalculated upward to compensate for the money that was withheld.

24. **I'm 50. Will Social Security be there when I retire?**

    The Social Security trust fund, where accumulated assets are held, currently contains about $2.5 trillion. According to the system's board of trustees, that money and continuing tax contributions will allow payment of all benefits at current rates until 2037. After that, there still will be enough tax revenue coming in to pay about 78 percent of benefits. Congress is being urged to make financial fixes to Social Security to ensure it will be there for you.

25. **I know I can start collecting Social Security at age 62. But should I?**

    That depends. If you're healthy and can afford it, you should consider waiting until you reach your full retirement age of 66, or even 70. Here's why. By law, the age when workers can qualify for full benefits is gradually increasing, from 65 to 67. (It will be 67 for anyone born after 1960.) If you claim benefits before reaching full retirement age, they'll be reduced. That's because the goal set by Congress is to pay the same lifetime benefits to an individual regardless of when they're initially claimed. So let's say you claim benefits at age 62 and get $1,000 a month. If you can wait until you're 66, you'll get at least 33 percent more ($1,333). And if you can wait until you're 70, you'll get at least 75 percent more ($1,750). Social Security determines the amount of your benefits based, in part, on your highest 35 years of earnings. So you may get a larger monthly benefit if your extra years of work are your top earning years.

Critical Thinking

1. Should the surplus of funds in the social security account be used by the federal government to reduce the deficit and balance the budget?

2. Can a person receive a social security and an unemployment check at the same time?

3. Is it possible for a wife to receive her husband's social security benefits after his death?

STAN HINDEN is a retired Washington Post financial writer and author of How to Retire Happy: The 12 Most Important Decisions You Must Make Before You Retire.

Paying for Retirement: Sex Differences in Inclusion in Employer-Provided Retirement Plans

ROSEMARY WRIGHT

As the oldest of the Baby Boom cohort in the United States reaches age 65 in a time of economic uncertainty, the amount and the security of retirement income are of critical interest to workers, employers, and scholars. More than 70 million people were born between 1946 and 1964 (Rogerson & Kim, 2005). The availability of private retirement income to this large cohort has a major impact at the policy level, including in the evaluation of the long-term viability of Social Security, the provision of government benefits for health and long-term care, and tax policy (Butrica, Murphy, & Zedlewski, 2010; Johnson, Uccello, & Goldwyn, 2005). Additionally, the availability of retirement income drives important life decisions for individuals, such as how long to work, how to prepare for financial contingencies in later life, and estate planning (Cahill, Giandrea, & Quinn, 2006; Johnson, 2009). These issues are especially important for women who, despite lengthening life spans for both men and women, are likely to outlive men and therefore are likely to have a longer period of retirement to finance than men.

The current study applied the theoretical frameworks of two 1995 studies of pension benefits and retirement income of retirees (DeViney, 1995; DeViney & Solomon, 1995) to a study of availability of employer retirement benefits to a sample of Baby Boom workers. The 1995 studies used independent variables that can be clustered into three theory types: structural theories, individual-level theories, and the life course perspective. The current study applied the same three theory types and used variables that were the same or proxies for most of the variables in the 1995 studies. The goals were (a) to determine if there are sex differences in employer retirement benefit availability within the Baby Boom cohort, (b) to determine if the three theory types are valuable as predictors of employer retirement benefit availability for the Baby Boom cohort, and (c) to examine the differences between the sample of retirees from the 1995 studies and the Baby Boom sample used in the current study in order to determine if there have been changes in availability of employer retirement benefits and changes in the

impact of predictor variables since the time of retirement of the older cohort. In addition, three new variables were added to examine the impact of significant social and economic changes since the 1995 studies: immigrant status, government employment, and the presence of young children in the worker's home.

Employer-provided retirement plans are a key component of private retirement income. Originally, these plans were defined benefit plans, in which the employer funds and manages a plan that guarantees a specified payment to participants upon retirement. In the late 1970s, tax code changes allowed the development of defined contribution plans, individual retirement plans that define the amount of contribution but do not guarantee the amount of the benefit (Beckmann, 2006). These are often funded and managed by the worker, so were embraced by employers as a way to provide a valuable benefit to more workers at lower cost. In 2010, only 20% of workers in the private sector were eligible for defined benefit plans but 59% were eligible for defined contribution plans (Bureau of Labor Statistics [BLS], 2010). However, often neither type of plan is offered in certain service-providing industries, in small firms, to part-time workers, or to workers in lower paid jobs (BLS, 2010; Costo, 2006). The National Retirement Risk Index projects that half the households in the United States will not have enough retirement income to support their preretirement standard of living (Munnell, Webb, & Golub-Sass, 2009).

Three Theory Types

Structural theories attribute differences in income to work structures that are external to and uncontrollable by the worker. Dual economy models divide industries into core and periphery sectors, which differ by size, centrality to a national economy, capital access, cost structure, organizational structure complexity, and type of business (Averitt, 1968; Beck, Horan, & Tolbert, 1978; Fields, 2007). Labor market segmentation models divide occupations into primary and secondary segments, which differ by level of education and skill required, wage and benefit levels, working conditions, and job stability (Doeringer

& Piore, 1975; Hudson, 2007; Kalleberg & Sorensen, 1979). In both these structural models, there is a relationship between sex and worker position. Both marriage and parenthood can have an impact on a worker's industry or occupation. Because women often have responsibility for child care, domestic labor, and caregiving, they may have delays and interruptions in education and careers and as a result are more likely than men to be employed in secondary segment jobs in periphery industries with less access to retirement benefits.

Individual-level theories relate income to factors that the individual can control. Human capital theory suggests that a worker's investment in education, training, or accumulation of work experience will lead to an improvement in income or benefits (Becker, 1962; Ben-Porath, 1967; Schultz, 1961). Rational choice theory predicts that people will act rationally to optimally satisfy their preferences (Zafirovski, 1999). If the individual has complete information about a work or personal choice, a decision will lead to the best outcome, but in the absence of complete information, risk must be estimated (Aguiar & de Francisco, 2009). Life course events have an impact on the ability to accumulate human capital as well as on the risk associated with a choice. For example, the decision to have children may require a calculation of the risk to a career and future earnings. Because of sex differences in the likely outcomes of decisions such as these, the risk level is different for men and women.

The life course perspective allows for the consideration of social, cultural, and historical contexts in which people live. This perspective focuses on the events, transitions, and trajectories of a life (George, 1993; Hatch, 2000; Hogan, 1978), and within this framework, many factors differentiated by sex emerge. Transitions are tied to age and event sequences that are socially or culturally expected, such as marriage, parenthood, and retirement (George, 1993; Hatch, 2000). Interruptions in a sequence may occur due to unpredictable events such as war or an economic depression (George, 1993; Moen & Orrange, 2002). Life course trajectories are affected not only by events but also by social structure, including race, ethnicity, and sex, which can result in lower levels of human capital, lower earnings, and less stable employment (Angel, Jiménez, & Angel, 2007; Ferraro & Shippee, 2009). Interruptions introduce risk into the career trajectory by changing its direction and slope, and these interruptions result in inequalities that accumulate over the life course (Ferraro & Shippee, 2009). Risk is cumulative because the trajectory may not return to its original direction after each transition (Ferraro, Shippee, & Schafer, 2009; Holden & Fontes, 2009). For women, this may result in being sorted into jobs that are unlikely to provide retirement benefits: part-time jobs, nonprofessional service jobs, and jobs in secondary sector industries. However, sorting alone does not explain all sex differences in retirement coverage. If a woman is covered by any retirement plan, there is a risk that her life course will have a negative impact as a result of "invisible" gender bias in the plan, such as in rules regarding vesting, seniority rights, and continuous service (Quadagno, 1988; Richardson, 1999; Shuey & O'Rand, 2004). Additionally, although the percentage of earnings contributed to defined contribution plans may be similar between men and women, women contribute fewer dollars because their earnings are lower and as a result draw a smaller amount in retirement benefits when they retire (Calasanti, 2010).

Key Prior Studies

Two earlier studies examined sex differences among retired workers in the receipt of non-Social Security retirement benefits (DeViney, 1995) and in the level of retirement income (DeViney & Solomon, 1995). These studies used data from the 1982 Social Security Administration Master Beneficiary Record of benefit recipients from mid-1980 to mid-1981, with the youngest retirees born close to the First World War. Both studies examined structural, individual, and life course variables as possible predictors of outcomes. The first study found that women were much less likely than men to receive retirement plan payments (DeViney, 1995). Variables that increased the odds of receiving retirement plan payments were core industry employment, educational level, and on-the-job experience. Variables that reduced the odds of receiving retirement benefits included marital status and children. Although children reduced the odds of receiving a retirement benefit for both men and women, marital status had a different effect for men and women. A continuous marriage increased the odds of receiving retirement benefits for men but reduced the odds for women.

The second study examined the relationship of the same variables to income from all sources for the respondent and the respondent's spouse (DeViney & Solomon, 1995). This study found that women retirees received significantly less income than men. Educational level had the greatest impact on retirement income for both sexes and marital status had the second largest impact. For men, current marital status was the most important predictor: Men who were divorced or widowed received lower retirement income than those who were married. However, continuous marriage to the same person had the greatest positive effect on women's retirement income.

The 1995 studies used samples of respondents the youngest of whom would have been born around the time of the First World War. This universe of retirees is a much smaller group than the cohort of workers born from 1946 through 1964. Longer life spans for this large newer cohort will mean a longer period of retirement to fund, especially for women who still generally live longer than men. Work, social, and economic environments for this group of workers are much different than for the retirees in the earlier studies: there are more women in the workforce, workers have more education, industrial employment has been dramatically reduced, and technology has emerged as a powerful engine of economic growth. This study used the theoretical frameworks of the 1995 studies to assess their impact on retirement plan inclusion today for workers born during the Baby Boom as well as on sex differences in retirement plan inclusion. There were two primary research questions: Are there significant sex differences in the likelihood of (a) working for an employer who has a retirement plan and (b) inclusion in the employer's retirement plan? Additionally, the study examined whether these frameworks were useful predictors of employer retirement plan availability and inclusion for Baby Boom workers and how these results compared with the 1995 studies.

Methods
Data and Sample

The data set used in this study is the Current Population Survey (CPS) 2009 Annual Social and Economic Supplement conducted by the United States Bureau of the Census for the Bureau of Labor Statistics (United States Department of Labor, 2002). The CPS provides monthly labor force data as well as supplemental data on work experience, income and benefits, and migration. Because the population of interest for this study is workers in the Baby Boom cohort, the sample has been restricted to respondents born in years 1946 through and including 1964 who self-identify as working for pay full time for the full year. The full sample for this study consists of 23,423 full-time full-year workers (see Table 1 for complete analysis). Workers in this sample whose employers had a retirement plan were selected for the analysis of the likelihood of being included in that plan. This group comprises 15,819 full-time full-year workers.

Table 1   Descriptive Statistics for Respondents' Characteristics

	Full sample (N = 23,423)	Male (n = 12,514)	Female (n = 10,909)
Likelihood of employer having a retirement plan			
% Minority	22.09	21.74	22.48
Age in years (mean)	52.33	52.33	52.34
% Employed in core industry	22.00	32.00	11.00
% Employed in primary occupational sector	58.85	64.77	52.12
% Employed in female-predominant occupations	46.00	21.29	74.47
Educational level			
Less than high school (%)	7.50	9.00	5.80
High school diploma (%)	30.60	31.00	30.20
Some college (%)	29.10	27.40	31.10
4-Year college degree (%)	20.40	20.40	20.40
Graduate degree (%)	12.40	12.20	12.70
% With children under 18	26.36	29.52	22.77
% Married	69.44	75.60	62.44
% Ever married	21.07	15.43	27.47
% Never married	9.49	8.97	10.08
% Children under six	4.90	5.81	3.87
% Immigrant	13.59	14.70	12.34
% Government worker	20.48%	17.26%	24.14%

	Full sample (N = 15,819)	Male (n = 8,322)	Female (n = 7,497)
Likelihood of respondent being included in employer retirement plan			
% Minority	18.85	18.31	19.44
Age in years (mean)	52.37	52.33	52.42
% Employed in core industry	21.00	31.00	10.00
% Employed in primary occupational sector	63.04	68.90	56.68
% Employed in female-predominant occupations	47.89	22.86	75.01
Educational level			
Less than high school (%)	4.40	5.30	3.30
High school diploma (%)	29.20	29.70	28.70
Some college (%)	29.90	28.40	31.50
4-Year college degree (%)	21.70	22.00	21.40
Graduate degree (%)	14.80	14.50	15.10
% With children under 18	25.10	28.50	21.30
% Married	70.51	77.25	63.21
% Ever married	20.57	14.68	26.94
% Never married	4.46	8.07	9.84
% Children under 6	4.46	5.32	3.53
% Immigrant	9.29	9.73	8.82
% Government worker	27.32	23.66	31.28

Dependent Variables

The first dependent variable is a binary variable in which 1 represents the respondent's employer having a retirement plan. This variable determines whether respondents are sorted into the next sample: The respondent is included in the next analysis only if the employer offers a retirement plan. The second dependent variable is a binary variable in which 1 represents the respondent's inclusion in the employer's plan.

Independent Variables

Because a different data set was used for the 1995 studies, the variables available in the CPS are in some cases not exact matches. As a result, most of the independent variables for this study were chosen to approximate as closely as possible those used by the prior studies.

The primary independent variable of interest in this study is sex (1 = *female*). In addition to sex, two control variables are included. Minority status is a binary variable (1 = *minority*) that is created from race and ethnicity variables in the CPS and sorted into minority and nonminority groups by mean annual earnings using a post hoc Scheffé analysis. This analysis showed no significant difference in mean annual earnings between White and Asian respondents but a significant difference between the income of White and Asian respondents and the earnings of all other respondents. As a result, White and Asian respondents were sorted as nonminority, and all others were sorted as minority. Age is a continuous variable ranging from age 45 to 63.

Three binary variables are used to approximate DeViney's (1995) structural theory variables. First, the industry of the respondent's last job is used to represent employment in a core industry. In the CPS, these industries are agriculture, mining, construction, and manufacturing. Industrial location is a nominal variable in the CPS. For this study, the variable was collapsed and recoded as a binary variable (1 = *core industry employment*). Second, the occupation of the respondent's last job is the variable used to represent employment in the primary occupational segment. This segment includes jobs that have high skill and education requirements, such as management, technical, professional, and highly skilled labor positions. Occupational location is a nominal variable in the CPS. This variable was collapsed and recoded as a binary variable (1 = *primary occupational segment employment*). Finally, a variable representing occupational sex segregation (OSS) is used to identify whether the respondent works in a job with overrepresentation of women. OSS is an index variable with values ranging from 0 to 2.00. A value of 1 indicates equal representation of men and women in an occupation. A score lower than 1 indicates an overrepresentation of men in the occupation and a score higher than 1 indicates an overrepresentation of women in the occupation. This variable was recoded into a binary variable (1 = OSS > 1).

Educational level is used to represent human capital investment. In the CPS, educational attainment is captured as an ordinal-level variable with 16 levels. For this study, the education variable was recoded into a five-level ordinal variable with levels representing less than high school, high school graduate, some college, bachelor's level college degree, and graduate-level college degree.

Variables representing life course factors in this study are marital status and children under 18 years of age. Marital status was recoded from a seven-level nominal variable into a three-level nominal variable representing never married, married, and ever married. Ever married includes respondents who are widowed, divorced, or separated. These three levels were recoded into three binary variables (1 = *never married, married, ever married*). The presence of children under 18 years old is represented in the CPS by a continuous variable representing the number of related persons in the household who are under 18 years of age. This variable was recoded into a binary variable (1 = *presence of children under 18*).

Three variables were added for exploratory purposes to represent significant social and economic changes since the 1995 studies. First, a binary variable representing children in the household under 6 years of age (1 = *presence of children under 6*) is included to capture any effect of later-in-life marriage and child rearing or grandparents raising grandchildren (National Center for Health Statistics, 2009; Simmons & Dye, 2003). Second, because of the large increase in immigration into the United States in the last 20 years (Gibson & Jung, 2006), a binary variable representing immigration status (1 = *not born in the United States*) is included to determine any effects on access to retirement plans for workers not born in the United States. Finally, because of the shift in union membership from industrial workers to public employees (United States Bureau of Labor Statistics, 2010), a binary variable representing status as a government employee (1 = *government worker*) is included.

Design and Statistical Analyses

This study is a secondary data analysis of cross-sectional data from the 2009 CPS. Standard weights are provided within the CPS, but relative weights were calculated and imposed in order to ensure that the sample size and distribution remained consistent with the target population. The relative weight was calculated by dividing the standard weight by its mean. The Statistical Package for Social Sciences software (version 17.0) was used to perform the statistical analyses.

Preliminary chi-square tests were performed to establish whether relationships exist between sex and (a) whether an employer provides a retirement plan and (b) whether the respondent is included in the retirement plan (Tables 2 and 3).

Table 2　Employer Provides Retirement Plan

	Female	Male	Total
No (%)	31.60	34.80	
Yes (%)	68.40	65.20	
n	12,462	10,961	23,423

Note. chi-square = 27.219, *df* = 1, *p* < .001.

Table 3 Respondent Included in Employer Retirement Plan

	Female	Male	Total
No (%)	8.90	7.60	
Yes (%)	91.10	92.40	
n	7,501	8,127	15,628

Note. chi-square = 9.096, $df = 1$, $p < .01$.

Because the dependent variables are binary in nature (employer has a retirement plan or not and inclusion in a retirement plan or not), logistic regression was used with both the full sample and with men and women separately to test how well the independent variables predicted the likelihood of the employer having a retirement plan and, if the employer provided a plan, the likelihood of the respondent being included (Tables 4 and 5). A z statistic was calculated to determine whether significant differences exist between men and women respondents in the regression results. The assumption of independence of observations was tested and met. No outliers were found.

Results
Respondent Characteristics

Descriptive statistics for the samples are provided in Table 1. Of the full sample of 23,423 workers, 53.4% are men and 46.8% are women; 15,819 workers, about 67% of the full sample, worked for employers who provided a retirement plan. Of the second sample, 52.6% are men and 47.4% are women. The average age of men and women in both samples is about 52 years.

Likelihood of Working for Employer With a Retirement Plan

A preliminary chi-square analysis (Tables 2 and 3) found that more than two thirds of women respondents worked for an employer with a retirement plan. This is a higher proportion than for men, and this difference is significant. Logistic regressions for the employer having a retirement plan were conducted for the full sample and for men and women separately. There was a significant positive relationship between being a woman and working for an employer who has a retirement plan (Table 4). Overall, women were 1.1 times more likely than men to work for an employer with a retirement plan. However,

Table 4 Logistic Regression for Respondent's Employer Having a Retirement Plan

Variables	Full sample[a]			Male[b]			Female[c]			
	B	SE	Odds ratio	B	SE	Odds ratio	B	SE	Odds ratio	z[d]
Control variables										
Female	0.097**	0.036	1.101							
Minority	−0.258***	0.038	0.772	−0.172**	0.053	0.842	−0.354***	0.054	0.702	2.405*
Age	−0.008**	0.003	0.992	−0.018***	0.004	0.982	0.000	0.005	1.000	—
Structural factors variables										
Core industry	0.202***	0.038	1.224	0.246***	0.046	1.279	0.158**	0.069	1.171	1.061
Primary occupational sector	0.229***	0.032	1.250	0.191***	0.044	1.211	0.280***	0.047	1.323	−1.382
Occupational sex segregation	0.062	0.036	1.040	0.142**	0.053	1.152	−0.012	0.051	0.988	—
Individual factors variable										
Educational level	0.202***	0.015	1.224	0.232***	0.020	1.261	0.159***	0.023	1.173	2.395*
Life course variables										
Children under 18	−0.198***	0.038	0.820	−0.191***	0.052	0.827	−0.249***	0.058	0.779	0.745
Married	0.224	0.051	1.252	0.397***	0.072	1.488	0.042	0.075	1.042	—
Ever married	0.080	0.057	1.083	0.129	0.082	1.137	−0.004	0.080	0.996	—
New variables										
Children under 6	0.099	0.073	1.104	0.065	0.093	1.067	0.148	0.119	1.159	—
Immigrant	−0.783***	0.043	0.457	−0.856***	0.058	0.425	−0.712***	0.064	0.491	−1.667
Government worker	1.525***	0.050	4.595	1.631***	0.076	5.111	1.454***	0.068	4.280	1.736
Constant	0.121	0.174	1.129	0.388	0.234	1.475	0.092	0.261	1.097	—

Note. Omnibus model $\chi^2_{\text{full sample}}(13) = 2662.22$, $p < .001$; omnibus model $\chi^2_{\text{male}}(12) = 1490.94$, $p < .001$; omnibus model omnibus model $\chi^2_{\text{female sample}}(12) = 1192.10$.
[a]Full sample $N = 23,423$.
[b]Male $N = 12,514$.
[c]Female $N = 10,909$.
[d]z calculated between significant male and female B.
*$p < .05$. **$p < .01$. ***$p < .001$.

Table 5 Logistic Regression for Respondent Being Included in Employer Retirement Plan

Variables	Full sample[a]			Male[b]			Female[c]			z[d]
	B	SE	Odds ratio	B	SE	Odds ratio	B	SE	Odds ratio	
Control variables										
Female	−0.057	0.071	0.945							
Minority	−0.312***	0.073	0.732	−0.350***	0.106	0.704	−0.275**	0.102	0.760	−0.510
Age	0.018**	0.006	0.005	0.003	0.009	1.003	0.028**	0.009	1.029	—
Structural factors										
Core industry	0.413***	0.081	1.511	0.337**	0.099	1.401	0.525***	0.146	1.690	−1.066
Primary occupational sector	0.214**	0.064	1.238	0.281**	0.093	1.325	0.152	0.091	1.165	—
Occupational sex segregation	0.002	0.072	1.002	0.045	0.110	1.046	−0.003	0.097	0.997	—
Individual factors										
Educational level	0.278***	0.031	1.320	0.254***	0.044	1.289	0.296***	0.046	1.345	−0.660
Life course factors										
Children under 18	0.051	0.082	1.052	0.070	0.118	1.073	−0.030	0.114	0.970	—
Married	0.484***	0.097	1.623	0.577***	0.144	1.780	0.412**	0.132	1.510	0.845
Ever married	−0.027	0.103	0.974	−0.163	0.155	0.850	0.047	0.139	1.048	—
New variables										
Children under 6	−0.062	0.152	0.940	−0.264	0.196	0.768	0.208	0.242	1.231	—
Immigrant	−0.122	0.098	0.886	−0.175	0.137	0.840	−0.055	0.141	0.946	—
Government worker	1.123***	0.093	3.074	0.929***	0.134	2.532	1.293***	0.129	3.644	−1.957*
Constant	0.028	0.349	1.028	0.852	0.498	2.345	−0.626	0.490	0.535	—

Note. Omnibus model $\chi^2_{\text{full sample}}(13) = 519.42$, $p < .001$; omnibus model $\chi^2_{\text{male}}(13) = 239.56$, $p < .001$; omnibus model $\chi^2_{\text{female sample}}(13) = 1192.10$, $p = .001$.
[a]Full sample $N = 15,819$.
[b]Male $N = 8,322$.
[c]Female $N = 7,497$.
[d]z calculated between significant male and female B.
*$p < .05$. **$p < .01$. ***$p < .001$.

minority women and currently married women were significantly less likely to work for an employer with a retirement plan than their male counterparts. Minority status had a significant negative impact on the likelihood of working for an employer with a retirement plan for the full sample and for men and women separately, with the overall odds being about three fourths the odds for nonminorities.

Both core industry and primary occupational sector employment were significant positive predictors of the employer having a retirement plan for the full sample and for men and women separately, with workers in these segments being more than 1.2 times as likely as workers not in these segments to work for an employer with a retirement plan. OSS was found to be a significant positive predictor of the employer having a retirement plan for men but not for women.

Educational level was a significant positive predictor of the employer having a retirement plan for the full sample and for both men and women. The likelihood of working for an employer with a retirement plan increased by almost 1.3 times for men and almost 1.2 times for women for each additional level of educational attainment. Because educational attainment often functions as a gateway to better jobs and higher

pay, especially within human capital theory, the relationship between education and minority status, core industry employment, primary occupational sector employment, immigrant status, and government worker status was also examined for differences between binary segments (both 1 and 0). Although educational level was a significant predictor of working for an employer with a retirement plan in all five variables, government worker status was the only variable among the five for which there was no significant difference between workers in both binary segments in the impact of educational attainment upon working for an employer with a retirement plan (see Tables 6 and 7). Educational attainment gave the biggest boost to minorities, with an odds ratio (OR) of 1.35 of working for an employer with a retirement plan compared with 1.19 for nonminorities, and to foreign-born respondents, with an odds ratio of 1.34 compared with 1.20 for non–foreign-born respondents.

Children under the age of 18 years had a significant negative impact, with the overall odds of working for an employer with a retirement plan for the full sample and for men with children under 18 about 80% of their counterparts without younger children. For women, the odds are even lower. Being currently married had a significant impact on the likelihood of working

Table 6 Logistic Regression for Respondent's Employer Having a Retirement Plan (Education × Selected Variables)

Selected variables	B_0	SE	Odds ratio	B_1	SE	Odds ratio	z
Minority[a]	0.174***	0.017	1.190	0.303***	0.031	1.354	−3.649***
Core industry[b]	0.179***	0.017	1.196	0.259***	0.031	1.295	−2.263*
Primary occupational sector[c]	0.104***	0.024	1.109	0.252***	0.019	1.287	1.146
Immigrant[d]	0.181***	0.016	1.199	0.294***	0.034	1.342	−4.835***
Government worker[e]	0.213***	0.016	1.238	0.155**	0.048	1.168	−3.007**

[a]1 = minority, 0 = nonminority.
[b]1 = employed in core industry, 0 = not employed in core industry.
[c]1 = employed in primary occupational sector, 0 = not employed in primary occupational sector.
[d]1 = foreign born, 0 = not = foreign born.
[e]1 = employed by a government, 0 = not employed by a government.
*p < .05. **p < .01. ***p < .001.

Table 7 Logistic Regression for Respondent Being Included in Employer Retirement Plan (Education × Selected Variables)

Selected variables	B_0	SE	Odds ratio	B_1	SE	Odds ratio	z
Minority[a]	0.279***	0.037	1.322	0.267***	0.062	1.306	0.166
Core industry[b]	0.278***	0.035	1.321	0.282***	0.074	1.326	−0.049
Primary occupational sector[c]	0.230***	0.050	1.259	0.317***	0.041	1.373	−1.345
Immigrant[d]	0.309***	0.034	1.362	0.079	0.082	1.082	2.591**
Government worker[e]	0.289***	0.034	1.335	0.208**	0.088	1.231	0.859

[a]1 = minority, 0 = nonminority.
[b]1 = employed in core industry, 0 = not employed in core industry.
[c]1 = employed in primary occupational sector, 0 = not employed in primary occupational sector.
[d]1 = foreign born, 0 = not = foreign born.
[e]1 = employed by a government, 0 = not employed by a government.
*p < .05. **p < .01. ***p < .001.

for an employer with a retirement plan for men only, with the odds being almost 1.5 times greater for married men than for nonmarried men.

Immigrant status was a significant negative predictor of working for an employer with a retirement plan for the full sample and for both men and women. In all cases, foreign-born workers were less than half as likely as non–foreign-born workers to work for an employer with a retirement plan. By contrast, government worker status was a significant positive predictor of working for an employer with a retirement plan for both the full sample and for both men and women. In all cases, government workers were more than four times as likely as nongovernment workers to work for an employer with a retirement plan.

Likelihood of Inclusion in Employer's Retirement Plan

A chi-square analysis (Tables 2 and 3) showed that, although a slightly higher proportion of women than men respondents worked for an employer with a retirement plan, a slightly smaller proportion of women were included in a plan. Logistic regressions for being included in the employer's retirement plan were conducted for the full sample and for men and women

separately. Although the logistic regression showed a slightly negative impact of being a woman on inclusion in a retirement plan, this result was not significant, and the odds were only slightly less for women than for men of inclusion (Table 5). Significant differences between men and women were found only on one variable: government worker status. This variable had the greatest positive impact on inclusion of any variable in the study, and the difference between men and women was a positive one for women. Minority status had a significant negative impact on being included in the employer's retirement plan in all cases. Age was a significant positive predictor of inclusion for the full sample and for women, but not for men.

Employment in a core industry was a significant predictor of inclusion in a retirement plan for the full sample. Women in the industrial sector were more than 1.5 times more likely than women not employed in this sector to be included in a retirement plan, and men were more than 1.4 times likely than men not employed in this sector to be included in a plan. Employment in the primary occupational sector was a significant predictor of inclusion in the full sample and for men, but not for women, although workers in this segment all have greater odds of inclusion than workers not in this segment.

Educational level was a significant predictor of inclusion in the employer's retirement plan in all groups. All workers were about 1.3 times more likely to be included in a retirement plan for every additional level of educational attainment. Again, educational attainment was examined in more detail for its impact on inclusion in an employer-provided retirement plan (see Tables 6 and 7). The same five variables were examined for a relationship between educational attainment and inclusion: minority status, core industry employment, primary occupational sector employment, immigrant status, and government worker status. In this analysis, the only variable for which educational attainment was not a significant predictor of inclusion in a retirement plan was immigrant status, with an odds ratio of inclusion for foreign-born respondents of 1.08 compared with 1.36 for those who were not foreign born. Among these five variables, only immigrant status showed a significant difference between binary segments in the impact of educational attainment on inclusion in a retirement plan.

The only life course variable to have a significant impact on the likelihood of inclusion in the employer's retirement plan was being currently married. Married men were almost 1.8 times as likely as unmarried men to be included and married women were about 1.5 times as likely as unmarried women to be included.

The only new variable to have a significant impact on respondent inclusion in an employer retirement plan was government worker status, and this was the only variable to show a significant difference between men and women. Government workers were much more likely than nongovernment workers to be included in their employer's retirement plan. Male government workers were more than 2.5 times as likely and women government workers were more than 3.5 times as likely as nongovernment workers to be included. This variable had by far the largest impact on the likelihood of a respondent being included in an employer retirement plan of any other variable in the study.

Discussion

Overall, the results of this study are good news. Results point to little difference between working women and men in the Baby Boom cohort in either working for an employer with a retirement plan or being included in the employer's retirement plan. A much larger proportion of both men and women were included in their employer's retirement plan in this study (91.1% of women and 92.4% of men) than those receiving a pension in DeViney's study (34% of women and 49% of men). This may be a result of an increase in the types of retirement plan instruments that are now available for younger workers as well as differences in the employment situations of younger men and women compared with DeViney's sample of retired workers.

Likelihood of Employer Having a Retirement Plan

Only two variables in the regression for the employer having a retirement plan showed a significant difference between men and women: minority status and educational level (Table 4). The most striking differences are those for minority workers and for

workers who are married. For minority workers, both men and women have less likelihood than nonminority workers of working for an employer with a retirement plan. Overall, this may indicate sorting of minority workers into peripheral industries or secondary occupations where employers are less likely to offer this benefit. For men, the penalty is significantly less than for women, so female minority workers may be most likely to be sorted into industries or occupations that have the least likelihood of retirement benefits. However, for minorities, the significant bump in odds of working for an employer with a retirement plan as educational attainment increases indicates access to industries or occupations for which more education means more retirement benefits.

Among married workers, men have a much higher likelihood of working for an employer with a retirement plan compared with their unmarried counterparts than women. Married women have almost even odds compared with their unmarried counterparts. These are important findings because of the different questions they raise for men and women: Are men who are married sorted into industries or occupations with better benefits because they have wives who shoulder more of the household duties which allow men more freedom for career building? Does the even likelihood for women who are married and not married reflect social changes in which women are no longer penalized for life course demands? These questions are even more interesting when looking at whether workers are included in retirement plans.

Among the variables similar to those used by DeViney, those that are most predictive of whether the respondent's employer has a retirement plan are core industry or primary occupational sector employment, educational attainment, and marital status. These results provide support for parts of all three theoretical frameworks. Of the new variables, government employment has by far the most impact on whether the employer has a retirement plan and is the most important predictor of a positive outcome of any variable in the study. Because government employment is embedded within both the industry and occupational variables of the structural framework, this result demonstrates at least part of the reason the structural theories are supported.

Likelihood of Inclusion in an Employer Retirement Plan

In the analysis of inclusion in an employer retirement plan, only one variable shows a sex difference: government worker status. In this case, women have better outcomes than men. Many occupations into which women are traditionally sorted are in the public sector: teachers and other education professionals, librarians, health care providers, and clerical occupations. Because most public employers offer retirement plans, public employment provides an almost certain avenue to retirement benefits for women in these jobs.

The study variables with significant impact on inclusion in retirement plans are minority status, core industry employment, primary occupational sector employment (except for women), educational attainment, marital status, and government employment. Again, these results provide partial support for the three theoretical frameworks. Minority status reduced the likelihood of being included in the employer's pension plan for both men and women compared with nonminority workers. In DeViney's study, minority status had a negative impact on the receipt of pension benefits for men only. The result in the current study may reflect changes in economic structure or social conditions since the retirement of workers in DeViney's sample that have resulted in minority women becoming more disadvantaged with regard to retirement benefits.

Core industry employment, while a significant predictor of inclusion in the current study, is less important than it was for DeViney's respondents, for whom it was the most important predictor of the receipt of a private pension. The decline in employment and in union membership in core industries since the retirement of DeViney's respondents likely explains part of this difference. Educational attainment is much more important as a predictor variable in this study than for DeViney's study, which presumably reflects higher educational attainment among the younger group of respondents in this study compared with the older retired workers in the earlier study.

In the current study, being married has a significant positive impact on the likelihood of being included in a retirement plan for both men and women, although the impact for men is slightly higher than for women in comparison to their nonmarried counterparts. In DeViney's study, only men had a positive outcome on this variable. Additionally, DeViney's study found a significant negative impact on pension receipt of having children for both men and women. However, none of the results related to children and inclusion in the current study were significant. The results in the current study may indicate social changes that have accepted women in the workforce and pursuing careers since the time of the DeViney's study. However, there may be differences in inclusion based upon the number of children rather than just the presence of children. It seems likely that a larger number of children might have an impact on the ability of the worker, especially a woman worker, to maintain either full-time full-year employment or certain types of employment which are most likely to provide retirement plans. It would be interesting to determine whether the number of children is a differentiating variable for men and women for retirement plan inclusion.

Finally, in the current study, government employment has by far the greatest impact on inclusion in a retirement plan of any variable. Government employment was not examined in the DeViney's study, so no direct comparison can be made. However, the size of impact of this variable indicates that the model of structural, individual, and life course factors as predictors of retirement benefits is incomplete without including a variable that explicitly represents government employment, even if aspects of government employment are embedded within other variables.

Are the Three Theoretical Frameworks Relevant to Baby Boom Retirement?

The underlying assumptions of many structural theories have been weakened by economic transitions in the United States. Economic changes in this country since Averitt's (1968) definition of a dual industrial economy have had a dramatic impact

on what industries are "core" to the economy. Many industries considered to be the backbone of the economy have shrunk or disappeared as major employers, including heavy manufacturing, materials fabrication, and agriculture and mining. Industries that were of marginal importance or did not exist during the childhoods of workers born during the Baby Boom are now critical to the health of the economy and therefore have become core: financial firms, technology, real estate, and large retailers. Additionally, the rise of government employment has changed the face of union membership. Most union members are now employed in the public sector rather than the private sector, so the government is now the industrial group whose workers stand to gain the most in retirement security from benefits such as retirement plans that derive from union membership. Although core industry employment as defined in this study and DeViney's study remains significant in predicting retirement benefits, it does not accurately reflect the core industrial structure of the economy today. Labor market segmentation theory with its focus on high-skill, highly educated workers having the best opportunities for pay and benefits continues to be relevant to workers born during the Baby Boom. Overall, this cohort is more highly educated than any birth cohort of workers in the past, and because of the industrial shift away from production work toward knowledge work, many workers born during the Baby Boom have been well positioned to take advantage of availability of occupations that pay well and provide strong retirement benefits.

Individual-level theories remain well supported. Human capital theory with its emphasis on "the imbedding of resources in people" (Becker, 1962, p. 9) is supported by this study's strong positive findings on the relationship of educational attainment to employer-provided retirement plans. As a result of formalization of human resources practices and legal requirements, human capital requirements have become tightly linked to occupations through job descriptions, which almost universally include a section on required skills, knowledge, and abilities. However, human capital consists of more than education. Schultz (1961) proposed five types of human capital: investment in better health, formal education, on-the-job training, study programs outside the workplace, and migration to better job opportunities. It seems likely that using only one variable to represent human capital investment understates the importance of the impact of these theories on Baby Boom workers and retirement security, especially for workers who are resource disadvantaged. Rational choice theory should predict that if investment in human capital results in greater retirement security, and if retirement security is important to a worker, then the worker will invest in increases in human capital. However, if resources are scarce, will the worker choose to invest in more education at the risk of being unable to care for a family member? A "thick" model of rational choice includes choice based upon beliefs, values, and desires (Hechter and Kanazawa, 1997), and this may be the best explanation for making what appears to be a nonrational choice with regard to retirement security.

The results of this study also support at least part of the life course perspective as a theoretical framework for Baby Boom workers. Marriage is a key life course event and is shown in this study to have a positive impact for men on working for an employer with a retirement plan and a positive impact for both men and women on inclusion in a retirement plan. For this cohort, having children under the age of 18 years was not significant for either men or women for inclusion in a retirement plan but had a significant negative effect for both men and women on working for an employer with a retirement plan. This may demonstrate a cultural shift that spreads the responsibility for children between both parents or the impact of a higher divorce rate and the resulting dislocations relating to managing children from two different households. In any event, this result may illustrate that disruptions to the life course create the risk of being sorted into jobs or industries that are unlikely to provide access to employer retirement plans. However, it seems possible that the most important impact of the life course perspective exists at the intersection of vulnerabilities: women with children and adult caregiving responsibilities, minority and immigrant workers without higher education, and other points where social structure interacts with the life course trajectory to create multiple jeopardies and cumulative inequality as described by Angel, Jimenez, and Angel (2007) and Ferraro and Shippee (2009). Workers born during the early Baby Boom are old enough that the cumulative risks resulting from these vulnerabilities have had an irreversible negative impact on their retirement security.

Limitations

This study was intended to allow some assessment of change in inclusion in retirement benefit plans from 1980 to 2009. However, both the current study and the comparison studies used cross-sectional data sets of different cohorts of workers. As a result, it is important to note that this study is not a study of trends but a study of a different cohort using the same variable structure, with a nonstatistical comparison of an older cohort with a younger cohort.

In some cases, the variables used in the CPS do not directly compare with the variables available in the Social Security Master Beneficiary Record. In these cases, variables from the CPS were chosen to approximate those used by DeViney. In the CPS, employment in a core industry or in a primary occupational sector relates only to the longest job held in the most recent year of employment, but in the earlier study, these variables relate to the longest job held in the respondents' career. DeViney was also able to capture years of experience as an additional human capital variable by measuring the number of years employed in the longest held occupation, but there is no good proxy for experience in the CPS.

The dependent variables are different because the cohorts are of different ages: DeViney measured receipt of pension benefits by retired workers and the current study measured inclusion of younger workers in retirement plans. Both are intended to provide a measure of retirement security. However, due to terminology, it is difficult to ascertain whether pension benefits include only benefits from defined benefit plans. Other retirement instruments such as defined contribution plans or individual retirement accounts had been developed and adopted by some employers in the early 1980s, but they were not as common or widespread as they are today. If the current study examined only inclusion in defined benefit plans, it is likely that the proportion of employers with a retirement plan and the proportion of workers covered would be lower. Additionally, it is important to realize that not all retirement plans are equal: Inclusion in a retirement plan is not a guarantee of equal retirement security for all. Although defined contribution plans have allowed many more workers the opportunity to save for retirement, these plans have different levels of employer contributions and allow different levels of employee contributions. At lower income levels or at younger ages, employee contributions to a defined contribution plan may be difficult or seem unnecessary, so less retirement capital is built. Workers assume investment risk when they participate in a defined contribution plan, which means that their entire principal may be lost as a result of a bad choice or a down market. This study examines differences in inclusion in retirement plans, but its scope does not include assessing the adequacy of the plans in providing additional retirement security.

The selection of a sample of full-time, full-year workers limits the inferences that can be made about the availability of retirement benefits to the entire workforce. Not only are part-time workers less likely to be included in retirement plans of any kind, women have traditionally been more likely than men to work in part-time, nonstandard jobs because of life course events such as being a trailing spouse, child rearing, or adult caregiving. As a result, this group of workers is more at risk of retirement insecurity than the sample used in this study.

Finally, changes in U.S. economic conditions may not be accurately reflected in the current study. Because the data capture only the last year of employment, it is impossible to determine whether a worker has changed jobs or reentered the workforce after a period of unemployment. If this is the case, the worker may be included in a different employer's retirement plan. Because of this, the results may underestimate or overestimate the actual level of retirement security for this cohort.

Conclusion

Retirement security is critically important both as a matter of individual health and welfare and as a matter of public policy. The prospect of 70 million new healthy retirees over the next 20 years places sharp focus on the question of how to pay for more retirees living longer than any cohort in the past. Private retirement income is a critical part of that calculation, either through personal savings or employer-provided retirement plans.

This study examined sex differences in inclusion of Baby Boom workers in employer-provided retirement plans. Two major good news stories emerged from this study and comparison. First, a much larger group of workers is included in an employer's retirement plan in this study than received pension benefits in the 1995 study. This indicates an expansion of the types and availability of retirement benefits available to workers today and is a good sign for retirement security as Baby Boom workers begin to retire. Second, there were very few areas in which the likelihood of being included in a retirement plan differed by sex. It is hoped that this reflects a general shift toward women being less dependent on a husband's retirement income for security in old age.

However, this study also suggests some areas for further study. Minority workers have the lowest likelihood of being included in a retirement plan and the second lowest likelihood (after foreign-born workers) of working for an employer who has a retirement plan. Minority workers who are also immigrants have the lowest likelihood of working for an employer with a retirement plan. Although it appears that educational attainment may help sort minority and immigrant workers into jobs with employers who have retirement plans, other factors such as government employment or occupational sector of employment may determine whether these groups are included in a plan. The components of these results need to be examined in greater detail to determine where the differences with non-minority and nonimmigrant workers exist.

The high likelihood of public employees being included in a retirement plan also suggests further study on the impact of the reduction of these benefits. Current difficult economic conditions affecting national, state, and local governments have resulted in proposals that will reduce or eliminate many jobs and certain types of retirement benefits in the public sector. As a result, the economic security that is associated with public employment may be illusory. Further study is important to project the effects on workers and on other retirement and safety net programs if a large number of public employees have their retirement benefits reduced.

References

Aguiar, F., & de Francisco, A. (2009). Rational choice, social identity, and beliefs about oneself. *Philosophy of the Social Sciences, 39,* 547–571. doi:10.1177/0048393109333531

Angel, J. L., Jiménez, M. A., & Angel, R. J. (2007). The economic consequences of widowhood for older minority women. *The Gerontologist, 47,* 224–234. doi: 10.1093/geront/47.2.224

Averitt, R. T. (1968). *The dual economy: The dynamics of American industry structure.* New York: Norton.

Beck, E. M., Horan, P. M., & Tolbert, C. M., II (1978). Stratification in a dual economy: A sectoral model of earnings determination. *American Sociological Review, 43,* 704–720. Retrieved from www.asanet.org/journals/asr/

Becker, G. S. (1962). Investment in human capital: A theoretical analysis. *Journal of Political Economy, 70,* 9–49. doi: 10.1086/258724

Beckmann, A. (2006). *Access, participation, and take-up rates in defined contribution retirement plans among workers in private industry,* 2006. Washington, DC: United States Department of Labor. Retrieved from www.bls.gov/opub/cwc/cm20061213ar01p1.htm

Ben-Porath, Y. (1967). The production of human capital and the life cycle of earnings. *Journal of Political Economy, 75,* 352–365. Retrieved from www.journals.uchicago.edu/JPE/

Bureau of Labor Statistics. (2010). *Retirement benefits: Access, participation, and take-up rates, civilian workers, National Compensation Survey.* United States Department of Labor. Retrieved from www.bls.gov/ncs/ebs/benefits/2010/ownership/civilian/table02a.pdf

Butrica, B. A., Murphy, D. P., & Zedlewski, S. R., (2010). How many struggle to get by in retirement? *The Gerontologist, 50,* 482–494. doi:10.1093/geront/gnp158

Cahill, K. E., Giandrea, M. D., & Quinn, J. F. (2006). Retirement patterns from career employment. *The Gerontologist, 46,* 514–523. doi:10.1093/geront/46.4.514

Calasanti, T. (2010). Gender relations and applied research on aging. *The Gerontologist, 50,* 720–734. doi: 10.1093/geront/gnq085

Costo, S. L. (2006). Trends in retirement plan coverage over the last decade. *Monthly Labor Review, 129*(2), 58–64. Retrieved from http://bls.gov/opub/mlr/2006/02/art5full.pdf

DeViney, S. (1995). Life course, private pension, and financial well being. *American Behavioral Scientist, 39,* 172–185. doi:10.1177/000276429503900205

DeViney, S., & Solomon, J. C. (1995). Gender differences in retirement income: A comparison of theoretical explanations. *Journal of Women & Aging, 7,* 83–100. Retrieved from www.tandf.co.uk/journals/WJWA

Doeringer, P. B., & Piore, M. J. (1975). Unemployment and the 'dual labor market'. *National Affairs, 38,* 67–79. Retrieved from www.nationalaffairs.com/public_interest/detail/unemployment-and-the-dual-labor-market

Ferraro, K. F., & Shippee, T. P. (2009). Aging and cumulative inequality: How does inequality get under the skin? *The Gerontologist, 49,* 333–343. doi:10.1093/geront/gnp034

Ferraro, K. F., Shippee, T. P., & Schafer, M. H. (2009). Cumulative inequality theory for research on aging and the life course. In V. L. Bengston, D. Gans, N. M. Putney, & M. Silverstein (Eds.), *Handbook of theories of aging* (pp. 412–433). New York: Springer.

Fields, G. S. (2007). *Dual economy.* Retrieved from http://digitalcommons.ilr.cornell.edu/workingpapers/17/(http://digitalcommons.ilr.cornell.edu/workingpapers/l7/)

George, L. K. (1993). Sociological perspectives on life transitions. *Annual Review of Sociology, 19,* 353–373. doi:10.1146/annurev.so.19.080193.002033

Gibson, C., & Jung, K. (2006). *Historical census statistics on the foreign-born population of the United States: 1850–2000* (Working Paper No. 81). Retrieved from www.census.gov/population/www/documentation/twps0081/twps0081.pdf

Hatch, L. R. (2000). *Beyond gender differences: Adaptation to aging in life course perspective.* Amityville, NY: Baywood.

Hechter, M., & Kanazawa, S. (1997). Sociological rational choice theory. *Annual Review of Sociology, 23,* 191–274. doi:10.1146/annurev.soc.23.1.191

Hogan, D. P. (1978). The variable order of events in the life course. *American Sociological Review, 43,* 573–586. Retrieved from www.asanet.org/journals/asr/

Holden, K. C., & Fontes, A. (2009). Economic security in retirement: How changes in employment and marriage have altered retirement-related economic risks for women. *Journal of Women, Politics & Policy, 30,* 1731–197. doi: 10.1080/15544770902901817

Hudson, K. (2007). The new labor market segmentation: Labor market dualism in the new economy. *Social Science Research, 36,* 286–312. doi:10.1016/j.ssresearch.2005.11.005

Johnson, R. W. (2009). Family, public policy, and retirement decisions: Introduction to the special issue. *Research on Aging, 31,* 139–152. doi:l0.1177/0164027508328307

Johnson, R. W., Uccello, C. E., & Goldwyn, J. H. (2005). Who foregoes survivor protection in employer-sponsored pension annuities? *The Gerontologist, 45,* 26–35. doi:10.1093/geront/45.1.26

Kalleberg, A. L., & Sorensen, A. B. (1979). The sociology of labor markets. *Annual Review of Sociology, 5,* 351–379. doi:10.1146/annurev.so.05.080179.002031

Moen, P., & Orrange, R. M. (2002). Careers and lives: Socialization, structural lag, and gendered ambivalence. In R. Settersten, & T. Owens (Eds.), *Advances in life course research: New frontiers in socialization* (*Vol. 7,* pp. 231–260). London, UK: Elsevier Science.

Munnell, A. H., Webb, A., & Golub-Sass, F. (2009). *The national retirement risk index: After the crash* (Brief No. 9-22). Retrieved from http://crr.bc.edu/images/stories/Briefs/IB_9-22.pdf

National Center for Health Statistics. (2009). *Delayed childbearing: More women are having their first child later in life* (NCHS Data Brief No. 21). Retrieved from www.cdc.gov/nchs/data/databriefs/db21.pdf

Quadagno, J. (1988). Women's access to pensions and the structure of eligibility rules: Systems of production and reproduction. *Sociological Quarterly, 29,* 547–558. doi:10.1111/j.1533-8525.1988.tb01433.x

Richardson, V. (1999). Women and retirement. *Journal of Women and Aging, 11,* 49–66. Retrieved from www.tandf.co.uk/journals/WJWA

Rogerson, P. A., & Kim, D. (2005). Population distribution and redistribution of the Baby Boom cohort in the United States: Recent trends and implications. *Proceedings of the National Academy of Sciences of the United States of America, 102,* 15319–15324. doi:10.1073/pnas. 0507318102

Schultz, T. W. (1961). Investment in human capital. *American Economic Review, 51,* 1–17. Retrieved from www.aeaweb.org/aer/index.php

Shuey, K. M., & O'Rand, A. M. (2004). New risks for workers: Pensions, labor markets, and gender. *Annual Review of Sociology, 30,* 453–477. doi:l0.1146/annurev.soc.30.012703.110534

Simmons, T., & Dye, J. L. (2003). *Grandparents living with grandchildren: 2000* (Census 2000 Brief C2KBR-31). Retrieved from www.census.gov/prod/2003pubs/c2kbr-31.pdf

United States Bureau of Labor Statistics. (2010). *Union members summary* (Economic News Release USDL-11-0063). Washington, DC: United States Department of Labor. Retrieved from http://data.bls.gov/cgi-bin/print.pl/news.release/union2.nr0.htm

United States Department of Labor. (2002). *Current Population Survey technical paper 63RV: Design and methodology.* Retrieved from www.census.gov/prod/2002pubs/tp63rv.pdf

Zafirovski, M. (1999). Unification of sociological theory by the rational choice model: Conceiving the relationship between economics and sociology. *Sociology, 33,* 495–514. doi:10.1177/S0038038599000322

Critical Thinking

1. What were the most significant predictors of inclusion in a retirement plan for both men and women?

2. Were baby boomer women more or less disadvantaged than their counterparts in earlier studies?

3. What two major good news stories emerged from the most recent study of retirement benefits provided to baby boom workers?

Acknowledgments—The author thanks Dr. David W. Wright of Wichita State University for providing assistance with the Current Population Survey data set for this study and Dr. Twyla J. Hill of Wichita State University and Dr. Teresa S. Radebaugh of the Regional Institute on Aging at Wichita State University for their reviews of earlier drafts of this study and their very valuable suggestions for improvement.

Work/Retirement Choices and Lifestyle Patterns of Older Americans

HAROLD COX ET AL.

This study examined the work, retirement, and lifestyle choices of a sample of older Indiana residents. The six lifestyles examined in this study were:

1. *to continue to work full-time;*
2. *to continue to work part-time;*
3. *retire from work and become engaged in a variety of volunteer activities;*
4. *to retire from work and become involved in a variety of recreational and leisure activities;*
5. *to retire from work and later return to work part-time; and*
6. *to retire from work and later return to work full-time*

These findings indicate that health was not a critical factor in the older person's retirement decision, and that those who retired and engaged in volunteer or recreational activities were significantly more satisfied with their lives than those who continue to work. Those who retired and engaged in volunteer or recreational activities scored significantly higher on life satisfaction than those who had returned to work full or part-time. There was no significant difference between those who had retired and those who had continued working in terms of how they were viewed by their peers. Of those who retired and then returned to work, the most satisfied with their lives were the ones who returned to work in order to feel productive. Those least satisfied with their lives were the ones that returned to work because they needed money.

Introduction

There are basically six different choices of lifestyles from which older Americans choose when they reach retirement age. They can (1) continue to work full-time, (2) reduce work commitments but continue to work part-time, (3) retire from work and become engaged in a variety of volunteer activities that provide needed services but for which they will receive no economic compensation or (4) retire from work and become involved in a variety of recreational and leisure activities, (5) retire from work and later return to work part-time, (6) retire from work and return to work full-time.

There are a multitude of life experiences and retirement patterns that may ultimately lead older persons to choose among the diverse ways of occupying themselves during their later years. Some enjoy their work as well as the income, status, privilege, and power that go with full-time employment and never intend to retire. Some retire intending to engage in recreational and leisure activities on a full-time basis only to find this lifestyle less satisfying than they imagined and ultimately return to work. The need to feel productive and actively involved in life is often a critical factor inducing some retirees to return to work. Some retirees who have become widowed, divorced, or never married find themselves too socially isolated in retirement. They return to work either full-time or part-time because their job brings them into contact with a variety of people, and therefore they are less isolated. Thus, there are a variety of reasons why older persons may continue to work or to become active volunteers during their later years. On the other hand, many persons retire, dedicate themselves to recreation and leisure activities, and are most satisfied doing so.

The purpose of this study was to determine which of these six groups were better off in terms of their health, life satisfaction, retirement adjustment and the respect they received from their peers.

A second factor, which will be examined in this study, is the advisability for both government and industry of encouraging older workers to remain in the labor force longer. Changes in Social Security regulations after the year 2000 are going to gradually increase the age of eligibility for Social Security payment from 62 to 64 for early retirement and from 65 to 67 for full retirement benefits. Will changes in the age of eligibility for retirement income derived from Social Security regulations be good or bad for older Americans?

Review of Literature
Work

The meanings of such diverse activities as work, leisure, and retirement to a member of a social system are often quite complex. Paradoxically, the relevance of work and leisure activities for an individual is often intertwined in his or her thinking. Consequently, the concept of work or occupation has been difficult for sociologists to precisely define.

For some time sociologists have struggled to come up with an adequate definition of work. Dubin (1956), for example, defined work as continuous employment in the production of goods and services for remuneration. This definition ignores the fact that there are necessary tasks in society carried out by persons who receive no immediate pay. Mothers, fathers, housewives, and students do not receive pay for their valued activities.

Hall (1975) attempts to incorporate both the economic and social aspects of work in his definition: "An occupation is the social role performed by adult members of society that directly and/or indirectly yields social and financial consequences and that constitutes a major focus in the life of an adult." Similarly Bryant (1972) tries to include both the economic and social aspects of work life in his definition of labor: "Labor is any socially integrating activity which is connected with human subsistence." By *integrating activity* Bryant means sanctioned activity that presupposes, creates, and recreates social relationships. The last two definitions seem to take a broader view of work in the individual's total life. Moreover, they could include the work done by mothers, fathers, housewives, and students. The advantage of definitions that attach strong importance to the meaning and social aspects of a work role is that they recognize the importance of roles for which there is no, or very little, economic reward. The homemaker, while not receiving pay, may contribute considerably to a spouse's career and success. College students in the period of anticipatory socialization and preparation for an occupational role may not be receiving any economic benefits, but their efforts are crucial to their future career.

The most appropriate definitions of work, therefore, seem to be those that emphasize the social and role aspects of an occupation, which an individual reacts to and is shaped by, whether or not he or she is financially rewarded for assuming these roles. From the perspective of sociology, one's work life and the roles one assumes during the workday will, in time, shape one's self-concept, identity, and feelings about oneself, and therefore strongly affect one's personality and behavior. Moreover, from this perspective, the individual's choice of occupations is probably strongly affected by the desire to establish, maintain, and display a desired identity.

Individual Motivation to Work

Vroom (1964) has attempted to delineate the components of work motivation. The first component is wages and all the economic rewards associated with the fringe benefits of the job. People desire these rewards, which therefore serve as a strong incentive to work. Iams (1985), in a study of the post-retirement work patterns of women, found that unmarried women were very likely to work at least part-time after retirement if their monthly income was below $500. Hardy (1991) found that 80 percent of the retirees who later re-entered the labor force stated that money was the main reason they returned to work. The economic inducement to work is apparently a strong one.

A second inducement to work is the expenditure of physical and mental energy. People seem to need to expend energy in some meaningful way, and work provides this opportunity. Vroom (1964) notes that animals will often engage in spontaneous activity as a consequence of activity deprivation.

A third motivation, according to Vroom, is the production of goods and services. This inducement is directly related to the intrinsic satisfaction the individual derives from successful manipulation of the environment.

A fourth motivation is social interaction. Most work roles involve interaction with customers, clients, or members of identifiable work groups as part of the expected behavior of their occupants.

The final motivation Vroom mentions is social status. An individual's occupation is perhaps the best single determinant of his or her status in the community.

These various motivations for work undoubtedly assume different configurations for different people and occupational groups. Social interaction may be the most important for some, while economic considerations may be most important for others. For still others the intrinsic satisfaction derived from the production of goods and services may be all-important. Thus, the research by industrial sociologists has indicated that there are diverse reasons why individuals are motivated to work.

The critical questions for gerontologists is whether the same psychological and social factors that thrust people into work patterns for the major part of their adult life can channel them into leisure activities during their retirement years. Can people find the same satisfaction, feeling of worth, and identity in leisure activities that they did in work-related activities? Streib and Schneider (1971) think they can. They argue that the husband, wife, grandmother, and grandfather's roles may expand and become more salient in the retirement years. Simultaneously, public service and community roles become possible because of the flexibility of the retiree's time. They believe that the changing activities and roles, which accompany retirement, need not lead to a loss of self-respect or active involvement in the mainstream of life.

Retirement Trends

Demographic and economic trends in American society have resulted in an ever-increasing number of retired Americans. Streib and Schneider (1971) observed that for retirement to become an institutionalized social pattern in any society, certain conditions must be met. There must be a large group of people who live long enough to retire, the economy must be sufficiently productive to support segments of the population that are not included in the work force, and there must be some well-established forms of pension or insurance programs to support people during their retirement years.

There has been a rapid growth in both the number and percentage of the American population 65 and above since 1900.

In 1900, there were 3.1 million Americans 65 and over, which constituted four percent of the population. Currently, approximately 31 million Americans are in this age category, which makes up 12.5 percent of the population. While the number and proportion of the population over

Table 1 Civilian Labor Force Participation Rates: Actual and Projected*

	Men			Women		
Year	45–54	55–64	65 and Over	45–54	55–64	65 and Over
1950	95.8	86.9	45.8	37.9	27.0	9.7
1960	95.7	86.8	33.1	49.8	32.2	10.8
1970	94.2	83.0	26.8	54.4	43.0	9.7
1980	91.2	72.3	19.1	59.9	41.5	8.1
1986	91.0	67.3	16.0	65.9	42.3	7.4
1990*	90.7	65.1	14.1	69.0	42.8	7.0
2000*	90.1	63.2	9.9	75.4	45.8	5.4

Source: For the rates from 1950–1970: U.S. Department of Labor (1980:224). For the rates from 1980–2000: Bureau of Labor Statistics (unpublished data).
*Values are projections from the Bureau of Labor Statistics middle growth path.

65 have been increasing steadily, the proportion of those who remain in the work force has decreased steadily. In 1900, nearly two thirds of those 65 worked. Sammartino (1979) reports that by 1947 this figure had declined to 47.8 percent. By 1987 only 16.5 percent of those 65 and older were still in the work force. In the past 20 years the decline in labor force participation in later years has extended into the 55–64 year old age group. Clark (1988) observed that between 1960 and 1970 the labor force participation of men (55–64) dropped from 86.8% to 83%. By 1990 the labor force participation rate of men in this age group (55–64) had dropped to 65.1% (see Table 1). Table 1 indicates that the labor force participation rates of women 55–64 rose from 27% to 43% from 1950 to 1970 but has remained relatively stable since 1970. Thus, while the labor force participation rate of 55-years and -older women has remained relatively stable since 1970, the labor force participation rate of women 45–54 has grown from 54.4% in 1970 to 69% in 1990. It would appear from these figures that, while younger women are in increasing numbers entering the labor force, women 55 and above are following the same path as their male counterparts and choosing to retire early.

Similarly, there appears to be a somewhat greater convergence in the work and retirement patterns of men and women when comparing 1900 with 1970. The earlier pattern of work histories seemed to be for men to enter the work force earlier and retire later; women tended to enter later and retire earlier. Current trends indicate that women are entering the work force earlier and working longer.

Men, on the other hand, enter the work force later and retire earlier. Thus, the work histories of men and women are becoming very similar, although men as a group still have longer work histories than women. Today, more women are both entering the labor force and also remaining in the labor force throughout their adult lives.

The trend for both men and women for the past 30 years has been for larger numbers to choose to claim Social Security benefits prior to age 65. Allen and Brotman (1981) point out that in 1968, 48 percent of all new Social Security payment awards to men were to claimants under 65; by 1978 this figure had increased to 61 percent. In 1968, 65 percent of all new Social Security awards to women were to claimants under 65; in 1978, the figure was 72 percent.

Simultaneously, fewer persons are choosing to remain in the labor force beyond the age of 65. Soldo and Agree (1988) report that 62 percent of the men and 72 percent of the women who received Social Security benefits in 1986 had retired prior to age 65 and therefore were receiving reduced benefits. The General Accounting Office reports that almost two-thirds of those receiving private retirement benefits in 1985 stopped working prior to age 65. Of those who do remain in the labor force after age 65, Soldo and Agree (1988) report that 47 percent of the men and 59 percent of the women held part-time positions.

Quinn and Burkhauser (1990) report that probably the most critical factor in the decision to retire early is adequate retirement income. They found that between 1975 and 1990 the proportion of workers covered by two pension plans had risen from 21 percent to 40 percent. Moreover, Gall, Evans, and Howard (1997) report a number of studies that found that those with higher incomes, or at least adequate finances, were more satisfied with their life in retirement (Fillenbau, George, and Palmore 1985; Seccombe and Lee 1986; Crowley 1990; Dorfman 1992).

There is a multiplicity of problems confronting the individual at retirement: the lowering of income; the loss of status, privilege, and power associated with one's position in the occupational hierarchy; a major reorganization of life activities, since the nine-to-five workday becomes meaningless; a changing definition of self, since most individuals over time shape their identity and personality in line with the demands of their major occupational roles; considerable social isolation if new activities are not found to replace work-related activities; and a search for a new identity, new meaning, and new values in one's life. Obviously, the major reorganization of one's life that must take place at retirement is a potential source of adjustment problems. Critical to the adjustment is the degree to which one's identity and personality structure was attached to the work role. For those individuals whose work identity is central to their self-concept and gives them the greatest satisfaction, retirement will represent somewhat of a crisis. For others, retirement should not represent a serious problem.

Work and Retirement Patterns in Later Life

Beck (1983) identified three different work and retirement patterns of older persons which include:

1. the fully retired
2. the partially retired
3. the formerly retired

What could be added to Beck's pattern are "the never retired."

There are a number of different studies and authors who have attempted to identify the critical factor determining who will or will not work during their later years. Beck (1983) found that individuals with high job autonomy and high demand jobs were most likely to return to work after formal retirement. Those with the greatest financial need—service workers and laborers—were less likely to return to work despite financial limitations. Beck concludes that income was the critical factor in the motivation of workers who were very poor to return to work. Those in other income categories were less likely to return to work because of actual financial benefits as much as for other factors.

A number of other studies tended to support Beck's analysis of work and retirement patterns. Tillenbaum (1971) found that those with higher levels of education were more likely to continue working beyond age 65 or to return to work after retiring if they chose to do so. Quinn (1980) found the self-employed were much more likely to work beyond retirement age. Streib and Schneider (1971) found that white collar workers were significantly more likely than blue collar workers to return to work. They found no relationship between income and post-retirement work. Howell (1988) reports that those who formally retire and engage in no substantial work during the next three years are more likely to have been unemployed before retirement and to have lower incomes after retirement. They are also more likely to be nonwhite urban dwellers in poor health.

The past research has indicated then that those who either continue to work after retirement age or return to work after retiring are most likely to:

1. have stable employment patterns throughout their adult life;
2. be in white collar occupations;
3. have higher incomes;
4. have a higher number of years of education;
5. be self-employed.

Those least likely to either work after retirement age or return to work after retirement age:

1. those who experienced periods of unemployment throughout their adult life;
2. those in blue collar occupations;
3. those with low incomes;
4. those who have a lower number of years of education;
5. those who are of minority status (Tillenbaum 1971; Quinn 1980; Howell 1988).

These findings support the idea that many people who continue to work after retirement do so for other than financial reasons. If work was stable and both social and psychologically meaningful to the individual, he/she is much more likely to be found working during the retirement years.

As a rule, retirees do not return to jobs with low autonomy, poor working conditions, and difficult physical labor. Those who most need to continue working during the retirement years for financial reasons are least likely to be able to do so. This is most probably related to their inability to find gainful employment.

Volunteer Work in Retirement

Social integration refers to the individual being actively involved in a variety of groups and organization and thus integrated into the web of community activity. The active older person is likely to be involved in a variety of groups ranging from family to social clubs to church and community organizations. While work and career often place the individual in disparate groups and organizations throughout much of his/her adult life, active engagement in voluntary organizations is likely to keep the individual socially involved during their retirement years.

Moen, Dempster-McClain, and Williams (1992) report that studies as early as 1956 reporting that older persons participating in volunteer work on an intermittent basis and belonging to clubs and organizations were positively related to various measures of health. They concluded that occupying multiple roles in the community was positively related to good health.

A number of studies have found a positive relationship between social integration (in the form of multiple roles) and health in later life (Berkman and Breslow 1983; House, Landes, and Umberson 1988; Moen et al.; Williams 1992).

The researchers were unable to determine if multiple roles lead to improved health or if healthy people were more likely to engage in multiple roles. Moen et al. (1992), however, once again found that being a member of a club or organization appeared to be a critical factor in the current health of the individual, after previous health had been controlled. Paid work over the life course, while positively related to multiple roles in later life, was negatively related to measures of health. However, any volunteer activity at any time during adult life appears to promote multiple role occupancy, social integration, and health in later life.

Mobert (1983) observes that church affiliation itself was not considered a volunteer group or activity; however, membership in groups sponsored by the church such as choir, Old Timers, etc. was considered a volunteer activity. Moreover, church members generally remain active participants in church-related activities long after dropping participation from other voluntary associations (Gray and Moberg 1977). Markides (1983) and Ortega, Crutchfield, and Rusling (1983) argue that the church serves as a focal point for individual and community integration of the elderly and that this is crucial to their sense of well-being. Both of these studies found that church attendance was significantly correlated with life satisfaction.

Productivity in Later Life

Older workers who remain in the work force have been found to be just as productive as younger workers. An industrial survey conducted by Parker (1982) found that older workers were most often regarded as superior to younger workers. Adjectives used by employers to describe older workers were responsible, reliable, conscientious, tolerant, reasonable, and loyal. Older workers have greater stability, they miss work less frequently, change jobs less frequently, and are more dedicated and loyal to the employing organization. Welford (1988) found that performance on production jobs tends to increase with age. While this is true, employers generally offer incentive plans to encourage older workers to retire early. Older workers are generally higher on salary schedules, have accumulated more vacation time and fringe benefits. Thus, many employers see younger workers as cheaper. The fact that they are untested does not seem critical to the employer.

Fyock in discussing the early retirement policies of the 1970's states that:

> Employers liked it because it enabled them to hire and promote younger, more recently trained and lower paid workers. The public liked it because it didn't appear to cost anything and because at age 62 or earlier they could expect to retire; older workers for obvious reasons loved it. (Fyock 1991:422)

Fyock (1991) warns however that we currently have an aging work force and that in the near future employers may find it to their advantage to encourage older workers to remain in the work force longer. She believes that employers often find that retirement appeals to their best, instead of the most expendable, employee.

Projected job growth coupled with a declining number of younger workers has raised concern about possible labor shortages. If these projections prove accurate and labor shortages do develop, the answer to the problem would seem to be the retention of older workers—the very workers employers are currently encouraging to retire. Dennis (1986), Sheppard (1990), and Fyock (1991) all argue that an aging labor force can be a source of opportunity for employers. The smart employers, they believe, will be the ones who know how to take advantage of the opportunity.

McShulski (1997) reports the need for a "soft landing" program which eases older workers out of the labor force on a very gradual basis. Encouraging retiring employees to work a reduced number of hours and handle more limited duties for less pay, helps both the company and the employee. Future retirees can impart relevant job information to their coworkers and teach less experienced employees about specific tasks and customer needs. Thus, working for reduced hours and more limited responsibilities results in a gradual transition to retirement, which is good for the company and the employee according to McShulski.

Retirement Policies and Older Workers

Industrialized societies traditionally have low fertility rates and long life expectancy, resulting in an ever-growing number and percentage of our population that is over 65. Thus, industrialized nations very early began to shift social welfare programs from younger persons to older persons. Many economists are questioning the willingness of society to continue to support an ever-growing number of older persons through public-funded retirement incomes.

Initially, in 1935 when Social Security was passed, both management and labor were anxious to get older persons out of the labor force. Management believed that older workers were too expensive since they were high on salary schedules and had accumulated considerable fringe benefits. Labor unions believed that removing older workers would create jobs for younger workers. The public was happy since they were given economic help in support of their older family members and ultimately they looked forward to being able to retire themselves.

The post-WWII era saw major expansions in Social Security programs. Social Security was extended to cover nearly all wage earners and self-employed persons. The permissible retirement age was lowered to 62, and a national disability income program was added to Social Security. A legal interpretation of the Taft-Hartley Act resulted in private pension plans becoming legitimate items of collective bargaining. The result was that private pension plans have grown substantially from 1950 to present. As a result of these and related activities, a retirement norm has emerged in America. Most people now plan to retire and to live some part of their life out of the labor force.

Congress, with the passage of new Social Security legislation in 1983, began, for the first time, to question the desirability of removing seniors from the labor force. Concern about the financial solvency of the Social Security program led Congress and the President to increase Social Security taxes, to increase taxes on earned income of older persons, to tax Social Security benefits, and to raise the eligible age of Social Security benefits after the year 2000.

Retirement age will go up very gradually during the first quarter of the next century. Early retirement will be increased from 62 to 64 years of age. Full retirement will be increased from 65 to 67. Reduction in pension benefits for those who retire early will go up from 20% to 30% of their full retirement income. Those who stay at work after 65 will get a pension boost of 8% for each extra year of work instead of today's 3%.

The changes in Social Security benefits are clearly designed to encourage people to work longer and retire later. The question that remains, given the trend toward younger retirements, is will these changes really keep older workers in the work force longer or merely mean that more retirees will earn less and therefore more will fall below the poverty line.

Economists and labor planners have never been able to establish the fact that for every older worker who retires, a job is created for a younger worker. Changing technologies and the creation of new jobs have at different times created a greater or lesser demand for more workers. Morris (1986) states that:

If financial and social policy disincentives to employment could be reduced there is no prior reason to believe that the economy would be unable to expand gradually to accommodate more retired persons especially in part-time, self-employed, and service capacities (Morris 1986:291).

Morris (1986) argues that half of the Social Security recipients abruptly leave the labor force and the other half engage in some short-term labor force participation after they retire.

The critical question raised by Congress in changing Social Security benefits in 1983 is can government policies change the age at which people choose to retire. If the older person is to be encouraged to remain in the labor force longer, both the individual worker and the business/industrial community must be convinced of the advantages of keeping older persons in the labor force longer. There seems to be no question that older persons can be productive members of the labor force beyond the retirement age if they have the opportunity and choose to do so.

Hypothesis

1. Those working full-time or part-time will be in better health than those who have retired.
2. Those people who have retired will score higher on measures of life satisfaction than those working full or part-time.
3. Those retirees engaged in volunteer or leisure activities will score higher on measures of life satisfaction than those returning to work.
4. Those people working full-time or part-time during their later years will be more highly regarded by their peers.

Methodology

The questionnaire utilized in this study included the standard demographic variables, as well as measures of attitude toward retirement, the respondent's perceived state of health, life satisfaction, retirement adjustment, and his/her perceived status among friends.

The questionnaire was mailed to 597 members of the Older Hoosiers Federation and 200 Green Thumb workers in Indiana. The Older Hoosiers Federation is a volunteer groups of senior citizens who lobby for or against various state and federal legislation which they perceive would affect older Americans. They are primarily retired Americans over the age of 55. The Green Thumb workers are persons 55 and older who work on various parks, roads, and community projects. They are employed by the federal government in community service projects in order to raise their income above the poverty level. A limitation of this study is that the sample was an available sample and not a random sample. It was the best available sample that the researchers could find at this time. There were 342 valid returns, which represented 42.91% of those surveyed.

Findings

The first hypothesis stated that those persons working full or part-time will be in better health than those who are retired. This hypothesis was not supported by the data. As Table 2 indicates, calculating the mean score on the subjects' perceived state of health for those working full-time, those working part-time, those retired and engaged in volunteer activities, and those retired and engaged in leisure activities and then performing a one-way analysis of variance resulted in a finding of no significant difference in the means of the four groups. While past studies of when people retire have indicated that perceived health and subjects' belief that they have adequate income to retire are often identified as the critical variables in the decision of when to retire, that would not appear to be the case with this sample. There were no significant differences in the perceived state of health for those subjects who were working in comparison to those subjects who were retired (Table 2).

Table 2 One-Way Analysis of Variance: Mean Perceived Health Scores for Older Workers and Retirees

	Mean	N = 329
Work Full-Time	3.4706	51
Work Part-Time	3.2970	101
Retired/Engaged in Volunteer Activities	3.2867	143
Retired/Engaged Leisure Act.	3.2647	34

Source	D.F.	Sum of Squares	Mean Squares	F-Ratio	F-Probability
Between Groups	3	1.4682	.4891	.9956	.3951
Within Groups	325	159.6574	.4913		
Total	328	161.1246			

Table 3 One-Way Analysis of Variance: Mean Life Satisfaction Scores for Older Workers and Retirees

	Mean	N = 318
Work Full-Time	7.6372	49
Work Part-Time	7.1875	96
Retired/Engaged in Volunteer Activities	7.9928	139
Retired/Engaged in Leisure Activities	8.0000	34

Source	D.F.	Sum of Squares	Mean Squares	F-Ratio	F-Probability
Between Groups	3	40.4064	13.4688	8.2667	.0015
Within Groups	314	803.0056	2.5573		
Total	317	843.4119			

Table 4 One-Way Analysis of Variance: Mean Life Satisfaction Scores for Older Workers and Retirees

	Mean	N = 268
Returned to Work Full-Time	2.2000	5
Returned to Work Part-Time	2.0333	90
Retired/Engaged in Volunteer Activities	2.3885	139
Retired/Engaged in Leisure Activities	2.2941	34

Source	D.F.	Sum of Squares	Mean Squares	F-Ratio	F-Probability
Between Groups	3	6.9659	2.3220	5.9067	.0006
Within Groups	264	103.7804	.3931		
Total	267	110.7463			

Hypothesis Two stated that those persons who have retired will score higher on measures of life satisfaction than those who are working full or part-time. The mean scores on life satisfaction were calculated for those working full-time, those working part-time, those retired and engaged in volunteer activity, and those retired and engaged in leisure activity. The data indicated that those retired and engaged in volunteer activities and those retired and engaged in leisure activity scored significantly higher on measures of life satisfaction than those working either full or part-time (Table 3). The hypothesis was supported by the data (Table 3).

Hypothesis Three stated that those retirees engaged in volunteer or leisure activities will score higher on measures of life satisfaction than those who retired and then returned to work on a full-time or part-time basis. Mean life satisfaction scores were calculated for those who had retired and then returned to work full-time, those who had retired and then returned to work part-time, those who had retired and were engaged in volunteer activities, and those who had retired and were engaged in leisure activities. Those retired and engaged

in volunteer or leisure activity scored significantly higher on life satisfaction than those who had retired and returned to work full or part-time. As Table 4 indicates there were only five people in this sample who had retired and returned to work full-time. Returning to work full-time was rare in this sample of people.

Hypothesis Four stated that those retirees who returned to work full or part-time will be more respected by their peers than those who have retired and engaged in volunteer or leisure activities.

In terms of their perceived respect by friends, those retired and returning to work full-time scored highest with a mean of 3.0. Those who retired and were engaged in volunteer activities scored second with a mean of 2.86. Those who retired and were engaged in leisure activities scored third with a mean of 2.76. Those who had retired and returned to work part-time perceived they were least respected by their friends with a score of 2.68. While the analysis of variance did not find significant differences in these means at the .05 level of significance, they were

Table 5   One Way Analysis of Variance: Mean Scores for Perceived Respect of Older Workers and Retirees by Their Peers

	Mean	N = 277
Returned to Work Full-Time	3.00006	4
Returned to Work Part-Time	2.6869	99
Retired/Engaged in Volunteer Activities	2.8643	140
Retired/Engaged in Leisure Activities	2.7647	34

Source	D.F.	Sum of Squares	Mean Squares	F-Ratio	F-Probability
Between Groups	3	2.0236	.6745	2.4254	.0657
Within Groups	272	75.8326	.2778		
Total	276	77.8556			

Table 6   One Way Analysis of Variance: Mean Scores on Life Satisfaction Based on the Reasons Individuals Returned to Work

	Mean	N = 130
Needed the money	6.7027	74
Wanted to feel productive	8.2703	37
Lonely & bored	7.2632	19

Source	D.F.	Sum of Squares	Mean Squares	F-Ratio	F-Probability
Between Groups	2	60.6360	30.3180	10.7420	.0000
Within Groups	127	358.4410	2.8224		
Total	129	419.0769			

significant at the .07 level of significance. Since the .05 level of significance is the normal level of acceptance of the significance of difference between groups, this hypothesis was not supported by the data (Table 5).

In order to clarify how the retirees' decision to return to work would affect their life satisfaction, an additional calculation was done. One question asked those who had returned to work was why they had done so. The choices to this question were: I needed the money, I needed to do something that makes me feel productive, and I was lonely and bored and work gave me something interesting to do. Mean scores and measures of life satisfaction were calculated for each of these three groups (Table 6). The highest mean score was for the group who returned to work in order to feel productive, and their score was 8.27. The second highest mean score was for those who had returned to work because they were lonely and bored, and their score was 7.26. The lowest mean score on life satisfaction was 6.7 for those who had been forced to return to work because they needed the money (Table 6). Thus, most of the people that returned to work did so because they needed the money, but they were the least satisfied with their lives.

Conclusion

The data from this study indicate that those who retire and engage in volunteer or recreational activities score higher on measures of life satisfaction than those that never retired. Of those that retired and then returned to work, those that did so because they wanted to feel productive scored highest on life satisfaction. Those that returned to work because they needed the money scored lowest on life satisfaction.

These findings would suggest that if the goal of the federal government is to keep older people in the labor force longer, some means must be found by which the older workers are kept at jobs in which they feel productive and needed. For the business community to continue, primarily for economic reasons, to encourage older workers to retire from highly skilled jobs in which they are more productive than younger workers does not seem desirable.

One possible solution to this problem might be for the federal government to give a tax incentive to businesses employing older workers so that the economic advantage business sees for retiring older workers and employing younger ones would diminish.

A major break in the cost of employing older workers in business would be for the federal government to develop a national health insurance program. One of the major costs to the employer of older workers is the amount of money they must put into health insurance for them. For the federal government to assume this cost would be a major reduction in the business cost of continuing to employ older workers.

Perhaps businesses could continue to utilize the talents of older workers by developing reduced and flexible work schedules which would pay them a lower salary but keep them involved in critical tasks for the industry, as suggested by McShulski (1997).

Since the trend of the last thirty years has been for an ever increasing number of workers to retire prior to age 65, perhaps the government's attempts to keep people in the workforce longer by increasing the age at which they can draw a Social Security check will not be successful. It is possible that through private savings, private investment programs, and pension programs financed by their employers, older workers will continue to retire prior to age 65.

On the other hand, improving technology may mean that business and industry will need fewer employees to produce the nations' goods and services, and therefore they will continue to encourage their workers to retire at younger ages.

The complexity and unpredictability of the factors involved makes predicting future employment and retirement patterns for older Americans at best hazardous and at worst impossible. Observing the results of economic and political pressures placed on both business and government by an ever increasing number of the baby boom generation arriving at retirement age in the next 25 years should prove interesting.

References

Allen, Carole and Herman Brotman. 1981. *Chartbook on Aging.* Washington, D. C.: Administration on Aging.

Beck, S. 1983. "Determinants of Returning to Work after Retirement." Final Report for Grant No. 1R23AG035:65–101, Kansas City, MO.

Berkman, Lisa F. and Lister Breslow. 1983. *Health and Ways of Living: The Alameda Country Study.* New York: Oxford University Press.

Clark, Robert. 1988. "The Future of Work and Retirement." *Research on Aging* 10:169–193.

Clifton, Bryant. 1972. *The Social Dimensions of Work.* Upper Saddle River, NJ: Prentice Hall.

Crowley, J. E. 1990. "Longitudinal Effects of Retirement on Men's Well-Being and Health." *Journal of Business and Psychology* 1:95–113.

Dennis, Helen. 1986. *Fourteen Steps to Managing an Aging Work Force,* edited by Helen Dennis, Lexington, MA: Lexington Books.

Dorfman, L. T. 1992. "Academics and the Transition to Retirement." *Educational Gerontology* 18:343–363.

Dubin, Robert. 1956. "Industrial Workers' Word: A Study of the Central Life Interests of Industrial Workers." *Social Problems* 3:131–142.

Fillenbau, G. G., L. K. George, and E. B. Palmore. 1985. "Determinants and Consequences of Retirement." *Journal of Gerontology* 39:364–371.

Fyock, Catherine. 1991. "American Work Force Is Coming of Age." *The Gerontologist* 31:422–425.

Gall, Terry, David Evans, and John Howard. May 1997. "The Retirement Adjustment Process; Changes in Well-Being of Male Retirees Across Time." *The Journal of Gerontology* 52B(3):110–117.

Gray, Robert M. and David O. Moberg. 1977. *The Church and the Older Person,* revised edition. Grand Rapids, MI: Ermanns.

Hall, Richard. 1975. *Occupations and the Social Structure.* Englewood Cliffs, NJ: Prentice Hall.

Hardy, Melissa. 1991. "Employment After Retirement." *Research on Aging* 13(3):267–288.

House, James S., Karl R. Landes, and Debra Umberson. 1988. "Social Relationships and Health." *Science* 241:540–545.

Howell, Nancy Morrow. 1988. "Life Span Determinants of Work in Retirement Years." *International Journal of Aging and Human Development* 27(2):125–140.

Iams, Howard M. 1985 "New Social Security Beneficiary Women." Correlates of work paper read at the 1985 meeting of the American Sociological Association.

Markides, Kyrakos S. 1983. "Aging, Religiosity and Adjustment: A Longitudinal Analysis." *Journal of Gerontology* 38:621–625.

McShulski, Elaine. 1997. "Ease Employer and Employee Retirement Adjustment with 'Soft Landing' Program." *HR Magazine,* Alexandria: 30–32.

Mobert, David D. 1983. "Compartmentalization and Parochialism in Religion and Voluntary Action Research." *Review of Religious Research* 22(4):318–321.

Moen, Phyllis, Donna Dempster-McClain, and Robin Williams. 1992. "Successful Aging: A Life Course Perspective on Women's Multiple Roles and Health." *American Journal of Sociology* 97(6):1612–1633.

Morris, Malcolm. 1986. "Work and Retirement in an Aging Society." *Daedalus* 115:269–293.

Ortega, Suzanne T., Robert D. Crutchfield, and William A. Rusling. 1983. "Race Differences in Elderly Personal Well-Being, Friendship, Family and Church." *Research on Aging* 5(1):101–118.

Parker, Stanley. 1982. *Works and Retirement.* London: Allen & Unwin Publishers.

Quinn, Joseph and Richard Burkhauser. *1990 Handbook of Aging and the Social Sciences,* edited by Richard Beinstock and Linda K. Gorge. Academic Press.

Quinn, J. F. 1980. *Retirement Patterns of Self-Employed Workers in Retirement Policy on an Aging Society,* R. L. Clark ed., Durham, NC: Duke University Press.

Soldo, Beth J. and Emily M. Agree. 1988. *Population Bulletin* 43(3). Population Reference Bureau.

Sammartino, Frank. 1979. "Early Retirement." in *Monographs of Aging,* No. 1, Madison: Joyce MacBeth Institute on Aging and Adult Life, University of Wisconsin.

Seccombe, K. and G. R. Lee. 1986. "Gender Differences in Retirement Satisfaction and Its Antecedents." *Research on Aging* 8:426–440.

Sheppard, Harold. 1990. *The Future of Older Workers.* International Exchange Center on Gerontology, University of South Florida, Tampa. FL.

Streib, G. F. and C. J. Schneider. 1971. *Retirement in American Society.* Cornell University Press, Ithaca, NY.

Tillenbaum, G. C. 1971. "The Working Retired." *Journal of Gerontology* 26:1:82–89. U. S. Department of Labor, Civilian Labor Force Participation Rates: Actual and Projected 1980.

Vroom, Victor. 1964. *Work & Motivation.* New York: John Wiley.

Welford, A. T. 1988. "Preventing Adverse Changes of Work with Age." *American Journal of Aging and Human Development* 4:283–291.

Critical Thinking

1. Of the life choices a person could have at retirement age, which group scored highest on life satisfaction?
2. Of those who retired and returned to work, who were the most satisfied?
3. Which group scored lowest in life satisfaction after retirement?

UNIT 6

The Experience of Dying

Unit Selections

Learning Outcomes

After reading this Unit, you will be able to:

- Describe the role that social activities and contact with children has on the adjustment to late life widowhood.

- Identify the group of individuals who were found to have low levels of social engagement in widowhood.

- Describe the main function of denial in the grieving process.

- Explain why confusion is normal for those whose social world has been destroyed.

- List the areas of congruence regarding the end of life preferences between terminally ill people and their family caregivers.

- Identify the areas of incongruence between terminally ill people and their families.

- List the six thematic areas that people who are terminally ill spoke of concerning the parts of their lives over which they felt they had control.

- Indicate the two areas of control that severely ill people could not control.

Student Website

www.mhhe.com/cls

Internet References

Agency for Health Care Policy and Research
www.ahcpr.gov
Growth House, Inc.
www.growthhouse.org
Hospice Foundation of America
www.HospiceFoundation.org

Modern science has allowed individuals to have some control over the conception of their children and has provided people the ability to prolong life. However, life and death still defy scientific explanation or reason. The world can be divided into at least two categories: sacred and secular. The sacred (that which is usually embodied in the religion of a culture) is used to explain all the forces of nature and the environment that can neither be understood nor controlled. On the other hand, the secular (defined as "of or relating to the world") is used to explain all the aspects of the world that can be understood or controlled. Through scientific invention, more and more of the natural world can be controlled. It still seems highly doubtful, however, that science will ever be able to provide an acceptable explanation of the meaning of death. In this domain, religion may always prevail. Death is universally feared. Sometimes, it is more bearable for those who believe in a life after death. Religion offers a solution to this dilemma. In the words of anthropologist Bronislaw Malinowski (1884–1942):

Religion steps in, selecting the positive creed, the comforting view, the culturally valuable belief in immortality, in the spirit of the body, and in the continuance of life after death. (Bronislaw Malinowski, *Magic, Science and Religion and Other Essays,* Glencoe, IL: Free Press, 1948).

The fear of death leads people to develop defense mechanisms to insulate themselves psychologically from the reality of their own death. The individual knows that someday he or she must die, but this event is nearly always thought to be likely to occur in the far distant future. The individual does not think of himself or herself as dying tomorrow or the next day but years from now. In this way, people are able to control their anxiety about death.

Losing a close friend or relative brings people dangerously close to the reality of death. Individuals come face to face with the fact that there is always an end to life. Latent fears surface. During times of mourning, people grieve not only for the dead but also for themselves and for the finiteness of life.

The readings in this section address bereavement, grief, and adjustments to the stages of dying. In "A Longitudinal Analysis of Social Engagement in Late-Life Widowhood," Linda Isherwood, Debra King, and Mary Luszcz examine the extent to which social engagement contributed to the adjustment of bereaved family members following the death of a spouse. In "The Grieving Process," Michael Leming and George Dickinson list and describe the stages of grief that individuals typically experience following the death of a loved one.

© Getty Images/Mark Thornton

Daniel Gardner and Betty Kramer, authors of "End-of-Life Concerns and Care Preferences: Congruence among Terminally Ill Elders and Their Family Caregivers," attempt to distinguish the similarities and differences in the beliefs and preferences of these two groups. Tracy Schroepfer, Hyunjin Noh, and Melinda Kavanaugh examine the strategies and means dying persons use to maintain control of their lives in the final days in "The Myriad Strategies for Seeking Control in the Dying Process."

A Longitudinal Analysis of Social Engagement in Late-Life Widowhood

Linda M. Isherwood, Debra S. King, and Mary A. Luszcz

Widowhood is one of the major transitions faced in older age (McCallum, 1986) and is considered part of the normative aging process (Baltes & Baltes, 1990). Widowhood engenders a far greater impact on an individual than purely an emotional loss; the transition to widowhood also involves the adjustment to a new role as a single person and the subsequent changes in life that this entails (Carr & Utz, 2002). Social engagement—having close relationships and participating in social activities—strongly influences the ability of the widowed spouse to successfully adapt to widowhood (Bennett, Gibbons, & Mackenzie-Smith, 2010). Therefore, it is important to understand how relationships and social activities change as a consequence of widowhood, and the potential role that social engagement has in protecting widowed people from the strain of bereavement and promoting healthy aging.

Active social engagement has been shown to play an important role during later life and in models of healthy aging. Continuing active engagement in life, along with the avoidance of disease and disability, and the maintenance of cognitive and physical functioning, has been proposed as a vital component of healthy aging (Rowe & Kahn, 1998). With ageing, undesirable changes (or losses) relating to physical, psychological, and social domains become more prevalent (Baltes & Baltes, 1990). The more resources an individual has, including ongoing social resources such as strong social networks and opportunities for social activity, the better their ability to cope with the losses associated with older age (Baltes & Lang, 1997).

By definition, those who have been widowed have lost a key figure in their network of social partners, with potentially an associated reduction in social engagement. The central purpose of this article is to examine the changes in social engagement which occur over time among widowed older adults. Social contact during the earlier stages of bereavement tends to be focused on adult children (Guiaux, van Tilburg, & van Groenou, 2007) and is an important source of emotional support (Ha, 2010). Friends play a more important role in terms of contact and support later in widowhood (Guiaux et al., 2007; Ha, 2008) and this contact is often centered around social activities (Chambers, 2005). Our study examines two key aspects of social engagement: the extent of contact with children and participation in social activities during late-life widowhood.

It is particularly important to understand the social engagement experiences of older widowed men and women for their experiences are likely to be different from that of those widowed at younger ages. Unlike their younger counterparts, the older widowed person is more likely to also be coping with other concurrent stressors such as health concerns, reduced mobility, financial pressures, relocation, cognitive decline, and loss of friends or family members (Carr, 2006). The life-span developmental perspective—which provided the theoretical grounding for this study—emphasizes that transitions during the life course are shaped by contextual factors (Baltes, 1987). Therefore, concomitant changes relating to aging may also have implications for social engagement, and hence the experience of social engagement during late-life widowhood must be viewed against this background.

Relationships with family, friends, and the wider social network take on increased significance following the death of a spouse (Feldman, Byles, & Beaumont, 2000). Social contact with network members during widowhood is an important factor in the facilitation or impediment of successful adjustment to spousal bereavement (van Baarsen, van Duijm, Smit, Snijders, & Knipscheer, 2002). Frequency of contact with others has been associated with well-being in widowhood (Bisconti, Bergeman,

& Boker, 2006; Lund, Caserta, & Dimond, 1993) and a lack of social contact identified as a major risk factor for post-bereavement loneliness (Pinquart, 2003).

Two previous studies have examined longitudinal change in contact with the social network during widowhood. These studies produced equivocal results possibly due to methodological differences in their design. Guiaux and colleagues (2007) explored changes in contact and support with the social network before and after widowhood over a 10-year period with outcome data collected every 3 years. Immediately following their loss, widowed individuals reported higher levels of contact with their social network than their still-married peers, with contact peaking at 2.5 years after widowhood. In a study of 108 bereaved spouses interviewed six times in the first 2 years of widowhood, Lund and colleagues (1990) found that contact with family and close friends reached its highest point at 2 months post-bereavement; contact with the primary social network then fell after this point (particularly for older widowed males).

Social activities may also play an important role in the process of adaptation to widowhood. Social activities are those activities which are performed with others and, more than any other activity domain, have been associated with physical and emotional well-being (Adams, Leibbrandt, & Moon, 2011). Kleiber and colleagues (2002) propose that social activities have four different functions during negative life events: activities may act as a buffer; generate hope for the future; provide continuity; and play a central role in personal transformations. Participation in social activities during widowhood has been associated with lower levels of loneliness (Pinquart, 2003), guilt and sadness (Sharp & Mannell, 1996), enhanced morale and reduced stress (Patterson & Carpenter, 1994), and better physical and mental health (Janke, Nimrod, & Kleiber, 2008a). Older widowed individuals may be at risk of lower levels of social participation as significant declines in activity levels have been associated with aging (Bennett, 2005), in particular due to reduced financial status, shrinking of social networks owing to deaths of friends, deterioration in physical health (Bennett, 1997), and poorer perceived health status (Patterson, 1996).

There have been no consistent findings regarding the impact of widowhood on levels of social activity. Previous studies examining participation in social activities have differed considerably in their design, in particular in the timing of measurements, the use of a married control group, and whether pre-loss measures were collected. These studies also measured social activity in very different ways, which could account for the disparate findings. In a comparison of married and widowed older adults

and their participation in 20 different activities (solitary as well as social), Bennett (2005) found that widowhood (and especially recent bereavement) led to a decrease in overall levels of activity. Likewise, a study exploring patterns of leisure activity in a sample of recently widowed older adults (Janke, Nimrod, & Kleiber, 2008b) found that the majority of participants reduced their involvement in activities following widowhood.

Meanwhile, other studies have reported increased participation in social activities during widowhood. A study by Utz and colleagues (2002) comparing levels of formal and informal social participation of recently widowed and married participants found that frequency of informal activities increased after widowhood; widowed and married participants reported similar levels of formal activities. Donnelly and Hinterlong (2010), however, in a quasi-replication of the study by Utz et al., found that widowed individuals tended to increase participation in both informal and formal activities. A study examining leisure activity in a female sample aged 50 years or older (Janke et al., 2008a) found that while widowed women increased their involvement in all activities (except gardening) over time, married participants decreased their participation in most leisure activities.

The main purpose of this study was to explore the changes and continuities which occur in social engagement during late-life widowhood. Previous widowhood research has recommended the use of prospective longitudinal data, married control groups, and collecting data prior to widowhood to ensure that pre-loss characteristics and resources can be controlled (Carr & Utz, 2002). This study follows these recommendations. Previous longitudinal studies have reported differing findings with regard to trajectories of change in social engagement in late-life widowhood. To date, there has been no consensus regarding the relationship between widowhood and the frequency of contact and social activities in later life. Contact in widowhood (particularly during the early stages) tends to be focused on adult children (Guiaux et al., 2007). To our knowledge, there have been no previous studies examining trajectories of change in contact with children during widowhood.

The majority of longitudinal studies of bereavement have focused on the earlier stages of the widowhood transition and used data drawn over two or three occasions. Very little is known of the longer-term outcomes of widowhood with regard to changes in social contact and activities. This study provides an opportunity for an extended longitudinal investigation of social engagement in late-life widowhood as data are available from five occasions over a 16-year period, enabling an examination of social engagement in early and later widowhood.

The particular aspects of social engagement focused on in this study were personal and phone contact with children and participation in social activities. Two primary research questions were developed:

1. Do widowed and married participants exhibit different levels of contact with children and participation in social activities over time?
2. What are the predictors of contact with children and participation in social activities during late-life widowhood?

Method
Participants

Participants were drawn from the Australian Longitudinal Study of Ageing (ALSA). Commenced in 1992, the ALSA aims to enhance understanding of biological social, and psychological factors associated with age-related changes in the health and well-being of older people (aged 65 years and over). To date, the ALSA has collected 11 waves of data: six major waves comprised of in-depth face-to-face interviews, clinical assessments, and self-completed questionnaires; and five waves utilizing shorter telephone interviews. Data on personal and phone contact with children and participation in social activities collected over the first five major waves (T1 = 1992 − 1993, T3 = 1994 − 1995, T6 = 2000 − 2001, T7 = 2002 − 2003, T9 = 2007 − 2008) of the ALSA were used for the longitudinal analyses.

ALSA participants who, at baseline, were married and had at least one living child were included in the sample for this study ($N = 1,266$). The widowed sub-sample was comprised of 344 participants who experienced spousal loss after baseline. The married participant group ($N = 922$) were continuously married throughout their participation in the ALSA. On average, 2.27 observations were available for each married participant. Widowed participants had an average of 3.69 observations each, representing 9.38 years in study.

Measures
Dependent Variables

Personal contact with children—The frequency of personal contact with children was determined by the question "Think of your children and/or children-in-law who do not live with you. In the past 12 months, how often did you have personal contact with at least one of them?" Frequencies were coded never (0), less than once a month (1), almost once a month (2), two or three times a month (3), once a week (4), and more than once a week (5).

Phone contact with children—The frequency of phone contact with children was ascertained by the question

"Again, think of your children and/or children-in-law who do not live with you. In the past 12 months, how often did you have phone contact with at least one of them?" Frequencies were again coded never (0), less than once a month (1), almost once a month (2), two or three times a month (3), once a week (4), and more than once a week (5).

Social Activities—Questions regarding participation in social activities in the ALSA were derived from the Adelaide Activity Profile (AAP). The AAP is an instrument for the measurement of lifestyle activities of older people relating to domestic chores, household maintenance, service to others, and social activities (Clark & Bond, 1995). Participants were asked about their frequency of participation in eight social activities over the previous 3 months: voluntary or paid employment; inviting people to the home; telephone calls to friends or family; social activities at a center or club; attendance at religious services or meetings; outdoor social activities; recreational or sporting activities; going for a drive or outing. The scores from the individual questions were summed to create a total social activities score (0 to 24).

Predictor variables and covariates—A number of variables identified in previous widowhood studies were used as either predictors or control variables at different stages in the analyses. These variables included socio-demographic (sex, age, marital status, household income, education), physical health (number of chronic conditions, self-rated health), psychological health (cognitive impairment, depression), and social network variables (number of children, child in close proximity). Sex, age, and education (time-invariant predictors) were based on self-reported data at baseline. All other covariates (time-varying predictors) used in this study were measured at each of the five major waves. The coding for these variables is outlined in Table 1.

Statistical Analysis

Multi-level modeling (MLM) was used to investigate longitudinal change in contact with children and in social activities. MLM has several advantages over repeated measures statistical models: both within-individual change and between-individual differences can be modeled; the number of observations can vary across participants thus allowing for missing data; occasions of measurement do not need to be fixed but can vary in their timing; and both time-varying (measures collected repeatedly over time) and time-invariant (attributes which are stable and measured only once) predictors can be included in the model (Singer & Willett, 2003). MLM enables both fixed and random effects to be modeled. Fixed effects describe the average patterns of change within a population, while random effects enable

Table 1 Descriptive Statistics for Participants at Baseline

Variable	Classification	Widowed (n = 344)		Married (n = 922)	
		n	(%)	n	(%)
Sex	Male	113	32.8	571	61.9
	Female	231	67.2	351	38.1
Age	65-74	5	48.1	372	40.3
	75-84	222	42.0	444	48.2
	85 +	95	9.9	106	11.5
	Mean (SD)	76.25	(5.79)	76.96	(5.84)
Household income	≤ $12,000	61	17.7	144	15.6
	$12,000-$30,000	234	68.0	623	67.6
	> $30,000	30	8.7	91	9.9
	Missing	19	5.5	64	6.9
Education (age left school)	≤ 14 years	176	51.2	522	56.6
	> 14 years	164	47.7	394	42.7
	Missing	4	1.2	6	0.6
Chronic conditions	0-1	251	73.0	633	68.5
	2-3	85	24.7	278	30.1
	4 +	8	2.3	13	1.4
	Mean (SD)	1.03	(0.97)	1.14	(0.99)
Self-rated health	Excellent/very good	153	44.5	315	34.2
	Good	107	31.1	277	30.0
	Fair/poor	84	24.4	325	35.2
	Missing	0	0.0	5	0.5
CES-D	No depression (<16/40)	307	89.2	789	85.6
	Depression (≥ 16/60)	36	10.5	119	12.9
	Missing	1	0.3	14	1.5
	Mean	7.42	(7.14)	7.58	(7.15)
MMSE	No cognitive impairment (>23/30)	294	85.5	708	76.8
	Cognitive impairment (≤ 23/30)	47	13.7	197	21.3
	Missing	3	0.9	17	1.8
	Mean	27.04	(3.19)	26.06	(4.32)
Number of children	1	56	16.3	132	14.3
	2	112	32.6	329	35.7
	3	93	27.0	238	25.8
	4 +	83	24.1	223	24.1
	Mean (SD)	2.74	(1.32)	2.79	(1.46)
Child in close proximity	0 children	27	7.8	83	9.0
	≥ 1 child	317	92.2	839	91.0
	Missing	0	0.00	1	0.1

within- and between-person variance to be accounted for in the model.

Hox (2010) recommends that if categorical data has at least five categories and the distributions are symmetric, then the potential bias introduced to the model is small and multi-level modeling can be used. The outcome variables for contact with children were therefore treated as linear dependent variables in the multilevel analysis. All the MLM analyses were conducted using SPSS Version 17.0 Linear Mixed Models program.

Comparison of Widowed and Married Participants

In order to ascertain whether widowed and married participants exhibited different levels of contact with children and participation in social activities over time, a series of multi-level models were developed. A forward modeling approach was used with predictors added to the model in subsequent steps. Predictors were retained in the model if overall model fit was improved. In order to ascertain the model of best fit for each of the outcome variables, the deviance statistic (-2LL) of the current model was compared to that of the previous model.

An unconditional growth model (Singer & Willett, 2003) was initially developed containing the random and fixed effects of "time in study." Hence, both the average rate of change over time in social engagement and the between-person variability in this change could be modeled. "Time in study," which was 0 for each participant at baseline, enabled exploration of changes in social engagement with each additional year in study. The fixed effects of "widowed status" at each wave were then added into the model enabling comparisons in levels of social engagement of widowed and married participants over time. Dummy variables for marital status (Married = 0, Widowed = 1) were created for each occasion of measurement. A fixed quadratic function of time in study explored whether change was better represented using a more complex polynomial function of time rather than a linear model (Singer & Willett, 2003). A final model controlled for socio-demographic, health, and network variables in order to ascertain whether marital status was a significant predictor of social engagement.

Predictors of Change for Widowed Participants

The predictors of change in contact with children and participation in social activities during late-life widowhood were then explored. The analysis again began with an unconditional growth model containing the fixed and random effects of "time in study." However, in this analysis, "time in study" was centered on widowhood (where time = 0 was the date of widowhood for each participant) enabling changes in the social engagement variables for each additional year in study before and after widowhood to be identified. Predictors (fixed effects only) were then added to the model in order to ascertain whether they had a significant relationship with levels of social engagement during widowhood. The predictors were added individually beginning with the time-variant predictors (Hox, 2010). Finally, fixed quadratic functions of time in study were added to the model. Using the date of widowhood

as a breakpoint, "quadratic time before widowhood" and "quadratic time after widowhood" were calculated at each wave (Guiaux et al., 2007).

Results

Descriptive statistics for the widowed and married participants at baseline are presented in Table 1. The distribution of men and women according to marital status varied. Females comprised the majority (67.2%) of the widowed sub-sample while males formed the majority (61.9%) of the married participants, $\chi^2 (1, 1266) = 84.14$, $p < .001$, $phi = .26$. Although small, significant differences were found between the married and subsequently widowed participants at baseline. Widowed participants were significantly younger, $t = 2.73$ (618.28), $p = .006$, reported better self-rated health, ($\chi^2 (5, 1262) = 26.58$, $p < .001$, $phi = .15$, and exhibited higher cognitive performance, $t = -4.34$ (809.24), $p = <.001$.

The results from the multi-level models of best fit for each of the social engagement variables are reported in Table 2.

Personal Contact with Children

Comparison of Widowed and Married Participants

Preliminary models suggested that widowed participants had higher levels of personal contact with their children than their married counterparts. However, once the final quadratic model of best fit controlled for psychological and physical health, social network variables, and socio-demographic factors, the difference between widowed and married participants, $\gamma = 0.117$, $p = .099$, was no longer significant, indicating that marital status is not predictive of personal contact with children in later life. For the average participant, personal contact with children decreased significantly over time, $\gamma = -0.044$, $p = .002$, reaching a low point at 11.0 years in study after which contact began to increase.

Predictors of Change for Widowed Participants

The model of best fit introduced health, social network, and socio-demographic predictors into the linear multi-level model. Controlling for all the predictors in this model, the average participant had 4.145 units ($p < .001$) of personal contact with their children at the time of widowhood (where a score of 4 indicates weekly contact and 5 is more than once a week). This frequent level of personal contact did not change significantly over time, $\gamma = -0.002$, $p = .783$, suggesting that fact-to-face contact with children does not vary with the length of widowhood.

Close proximity to children, $\gamma = -1.869$, $p < .001$, was the only predictor significantly related to personal

Table 2 Social Engagement—Multi-Level Models of Best Fit

Parameters	Comparison between widowed and married participants		
	Personal contact[a]	Phone contact[a]	Social activities[b]
Fixed effects			
Intercept	3.913***	4.213***	6.517***
Time in study	−0.044**	−0.068***	−0.059**
Widowed status	0.117	0.154*	1.376***
Quadratic time in study	0.002*	0.004***	—
Random effects			
Variance residual	0.611***	0.663***	5.177***
Variance intercept	0.747***	0.731***	6.953***
Variance slope	0.004***	0.001	0.027***
Covariance	−0.026***	−0.014*	−0.148**
Model fit			
-2LL	7335.420	7342.084	12700.735
df	18	18	17

Parameters	Predictors of change for widowed participants		
	Personal contact[c]	Phone contact[c]	Social activities[d]
Level-1 fixed effects			
—Intercept	4.145***	4.336***	7.357***
Time in study	−0.002	−0.009	0.197***
Cognitive impairment	0.067	−0.150	−0.969*
Depression	−0.078	0.026	−0.856*
Self-rated health	—	—	−0.464**
Chronic conditions	—	—	—
Close proximity to children	−1.869***	—	—
Number of children	—	—	—
Income	−0.031	0.100*	0.025
Quadratic time before widowhood	—	—	0.020**
Quadratic time after widowhood	—	—	−0.017**
Level-2 fixed effects			
Sex	—	−0.438***	−0.529
Age	—	—	−0.115***
Education	−0.093	0.047	0.955**
Random effects			
Variance residual	0.643***	0.599***	5.751***
Variance intercept	0.555***	0.618***	5.954***
Variance slope	0.004**	0.001	0.021*
Covariance	−0.007	−0.003	−0.052
Model fit			
-2LL	2723.162	2616.007	4718.699
df	11	11	15

Note: *df* indicates the number of parameters used in the model.

[a] Model included the fixed and random effects of time in study, the fixed effects of widowed status and quadratic time in study, and also controlled for socio-demographic, health, and network variables.

[b] Model included the fixed and random effects of time in study, the fixed effects of widowed status and also controlled for socio-demographic, health, and network variables.

[c] Model included the fixed and random effects of time in study and the fixed effects of socio-demographic, health, and network predictors.

[d] Model included the fixed and random effects of time in study, the fixed effects of quadratic time before and after widowhood, and the fixed effects of socio-demographic, health, and network predictors.

*$p < .05$, **$p < .01$, ***$p < .001$.

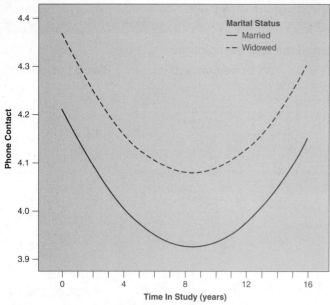

Figure 1 Average change in phone contact with children for married and widowed participants.

contact with children. Hence widowed participants with at least one child living within an hour's travel had considerably higher levels of personal contact with their children.

Phone Contact with Children
Comparison of Widowed and Married Participants

After controlling for health, socio-demographic, and network variables, the quadratic model of best fit showed a small but significant difference between widowed and married participants in level of phone contact, $\gamma = 0.154, p = .024$, indicating that widowhood is associated with more phone contact with children than remaining married. The trajectories of change in phone contact for married and widowed participants are shown in Figure 1. Phone contact with children significantly decreased over time ($\gamma = -0.068, p < .001$), reaching a low-point for the average participant at 8.5 years in study, after which contact started to increase again.

Predictors of Change for Widowed Participants

Controlling for the predictors in the linear model of best fit, the average participant had 4.336 units ($p < .001$) of phone contact with their children at the time of widowhood. Change in phone contact over time was not significant, $\gamma = -0.009, p = .125$, suggesting that the frequency of phone contact does not change during the different phases of widowhood.

Income, $\gamma = 0.100, p = .047$, and sex, $\gamma = -0.438, p = < .001$, were found to be significant predictors of phone contact with children during widowhood. Having a higher

income or being female were both predictive of higher levels of phone contact with children.

Social Activities
Comparison of Widowed and Married Participants

The model of best fit suggested that the average married participant had a social activities score of 6.517 ($p < .001$) at baseline, reducing by 0.059 ($p = .001$) with each passing year. Widowed participants on average scored 1.376 ($p < .001$) higher on the social activities scale compared to married participants, suggesting that widowhood is associated with more participation in social activities in older age.

Predictors of Change for Widowed Participants

Controlling for the predictors in the quadratic model of best fit, the average participant had a social activities score of 7.357 ($p < .001$) at the time of widowhood. With each additional year after widowhood, social activities increased by 0.197 ($p < .001$). The quadratic parameters for time before and after widowhood were both significant, $\gamma = 0.020, p = .001$; $\gamma = -0.017, p = .009$, indicating that the increase in social activities tapered off with time after widowhood. Figure 2 illustrates the average trajectory in social activities score during the transition to widowhood. Before widowhood, social activities were lowest at 4.9 years prior to bereavement. Activities then increased until 5.8 years after widowhood when participation began to decrease again.

Cognitive impairment, $\gamma = -0.969, p = .013$, depression, $\gamma = -0.856, p = .010$, self-rated health, $\gamma = -0.464, p = .002$, age, $\gamma = -0.115, p < .001$, and

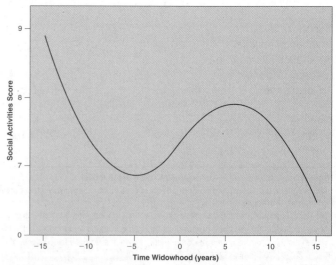

Figure 2 Average change in social activities score during widowhood.

education, $\gamma = 0.955$, $p = .004$, were all found to be significant predictors of participation in social activities during widowhood. Thus, having an absence of cognitive impairment and depressive symptomatology, better self-rated health, being younger, and having a higher level of education were associated with greater levels of social activity during widowhood.

Discussion

This study explored the levels and predictors of social engagement during late-life widowhood. As the results indicate, levels of social engagement remain high during older age and the transition to widowhood served to enhance phone contact with children and participation in social activities.

Contact with Children

Comparisons between widowed and married participants indicated that frequency of phone contact with children was greater for the widowed participants. Both married and widowed participants were found to have similarly high levels of face-to-face contact with their children. These results concur with the findings or Guiaux and colleagues (2007) that widowed individuals have higher levels of overall contact with their children compared to married older adults. However, Guiaux et al. used a measure of total contact with children in their study and did not differentiate between personal and phone contact. The current study, while showing that contact with children may increase overall with widowhood, also suggests that there are differences in the trajectories of personal and phone contact in later life. Hence, it is important to distinguish the nature of the contact.

Around the time of widowhood, participants reported on average high levels of both personal and phone contact with their children. Neither type of contact was shown to change significantly over time, indicating that the length of widowhood does not have an impact on the intensity of contact with children. The consistency of contact with children during widowhood found in this study differs from the findings or previous studies which have shown increased levels of contact with the social network during widowhood (Lund et al., 1990; Guiaux et al., 2007). However, it is difficult to fully compare the results of the current study with these previous studies given the methodological differences between them. Socio-emotional selectivity theory proposes that older adults place an increasing focus on close relationships (Carstensen, 1992). Our findings of sustained high levels of contact with children throughout widowhood confirm the importance of the parent-child relationship during this transition.

Nonetheless, these average effects varied as a function of other individual difference factors which were shown to influence the amount or type of contact. Living in close proximity to at least one child was found to significantly predict the level of personal contact with children, while having a higher income and being female were significant predictors of higher levels of phone contact. Previous research with an older cohort has suggested that wives tend to act as "kin-keeper" during a marriage facilitating social interactions for the couple and that widowed men may consequently be at more risk of social isolation (Chipperfield & Havens, 2001). Our findings concur that males, as well those from lower socio-economic groups, and individuals who do not have a child living nearby may experience lower levels of social contact during widowhood.

Social Activities

Longitudinal comparisons of married and widowed individuals revealed that becoming widowed leads to a significant increase in the extent of participation in social activities. This confirms the results of previous studies (Donnelly & Hinterlong, 2010; Janke et al., 2008a; Utz et al., 2002) which also found that widowed individuals had higher levels of participation in social activities. However, these studies only examined social activities during earlier stages of widowhood (18 months and up to 3 years and 5 years post-bereavement respectively); moreover, the study by Janke and colleagues (2008a) used an exclusively female sample. The current study, by examining the experiences of older widowed males and females up to 15 years post-widowhood, enables a longer-term view of social activity following spousal bereavement.

Participation in social activities during widowhood was shown to increase initially with each year after bereavement, reaching a peak at 5.8 years after which time participation began to fall. Age, poorer self-rated health, cognitive impairment, depression, and lower levels of education were all found to be detrimental to participation rates in social activities. Hence, as Bennett (2005) suggests, the very old (who are more likely to be suffering from cognitive decline and physical and mental health problems) may be less able to participate in social activities with others during widowhood.

The results should be interpreted in the context of several limitations. Timing between data collection was not uniform and varied between 2 to 6 years. The larger time intervals may have masked shorter-term fluctuations in social engagement, particularly during the initial stages of widowhood. This study focused on contact with children following spousal bereavement; contact with members of the wider social network was unable to be ascertained as the relevant data was not collected at all time points of the ALSA. An overall measure of social activity was used in the study. We were therefore unable to differentiate whether change occurred in the frequency of particular social activities over time, that is, between levels of participation in formal and informal activities.

These limitations are counterbalanced by the strengths of the study. The data on social engagement was drawn from a population-based study over a 16-year period which, to our knowledge, provides the longest exploration of social engagement in widowhood. Our findings thus enhance understanding of the longer-term impact of widowhood on levels of social engagement. Trajectories of change in contact with children during the transition to widowhood were examined for the first time, differentiating between personal and phone contact. By only including participants who were married at baseline, the study was able to control for pre-loss characteristics. A large sample of older adults was used with a wide age range (65-94 years at baseline) and length of widowhood (up to 15 years).

The results of this study showed that the transition to widowhood is characterized by enhanced levels of social engagement. Frequency of phone contact with children and participation in social activities were shown to be higher for the widowed participants in this study; and social participation increased during the first 6 years of widowhood. High levels of social engagement during widowhood may not only assist individuals in successfully overcoming the challenges of spousal bereavement but may also enhance healthy aging.

However, opportunities for social engagement in widowhood were not found to be uniform. In particular, the very-old, males, and those in lower socio-economic groups, in poorer health, or without a child living nearby may have restricted opportunities for social contact and activities in widowhood and thus be more vulnerable to social isolation. It is important that practitioners identify those bereaved individuals who may be more at risk of lower levels of social engagement. Promoting opportunities for contact and social activity could have a positive impact on older adults' adjustment to widowhood and provide enhanced opportunities for healthy aging.

References

Adams, K. B., Leibbrandt, S., & Moon, H. (2011). A critical review of the literature on social and leisure activity and wellbeing in later life. *Ageing & Society, 31,* 683–712.

Baltes, P. B. (1987). Theoretical proposition of life-span developmental psychology: On the dynamics between growth and decline. *Developmental Psychology, 23,* 611–626.

Baltes, P. B., & Baltes, M. M. (1990). Psychological perspectives on successful aging: The model of selective optimization with compensation. In P. B. Baltes & M. M. Baltes (Eds.), *Successful aging: Perspectives from the behavioral sciences* (pp. 1–34). Cambridge: The Press Syndicate of Cambridge University.

Baltes, M. M., & Lang, F. R. (1997). Everyday functioning and successful aging: The impact of resources. *Psychology and Aging, 12,* 433–443.

Bennett, K. M. (1997). A longitudinal study of wellbeing in widowed women. *International Journal of Geriatric Psychiatry, 12,* 61–66.

Bennett, K. M. (2005). Psychological wellbeing in later life: The longitudinal effects of marriage, widowhood and marital status change. *International Journal of Geriatric Psychiatry, 20,* 280–284.

Bennett, K. M., Gibbons, K., & Mackenzie-Smith, S. (2010). Loss and restoration in later life: An examination of dual process model of coping with bereavement. *Omega, 61,* 315–332.

Bisconti, T. L., Bergeman, C. S., & Boker, S. M. (2006). Social support as a predictor of variability: An examination of the adjustment trajectories of recent widows. *Psychology and Aging, 21,* 590–599.

Carr, D. (2006). Methodological issues in studying late life bereavement. In D. Carr, R. M. Nesse, & C. B. Wortman (Eds.), *Spousal bereavement in late life* (pp. 19–48). New York: Springer.

Carr, D., & Utz, R. (2002). Late-life widowhood in the United States: New directions in research and theory. *Ageing International, 27,* 65–88.

Carstensen, L. (1992). Social and emotional patterns in adulthood: Support for socioemotional selectivity theory. *Psychology and Aging, 7,* 331–338.

Chambers, P. (2005). *Older widows and the lifecourse: Multiple narratives of hidden lives.* Aldershot: Ashgate Publishing Ltd.

Chipperfield, J. G., & Havens, B. (2001). Gender differences in the relationship between marital status transitions and life satisfaction in later life. *Journal of Gerontology: Psychological Sciences, 56B,* 176–186.

Clark, M. S., & Bond, M. J. (1995). The Adelaide Activities Profile: A measure of the lifestyle activities of elderly people. *Aging: Clinical & Experimental Research, 7,* 174–184.

Donnelly, E. A., & Hinterlong, J. E. (2010). Changes in social participation and volunteer activity among recently widowed older adults. *The Gerontologist, 50,* 158–169.

Feldman, S., Byles, J. E., & Beaumont, R. (2000). 'Is anybody listening?' The experiences of widowhood for older Australian women. *Journal of Women & Aging, 12,* 155–176.

Guiaux, M., van Tilburg, T., & van Groenou, M. B. (2007). Changes in contact and support exchange in personal networks after widowhood. *Personal Relationships, 14,* 457–473.

Ha, J. (2008). Changes in support from confidants, children, and friends following widowhood. *Journal of Marriage and Family, 70,* 306–318.

Ha, J. (2010). The effects of positive and negative support from children on widowed older adults' psychological adjustment: A longitudinal analysis. *The Gerontologist 50,*471–481.

Hox J J. (2010). *Multilevel analysis: Techniques and application.* New York: Routledge.

Janke, M. C, Nimrod, G., & Kleiber, D. A. (2008a). Leisure activity and depressive symptoms of widowed and married women in later life. *Journal of Leisure Research, 40(2),* 250–266.

Janke, M. C, Nimrod, G., & Kleiber, D. A. (2008b). Reduction in leisure activity and well-being during the transition to widowhood. *Journal of Women and Aging, 20,* 83–98.

Kleiber, D. A., Hutchinson, S. L., & Williams, R. (2002). Leisure as a resource in transcending negative life events: Self-protection, self-restoration, and personal transformation. *Leisure Sciences: An Interdisciplinary Journal, 24,* 219–235.

Lund, D., Caserta, M., & Dimond, M. (1993). The course of spousal bereavement in later life. In M. Stroebe, W. Stroebe, & R. Hansson (Eds.), *Handbook of bereavement: Theory, research and intervention.* Cambridge: Cambridge University Press.

Lund, D. A., Caserta, M. S., van Pelt, J., & Gass, K. A. (1990). Stability of social support networks after late-life spousal bereavement. *Death Studies, 14,* 53–73.

McCallum, J. (1986). Retirement and widowhood transitions. In H. Kendig (Ed.), *Ageing and families: A support networks perspective.* Sydney: Allen & Unwin.

Patterson, I. (1996). Participation in leisure activities by older adults after a stressful life event: The loss of a spouse. *International Journal of Aging & Human Development, 42,* 123–142.

Patterson, I., & Carpenter, G. (1994). Participation in leisure activities after the death of a spouse. *Leisure Sciences, 16,* 105–117.

Pinquart, M, (2003). Loneliness in married, widowed, divorced, and never-married older adults. *Journal of Social and Personal Relationships, 20,* 31–53.

Rowe, J. W., & Kahn, R. L. (1998). *Successful aging.* New York: Pantheon Books.

Sharp, A., & Mannell, R. C. (1996). Participation in leisure as a coping strategy among bereaved women. In D. Dawson (Ed.), *Proceedings of the Eighth Canadian Congress on Leisure Research.* Ottawa, ON: University of Ottawa.

Singer, J. D., & Willett, J. B. (2003). *Applied longitudinal data analysis: Modeling change and event occurrence.* Oxford: Oxford University Press.

Utz, R. L., Carr, D., Nesse, R., & Wortman, C. B. (2002). The effect of widowhood on older adults' social participation: An evaluation of activity, disengagement, and continuity theories. *The Gerontologist, 42,* 522–533.

van Baarsen, B., van Duijn, M. A. J., Smit, J. H., Snijders, T. A. M., & Knipscheer, K. P. M. (2002). Patterns of adjustment to partner loss in old age: The widowhood adaptation longitudinal study. *Omega, 44,* 5–36.

Critical Thinking

1. How did the transition to widowhood affect the levels of social engagement of these individuals?

2. How did the social activities of widowed persons compare to those of married persons?

3. What is a major problem the older persons may experience if their level of social engagement declines during widowhood?

The Grieving Process

MICHAEL R. LEMING AND GEORGE E. DICKINSON

Grief is a very powerful emotion that is often triggered or stimulated by death. Thomas Attig makes an important distinction between grief and the grieving process. Although grief is an emotion that engenders feelings of helplessness and passivity, the process of grieving is a more complex coping process that presents challenges and opportunities for the griever and requires energy to be invested, tasks to be undertaken, and choices to be made (Attig, 1991, p. 387).

Most people believe that grieving is a diseaselike and debilitating process that renders the individual passive and helpless. According to Attig (1991, p. 389):

It is misleading and dangerous to mistake grief for the whole of the experience of the bereaved. It is misleading because the experience is far more complex, entailing diverse emotional, physical, intellectual, spiritual, and social impacts. It is dangerous because it is precisely this aspect of the experience of the bereaved that is potentially the most frustrating and debilitating.

Death ascribes to the griever a passive social position in the bereavement role. Grief is an emotion over which the individual has no control. However, understanding that grieving is an active coping process can restore to the griever a sense of autonomy in which the process is permeated with choice and there are many areas over which the griever does have some control. . . .

Coping with Grief

The grieving process, like the dying process, is essentially a series of behaviors and attitudes related to coping with the stressful situation of changing the status of a relationship. . . . Many have attempted to understand coping with dying as a series of universal, mutually exclusive, and linear stages. However, because most will acknowledge that not all people will progress through the stages in the same manner, we will list a number of coping strategies used as people attempt to resolve the pain caused by the loss of a significant relationship.

Robert Kavanaugh (1972) identifies the following seven behaviors and feelings as part of the coping process: shock and denial, disorganization, volatile emotions, guilt, loss and loneliness, relief, and reestablishment. It is not difficult to see similarities between these behaviors and Kübler-Ross's five stages (denial, anger, bargaining, depression, and acceptance)

of the dying process. According to Kavanaugh (1972, p. 23), "these seven stages do not subscribe to the logic of the head as much as to the irrational tugs of the heart—the logic of need and permission."

Shock and Denial

Even when a significant other is expected to die, at the time of death there is often a sense in which the death is not real. For most of us our first response is, "No, this can't be true." With time our experience of shock diminishes, but we find new ways to deny the reality of death.

Some believe that denial is dysfunctional behavior for those in bereavement. However, denial not only is a common experience among the newly bereaved, but also serves positive functions in the process of adaptation. The main function of denial is to provide the bereaved with a "temporary safe place" from the ugly realities of a social world that offers only loneliness and pain.

With time the meaning of loss tends to expand, and it may be impossible for one to deal with all of the social meanings of death at once. For example, if my wife dies, not only do I lose my spouse, but also I lose my best friend, my sexual partner, the mother of my children, a source of income, the person who writes the Christmas cards, and so on. Denial can protect me from some of the magnitude of this social loss, which may be unbearable at one point in time. With denial, I can work through different aspects of my loss over time.

Disorganization

Disorganization is that stage in the bereavement process in which one may feel totally out of touch with the reality of everyday life. Some go through the 3-day time period just prior to the funeral as if on "automatic pilot" or "in a daze." Nothing normal "makes sense," and they may feel that life has no inherent meaning. For some, death is perceived as preferable to life, which appears to be devoid of meaning.

This emotional response is also a normal experience for the newly bereaved. Confusion is normal for those whose social world has been disorganized through death. When my father died, my mother lost not only all of those things that one loses with a death of a spouse, but also her caregiving role—a social role and master status that had defined her identity in the 5 years that my father lived with cancer. It is only natural to experience confusion and social disorganization when one's social identity has been destroyed.

Volatile Reactions

Whenever one's identity and social order face the possibility of destruction, there is a natural tendency to feel angry, frustrated, helpless, and/or hurt. The volatile reactions of terror, hatred, resentment, and jealousy are often experienced as emotional manifestations of these feelings. Grieving humans are sometimes more successful at masking their feelings in socially acceptable behaviors than other animals, whose instincts cause them to go into a fit of rage when their order is threatened by external forces. However apparently dissimilar, the internal emotional experience is similar.

In working with bereaved persons over the past 15 years, I have observed that the following become objects of volatile grief reactions: God, medical personnel, funeral directors, other family members, in-laws, friends who have not experienced death in their families, and/or even the person who has died. I have always found it interesting to watch mild-mannered individuals transformed into raging and resentful persons when grieving. Some of these people have experienced physical symptoms such as migraine headaches, ulcers, neuropathy, and colitis as a result of living with these intense emotions.

Guilt

Guilt is similar to the emotional reactions discussed earlier. Guilt is anger and resentment turned in on oneself and often results in self-deprecation and depression. It typically manifests itself in statements like "If only I had . . . ," "I should have . . . ," "I could have done it differently . . . ," and "Maybe I did the wrong thing." Guilt is a normal part of the bereavement process.

From a sociological perspective, guilt can become a social mechanism to resolve the **dissonance** that people feel when unable to explain why someone else's loved one has died. Rather than view death as something that can happen at any time to any one, people can **blame the victim** of bereavement and believe that the victim of bereavement was in some way responsible for the death—"If he had been a better parent, the child might not have been hit by the car," or "If I had been married to him I might also have committed suicide," or "No wonder he died of a heart attack, her cooking would give anyone high cholesterol." Therefore, bereaved persons are sometimes encouraged to feel guilt because they are subtly sanctioned by others' reactions.

Loss and Loneliness

As we discussed earlier, loss and loneliness are the other side of denial. Their full sense never becomes obvious at once; rather, each day without the deceased helps us to recognize how much we needed and depended upon those persons. Social situations in which we expected them always to be present seem different now that they are gone. Holiday celebrations are also diminished by their absence. In fact, for some, most of life takes on a

"something's missing" feeling. This feeling was captured in the 1960s love song "End of the World."

> Why does the world go on turning?
> Why must the sea rush to shore?
> Don't they know it's the end of the world
> 'Cause you don't love me anymore?

Loss and loneliness are often transformed into depression and sadness fed by feelings of self-pity. According to Kavanaugh (1972, p. 118), this effect is magnified by the fact that the dead loved one grows out of focus in memory—"an elf becomes a giant, a sinner becomes a saint because the grieving heart needs giants and saints to fill an expanding void." Even a formerly undesirable spouse, such as an alcoholic, is missed in a way that few can understand unless their own hearts are involved. This is a time in the grieving process when anybody is better than nobody and being alone only adds to the curse of loss and loneliness (Kavanaugh, 1972, p. 118).

Those who try to escape this experience will either turn to denial in an attempt to reject their feelings of loss or try to find surrogates—new friends at a bar, a quick remarriage, or a new pet. This escape can never be permanent, however, because loss and loneliness are a necessary part of the bereavement experience. According to Kavanaugh (1972, p. 119), the "ultimate goal in conquering loneliness" is to build a new independence or to find a new and equally viable relationship.

Relief

The experience of relief in the midst of the bereavement process may seem odd for some and add to their feelings of guilt. My mother found relief in the fact that my father's battle with cancer had ended, even though this end provided her with new problems. I have observed a friend's relief 6 months after her husband died. This older friend of mine was the wife of a minister, and her whole life before he died was his ministry. With time, as she built a new world of social involvements and relationships of which he was not a part, she discovered a new independent person in herself whom she perceived was a better person than she had ever been.

Although relief can give rise to feelings of guilt, like denial, it can also be experienced as a "safe place" from the pain, loss, and loneliness that are endured when one is grieving. According to Kavanaugh (1972, p. 121):

> The feeling of relief does not imply any criticism for the love we lost. Instead, it is a reflection of our need for ever deeper love, our quest for someone or something always better, our search for the infinite, that best and perfect love religious people name as God.

Reestablishment

As one moves toward reestablishment of a life without the deceased, it is obvious that the process involves extensive adjustment and time, especially if the relationship was meaningful. It is likely that one may have feelings of loneliness, guilt, and disorganization at the same time and that just when one may experience a sense of relief something will happen to trigger a denial of the death. What facilitates bereavement and adjustment is fully experiencing each of these feelings as normal and realizing that it is hope (holding the grieving person together in fantasy at first) that will provide the promise of a new life filled with order, purpose, and meaning.

Reestablishment never occurs all at once. Rather, it is a goal that one realizes has been achieved long after it has occurred. In some ways it is similar to Dorothy's realization at the end of *The Wizard of Oz*—she had always possessed the magic that could return her to Kansas. And, like Dorothy, we have to experience our loss before we really appreciate the joy of investing our lives again in new relationships.

The Four Tasks of Mourning

In 1982 J. William Worden published *Grief Counseling and Grief Therapy,* which summarized the research conclusions of a National Institutes of Health study called the Omega Project (occasionally referred to as the Harvard Bereavement Study). Two of the more significant findings of this research, displaying the active nature of the grieving process, are that mourning is necessary for all persons who have experienced a loss through death and that four tasks of mourning must be accomplished before mourning can be completed and reestablishment can take place.

According to Worden (1982, p. 10), unfinished grief tasks can impair further growth and development of the individual. Furthermore, the necessity of these tasks suggests that those in bereavement must attend to "grief work" because successful grief resolution is not automatic, as Kavanaugh's (1972) stages might imply. Each bereaved person must accomplish four necessary tasks: (a) accept the reality of the loss, (b) experience the pain of grief, (c) adjust to an environment in which the deceased is missing, and (d) withdraw emotional energy and reinvest it in another relationship (Worden, 1982).

Accept the Reality of the Loss

Especially in situations when death is unexpected and/or the deceased lived far away, it is difficult to conceptualize the reality of the loss. The first task of mourning is to overcome the natural denial response and realize that the person is dead and will not return.

Bereaved persons can facilitate the actualization of death in many ways. The traditional ways are to view the body, attend the funeral and committal services, and visit the place of final disposition. The following is a partial list of additional activities that can assist in making death real for grieving persons.

1. View the body at the place of death before preparation by the funeral director.
2. Talk about the deceased and the circumstances surrounding the death.
3. View photographs and personal effects of the deceased.
4. Distribute the possessions of the deceased among relatives and friends.

Experience the Pain of Grief

Part of coming to grips with the reality of death is experiencing the emotional and physical pain caused by the loss. Many people in the denial stage of grieving attempt to avoid pain by choosing to reject the emotions and feelings that they are experiencing. Some do this by avoiding places and circumstances that remind them of the deceased. I know of one widow who quit playing golf and quit eating at a particular restaurant because these were activities that she had enjoyed with her husband. Another widow found it extremely painful to be with her dead husband's twin, even though he and her sister-in-law were her most supportive friends.

J. William Worden (1982, pp. 13–14) cites the following case study to illustrate the performance of this task of mourning:

> One young woman minimized her loss by believing her brother was out of his dark place and into a better place after his suicide. This might have been true, but it kept her from feeling her intense anger at him for leaving her. In treatment, when she first allowed herself to feel anger, she said, "I'm angry with his behavior and not him!" Finally she was able to acknowledge this anger directly.

The problem with the avoidance strategy is that people cannot escape the pain associated with mourning. According to Bowlby (cited by Worden, 1982, p. 14), "Sooner or later, some of those who avoid all conscious grieving, break down—usually with some form of depression." Tears can afford cleansing for wounds created by loss, and fully experiencing the pain ultimately provides wonderful relief to those who suffer while eliminating long-term chronic grief.

Adjust to an Environment in which the Deceased is Missing

The third task, practical in nature, requires the griever to take on some of the social roles performed by the deceased, or to find others who will. According to Worden (1982, p. 15), to abort this task is to become helpless by refusing to develop the skills necessary in daily living and by ultimately withdrawing from life.

I knew a woman who refused to adjust to the social environment in which she found herself after the death of her husband. He was her business partner, as well as her best and only friend. After 30 years of marriage, they had no children, and she had no close relatives. She had never learned to drive a car. Her entire social world had been controlled by her former husband. Three weeks after his funeral she went into the basement and committed suicide.

The alternative to withdrawing is assuming new social roles by taking on additional responsibilities. Extended families who always gathered at Grandma's house for Thanksgiving will be tempted to have a number of small Thanksgiving dinners after her death. The members of this family may believe that "no one can take Grandma's place." Although this may be true, members of the extended family will grieve better if someone else is willing to do Grandma's work, enabling the entire family to come together for Thanksgiving. Not to do so will cause double pain—the family will not gather, and Grandma will still be missed.

The final task of mourning is a difficult one for many because they feel disloyal or unfaithful in withdrawing emotional energy from their dead loved one. One of my family members once said that she could never love another man after her husband died. My twice-widowed aunt responded, "I once felt like that, but I now consider myself to be fortunate to have been married to two of the best men in the world."

Other people find themselves unable to reinvest in new relationships because they are unwilling to experience again the pain caused by loss. [A] quotation from John Brantner . . . provides perspective on this problem: "Only people who avoid love can avoid grief. The point is to learn from it and remain vulnerable to love."

However, those who are able to withdraw emotional energy and reinvest it in other relationships find the possibility of a newly established social life. Kavanaugh (1972, pp. 122–123) depicts this situation well with the following description.

At this point fantasies fade into constructive efforts to reach out and build anew. The phone is answered more quickly, the door as well, and meetings seem important, invitations are treasured and any social gathering becomes an opportunity rather than a curse. Mementos of the past are put away for occasional family gatherings. New clothes and new places promise dreams instead of only fears. Old friends are important for encouragement and permission to rebuild one's life. New friends can offer realistic opportunities for coming out from under the grieving mantle. With newly acquired friends, one is not a widow, widower, or survivor—just a person. Life begins again at the point of new friendships. All the rest is of yesterday, buried, unimportant to the now and tomorrow.

Critical Thinking

1. When one's identity and social order face the possibility of being destroyed by the death of a loved one, what are some of the most volatile reactions?

2. What are the results of feeling guilty when grieving over a loved one?

3. What are the four tasks of mourning according to Kavanaugh (1972)?

End-of-Life Concerns and Care Preferences: Congruence among Terminally Ill Elders and Their Family Caregivers

Daniel S. Gardner, PhD and Betty J. Kramer, PhD

Introduction

In the past several decades, it has become clear that there are substantial disparities between the way older Americans wish to die and the way their last days are realized. This discrepancy is due, in part, to well-documented gaps in the quality of care that people receive at the end of life (Field & Cassel, 1997; SUPPORT, 1995). Although most people prefer to die in their own homes (Higginson & Sen-Gupta, 2000; Tang & McCorkle, 2003; Thomas, Morris, & Clark, 2004), a majority of deaths occur in hospitals or nursing homes (Gallo, Baker, & Bradley, 2001; Pritchard, Fisher, Teno, Sharp, Reding, Knaus, et al., 1998). And despite considerable advances in medical and supportive approaches to pain management, a significant number of older adults with advanced and terminal illness experience serious pain and discomfort (SUPPORT, 1995; Teno, Clarridge, Casey, Welch, Wetle, Shield, et al., 2004). In an effort to better understand the needs and enhance the care of dying individuals and their families, end-of-life researchers have explored these and other disparities between end-of-life preferences and outcomes.

Barriers to quality end-of-life care include the unpredictable nature of terminal illness, communication difficulties in familial and social relationships, and the complex care needs of dying patients and their families (Kramer & Auer, 2005). Quality care is also hindered by systemic-level factors, including the emphasis on curative and life-sustaining intervention over quality of life and supportive care, health care financing and service delivery structures that move patients between multiple care settings with minimal coordination and poor continuity of care, a lack of providers trained in the fundamentals of palliative care (e.g., biopsycho-social-spiritual aspects of grief and loss, effective clinical communication, attention to family systems), and the absence of evidence-based practice knowledge in this area (Emanuel, von Gunten, & Ferris, 2000; Field & Cassel, 1997; Morrison, 2005). Further, end-of-life care models that represent the standard of care—hospice and palliative care—are underutilized and often inaccessible to the poor, racial and ethnic minorities, and elders with uncertain disease pathways.

Less is known about the subjective end-of-life experiences, concerns, and preferences of older patients and their family members (Cohen & Leis, 2002; Singer, Martin & Kellner, 1999; Vig, Davenport, & Pearlman, 2002). Recently there have been calls for research to better understand factors that affect patients' and families' perceptions of quality of life and quality of care at the end of life (Field & Cassel, 1997; Kramer, Christ, Bern-Klug, & Francoeur, 2005; NIH, 2004; SUPPORT, 1995). This study explores the challenges, concerns, and preferences of low-income elders receiving palliative care, and focuses on congruence and incongruence between the elders and their primary family caregivers.

Quality of Life and Care at the End of Life

The Institute of Medicine defined a "good death" as one with minimal suffering, which satisfies the wishes of dying patients and their families, while adhering to current medical, cultural and ethical standards (Field & Cassel, 1997). Researchers often operationalize a good death as the degree to which an individual's dying experiences correspond with their preferences for quality of life and quality of care at the end of life (Engelberg, Patrick, & Curtis, 2005). A growing literature has sought to shed light on the aspects of care that are most important to terminally ill elders and their family members (Heyland, Dodek, Rocker, Groll, Gafhi, Pichora et al., 2006; Laakkonen, Pitkala, & Strandberg, 2004).

When faced with advanced life-threatening illness, most people wish to be free of pain and symptoms (Heyland et al., 2006; Vig & Pearlman, 2004), to be treated with dignity and respect (Chochinov, Hack, Hassard, Kristjianson, McClement, & Harlos, 2002; Steinhauser, Christakis, Clipp, McNeilly, McIntyre, & Tulsky, 2000), and to maintain a sense of autonomy and control over their last days (Singer et al., 1999; McSkirmning, Hodges, Super, Driever, Schoessler, Franey, et al., 1999; Vig & Pearlman, 2004). Nearly all prefer to be informed of their prognoses and have time to put their affairs in order (Heyland et al., 2006; McCormick & Conley, 1995; Terry, Olson, Wilss, & Boulton-Lewis, 2006). Dying elders hope to avoid becoming burdens to their families (McPherson, Wilson, & Murray, 2007; Vig & Pearlman, 2004) and typically eschew the use of artificial means to prolong life (Heyland et al., 2006; Singer et al., 1999; see Steinhauser et al., 2000 for divergent findings). There is, however, a great deal of heterogeneity in what constitutes a "good death." Ultimately, end-of-life preferences are individual, dynamic and multidimensional, and vary across contexts such as age, gender, disease course, care setting, financial resources, and social and familial relationships (Thomas et al., 2004).

Congruence in Patient and Family Perspectives

During the course of advanced and terminal illness, elders increasingly rely on family members to identify and communicate their emotional and physical needs and concerns (McPherson, Wilson, Lobchuk, & Brajtman, 2008; Waldrop, Kramer, Skretny, Milch, & Finn, 2005). Much of the research on patients' end-of-life care preferences is also based on the report of family surrogates or healthcare proxies (Teno et al., 2004). However, the accuracy of family members' assessments of dying patients' concerns and preferences is uncertain. Studies have documented significant incongruence between patients and family members on their evaluations of quality of life (Farber, Egnew, Herman-Bertch, Taylor, & Guldin, 2003; McPherson & Addington-Hall, 2003), frequency and severity of pain and other physical and psychological symptoms (McPherson et al., 2008; Mularski, Curtis, Osborne, Engelberg, & Ganzini, 2004; Sneeuw, Sprangers, & Aaronson, 2002), and end-of-life preferences (Engelberg et al., 2005; Moorman & Carr, 2008; Shalowitz, Garrett-Myer, & Wendler, 2006; Steinhauser et al., 2000). Farber and colleagues (2003) describe these differences as reflecting the often highly divergent "cultural perspectives" of patients and their formal and informal caregivers around death and dying.

Although findings have been inconsistent, congruence in the end-of-life preferences and perceptions of elders and their family caregivers has been found to range from moderate to poor. There is some evidence of greater agreement around objective and measurable factors such as patient functioning and mobility, and less regarding subjective factors such

as pain and depression (Desbiens & Mueller-Rizner, 2000; Engelberg et al., 2005; McPherson & Addington-Hall, 2003; Tang & McCorkle, 2003). Congruence may be more likely when surrogate decision-makers are younger and female (McPherson & Addington-Hall, 2003; Zettel-Watson, Ditto, Danks, & Smucker, 2008), family income is higher (Desbiens & Mueller-Rizner, 2000), the illness is of longer duration, or the patient is closer to death (Sneeuw et al., 2002). Notably, there is evidence that families who have had explicit discussions about dying and the patient's wishes are more likely to agree with each other about end-of-life care preferences (Engelberg et al., 2005; Sulmasy, Terry, Weisman, Miller, Stallings, Vettese et al., 1998).

Despite gaps in our understanding of the correspondence between individual and family experiences of dying and preferences for end-of-life, very few studies have focused on congruence among paired patient-family caregiver dyads (Engelberg et al., 2005). And there remains a critical lack of knowledge about the shared and distinct challenges, concerns, and preferences of older adults and their family caregivers at the end of life (Vig et al., 2002). Empirical inquiry in this area may help to enhance familial understanding of older patients' concerns and the accuracy of surrogate decision-making, and to ultimately improve the quality of life at the end of life. The study described here uses qualitative methods to delve more deeply into the subjective experiences of terminally ill elders and their family caregivers, describe their end-of-life preferences and identify areas of congruence and incongruence.

Methods
Study Design

These data were collected as part of a larger longitudinal research study exploring the process and experience of end-of-life care provided to frail elders with advanced chronic disease enrolled in an innovative, fully "integrated" managed care program (Kramer & Auer, 2005). The design was an embedded case study (Scholz & Tietje, 2002), involving in-depth data collection with multiple sources of data. Case study research design makes it possible to examine processes, perceptions and outcomes regarding naturalistic phenomena of which the researcher seeks multiple perspectives (Yin, 2003). The results reported here address the congruent and incongruent end-of-life perceptions, challenges, concerns, and care preferences of elders and their primary family caregivers.

Research Site and Sample

Elder Care of Dane County, a not-for-profit organization, has provided community-based health and social services for older adults since 1976. The Elder Care Partnership (ECP) program, the largest program offered by this organization, provides comprehensive, fully integrated health, psychosocial, and long-term care to low-income frail elders. The program integrates practices that are consistent with clinical practice guidelines for quality palliative care (National Consensus Project, 2004). Detailed descriptions of the study and site can be found elsewhere (Kramer & Auer, 2005).

Study participants were purposefully selected by inter-disciplinary team members from the pool of elders (aged 65 years or older) enrolled in ECP. Enrollees had annual incomes below $10,000, seven to eight chronic medical conditions, and functional limitations in three or more Activities of Daily Living. Team members were asked to identify elders who were likely to die within 6 months, spoke English, were cognitively able to understand and respond to interview questions, and had a family member involved in their care. Once the elder completed consent procedures and agreed to participate, team members invited the identified primary family caregiver to participate in an interview with the Principal Investigator (PI; second author).

Data Collection

In-depth, semi-structured, face-to-face interviews, which ranged from 1 to 2 hours long, were conducted by the project PI, a university professor and Project on Death in America Social Work Leader. Elders and their identified family care-givers were interviewed separately at a time and place selected by the participant, most often in the participant's home. The interviews were not standardized in order to facilitate greater exploration of issues deemed most important to respondents (Padgett, 2008). Instead, each interview was structured around open-ended questions reflecting the study aims, including questions designed to explore the perceived challenges and concerns of the participants, their end-of-life preferences, and the extent to which they had discussed these issues with family members:

- What has been most difficult or challenging to you and your family members at this time?
- What are your [your family member's] concerns or worries?
- What is most important to you about the care you [your family member] receive[s] in your [their] last days?
- If you could plan it perfectly, what kind of death would you hope for [for the patient]? What would make a "good" death?

Additional questions and probes were used to explore participant preferences about the location of death, the desire for family members to be present, and the importance of family communication and saying "goodbye" during the elder's last days. In addition, the interviewer asked about the extent to which they had talked about the elders' end-of-life preferences, and their comfort or difficulty in doing so.

Data Analysis

All of the interviews were recorded on audiotape and transcribed verbatim, with participant consent. The researchers employed qualitative methods that entailed detailed readings and re-readings of each transcript, team coding, and thematic and conceptual analysis. Data analysis followed a form of *template analysis* (Crabtree & Miller, 1999) that begins with an a priori set of coding categories (i.e., a "template") based on the researchers' domains of interest (end-of-life challenges and worries or fears, care concerns, preferences, and family communication). Two researchers independently read the transcripts, identified segments that were relevant to the research domains, and used the preliminary coding template to search for and identify patterns and themes in the data. These themes were then tested within and across cases, and refined in order to generate broader and more integrated conceptual domains. Upon reaching theoretical saturation, a thematic conceptual matrix (Patton, 2002) was developed to examine the congruent (i.e., like) and incongruent (distinct) themes relevant to the domains of elder and family caregiver end-of-life challenges, concerns, and care preferences.

While no tests were conducted of inter-rater reliability, the research team employed several strategies to ensure analytic rigor. The protocol included: extended engagement, or the use of long interviews with extensive probing and clarification; independent team coding and peer debriefing; deviant case analysis in the development and testing of a final thematic schema; and careful auditing that involved documentation (including verbatim transcripts, field notes, and analytic memos) of the data collection and analytic process (Padgett, 2008).

Findings
Study Participants

Ten elders (five women and five men) and ten family care-givers (six women and four men) completed face-to-face interviews (see Table 1). The mean age of the elders was 85 years-old (range: 64-101), and family members were a mean 53 years-old (range: 47-67). Family caregivers included four daughters, three sons, one daughter-in-law, one grandson, and one wife. Nine of the dyads were non-Hispanic white, and one was African American. Elders were enrolled in the program an average of 2.6 years (range: 1.5-4), and all had multiple chronic health conditions. The most debilitating diagnoses included serious heart disease ($n = 5$), lung disease ($n = 3$), and cancer ($n = 2$). Five of the elders lived alone and five lived with their family caregivers (four with an adult child and one with a spouse).

Domains of Care

Four domains of end-of-life care framed the results of our analysis: a) the *challenges* or day-to-day difficulties related to the patient's terminal illness; b) participants' *worries* or fears about the patient's death and dying; c) *care concerns* regarding the patient's end-of-life care by formal and informal caregivers; and d) participants' hopes and preferences

Table 1   Elder and Family Caregiver Dyads

Elder	Family Caregiver
97-year-old African-American female with heart disease	47-year-old African-American grandson; single, live-in caregiver
86-year-old white female with lung disease	50-year-old white daughter; lives separately
89-year-old white male with heart disease	56-year-old white son; married, lives separately
82-year-old white female with lung cancer	52-year-old white daughter; single, lives separately
101-year-old white female with heart disease	67-year-old white son; single, live-in caregiver
84-year-old white male with heart disease	47-year-old white daughter; divorced, lives separately (in same town)
80-year-old white male with heart disease and accident-related injuries	48-year-old white daughter-in-law (married to step-son); lives separately
86-year-old white male with prostate cancer	56-year-old daughter; single, live-in caregiver
82-year-old white female with lung disease and accident-related injuries	48-year-old white son; married, lives with elder
64-year-old white male with lung disease	55-year-old white wife; live-in

Table 2   Congruence & Incongruence among Elders & Family Caregivers

Domain	Themes	Incongruent		Congruent
		Elder	**Family**	**Both**
Challenges	Experiencing decline			X
	Accepting dependence	X		
	Providing adequate care		X	
	Living with uncertainty			X
Worries	Pain & suffering			X
	Meeting elders' care needs		X	
	Becoming a burden	X		
	Anticipating the impact on survivors			X
Concerns about EOL Care	Receiving competent, consistent & responsive care			X
	Managing pain			X
	Being treated with dignity and respect			X
	Living while dying			X
A "Good Death"	Dying at home			X
	Dying quickly, without suffering			X
	Avoiding life support			X
	Being prepared	X		
	Addressing spiritual needs		X	

for a *good death*. These domains reflect a range of end-of-life concerns and preferences that were expressed and elaborated on by study participants, some of which are shared or congruent, and others which are distinct to either elders or their family members (see Table 2).

Challenges

Elders and their family caregivers identified four primary illness-related challenges they struggled with on a daily basis.

Experiencing Physical and Functional Decline

Elders spoke articulately about their efforts to participate in normal daily activities in the face of decreased energy and declining physical and functional capacities, as is illustrated here:

I like to walk. I can't get out and walk. I have to have a walker so sometimes the kids take me in a wheelchair and we can walk around the campgrounds, or we'll go down by the lake. I'd like to be able to walk, too. But I can't do it. I can't go up and down the stairs so I have to stay here and let somebody else go down and do my laundry. I haven't been down the stairs in the basement for two years. (83 year-old female elder)

I can't do the things I want to do, like mow the lawn or walk down the block. It's hard to breathe . . . Yeah, feels like you're ready to die—takes your breath right away from you. (64-year-old male elder)

Family caregivers also struggled with the changes in their loved ones' functioning, often within the context of lifelong relationships:

It's just that I can't be with him like I'd like to be . . . we've been married almost 37 years so it's a long time, and, just to see him going downhill like he is. (55-year-old wife)

Accepting Increasing Dependence

Closely associated with physical and functional decline, many elders struggled to contend with the diminished autonomy and increasing dependence on others:

I miss driving . . . I have to depend on other people and I was always so independent. It bothers me when I have to ask people to haul me around and pick me up, but they don't care, they don't say anything, but I—that's one thing that bugs me but I can't change it so I'll just go on the way it is. (80-year-old male elder)

Some family caregivers were aware that decreased autonomy could be challenging for the elders, but rather than viewing dependence as a challenge they emphasized the benefits of relying on others:

He was able to take his own baths and do everything and then wham-o, here he is. He's in bed all the time and somebody has to help him bathe or whatever . . . although I tell him it's *teamwork,* that we're doing this as a team. (56-year-old daughter)

Providing Adequate Care

Family caregivers spoke at length about caring for the elders, often emphasizing the challenges and responsibilities inherent in the role of family caregiver.

Basically, I'm her number one health advocate. I've had to deal with these situations where people didn't want [her] to go to the hospital and I knew she had to, or just on and on with different things that have happened. So, I just kind of focus on her. (48-year-old son)

The challenge of providing care was often experienced as stressful by family members, given the elder's changing medical needs and the complex nature of family history and relationships:

Part of my life is on hold right now because I'm staying here to take care of her. . . . I'm married and I have a wife and we want to enjoy our life together, so as painful as it is to see your parent leave your life, it's also going to be a big transition when I finally get on with my life . . . it's really a dichotomy because you feel selfish when you think about yourself and your own situation and what your preferences are and what you'd do if you were just living in your own house with your own family versus taking care of a parent. So, it's pretty hard. (48-year-old son)

Living with Uncertainty

Both elders and family caregivers talked about the difficulties they had in coping with their uncertain futures. Although all participants were aware that the elders had limited prognoses, many struggled with not knowing how and when their terminal decline would occur:

About death? I've had pains and stuff, you know, and I had to go to the hospital and all that. I don't know if I'm gonna come home again or not. You don't know that—if you're that bad—and these blood clots can move. They can hit you just like that and you're gone. (64-year-old male elder)

For me, it's never knowing when he's going into an attack, and if I'm at work . . . I told them at work—I said there'll be days when I can't come in because he isn't good, or I'll have to leave because something's gone wrong. (55-year-old wife)

Worries or Fears about Dying

Elders and family caregivers were encouraged to talk about their concerns, worries, and fears related to dying. In response to direct questions, most of the elders initially denied any fears of death or dying. As the interviews progressed, however, elders and family caregivers raised a variety of concerns about the future. Four areas of concern or worry were expressed by a majority of the participants.

Pain and Suffering

The principal concern shared by elders and family caregivers was that the elder would experience unmanageable pain or physical discomfort as they were dying.

I'm concerned about pain and cancer, I never had anyone in my family that's had cancer, my ideas of it are strictly from novels or movies, so they give you enough pain medication to control the pain then you're going to be nauseated and sleepy and even [lose] your mind, hallucinating even, so that's not something I look forward to. (82-year-old female elder)

I guess I'm . . . afraid of the pain, if she might have a lot of pain. I don't know, it really is kind of terrifying. I don't know what it's going to be like when the, if the cancer really hits. The best thing would be if she would die from some secondary, related, symptomatic illness like pneumonia or something. (52-year-old daughter)

Meeting Elders' Increasing Needs

Family caregivers were particularly worried about their capacity to respond to the intensifying needs of the elders, and that they might lack the necessary supports and resources to continue providing care at home. Several participants feared having to place elders in long-term care institutions in the future:

> I suppose my biggest concern . . . is that he will regress and have a physical deterioration that will make it virtually impossible for him to be able to continue in that apartment, making a full time placement in a nursing home type facility necessary. That's going to be hard in a lot of ways. There's the physical move and taking care of all the stuff that will need to be moved over there, and then there's just the emotional aspect for [Elder] in terms of being in a place where he just damn well doesn't want to be. (48-year-old daughter-in-law)

A related concern was that the elder might not be aware of—or might hide—signs of his or her decline.

> I think probably one of my biggest concerns with my mother is whether or not she'll be totally honest and recognize when something is really wrong. And so that, that's got me some concern to the point when she did fall the last time and she was in the nursing home . . . she had fallen a couple of times earlier in the week and hadn't told anybody that she had been dizzy and that she had fallen and if she, if she had told anybody either her home nurse or us, that that was going on, then we would have intervened, so it raised questions about whether or not she could be on her own or not. (50-year-old daughter)

Family caregivers often feared a sudden decline in the elder's health, and, in particular, "something happening with no one around." Several family members expressed anxiety and guilt about going to work or returning to their own homes, and leaving the elder in the care of others.

> Well, I worry every single day about her falling down and stuff like that, and what's going to be the next trigger that sends her back to the hospital for the next surgery that she can barely tolerate or not at all—that whole thing. (48-year-old son)

Becoming a Burden

A major concern of most of the elders was the fear of experiencing a long trajectory of decline, and becoming a burden on their families:

> Well, I'd like to go fast. I don't want to suffer a lot and make everybody else suffer a lot. That would be important. My husband had Alzheimer's and that was

just pathetic, watching him for ten years go downhill . . . most families now-a-days are half crazy with trying to make a living . . . they have to spend so much time with the woman working and the man working, and then to add the care of an elderly patient is just too much for them, it overburdens them so that they, the parent or the aunt or grandmother, whoever it is, begins to feel well I don't want to bother my children with this, I'll just let it go which is what I do to some extent. (82-year-old female elder)

Family caregivers did not share the concern that their elders were becoming burdens; most did not question their responsibility to provide care and support for the elders.

Anticipating Survivors' Wellbeing

Many elders worried about the needs and wellbeing of their families after their impending death. They were primarily concerned about family members' grief and ability to cope with the loss:

> Just to keep my daughter as calm as possible—that's the main thing. I don't want to upset her any more than I have to. What can you do? Your parents die, that's going to happen, so . . . there is nothing to be done about it but I want to, want her to be as calm as possible. (82-year old female elder)

One elder was also specifically anxious about the spiritual wellbeing of her children and grandchildren after she died:

> Well, to know that they're taken care of—their health and they're able to—their religion—stay with that. And then I hear about some of them giving up religion and they're all becoming atheists—it makes me feel kind of blue. I don't like to hear that. (101-year-old female elder)

Some elder participants worried more about practical concerns (e.g., medical bills, taxes, or loss of income) that would affect their loved ones. Many expressed regrets that they would not be around to look out for family members after death.

> Well, the thing I'd be concerned about is my wife and the kids, and the house and stuff, you know? All the bills should be paid, or whatever. Well, she'd be living here by herself, you know? And if she was taken care of, or whatever she has to do—I don't think she'd ever get remarried again, but I imagine it'd be tough for her to keep on rolling, keeping the house maybe. The taxes ain't cheap. (64-year-old male elder)

> I just hope that the kids will get along fine, and the grandkids, that's it. And hope the world straightens out a little bit better. All this terrorism and stuff, I don't like that but that's way beyond my help. (80-year-old male elder)

Family caregivers echoed these concerns with their own worries about life after the elder's death. Some concerns were about their anticipation of grief and loss, but several caregivers worried about pragmatic matters such as arranging funeral plans and paying bills.

[My fears are] stupid. [Laughs], My worries are about her funeral, okay? That it will come at a really bad time, like when I'm in the middle of three hundred and forty report cards and my house is a mess, you know, and that kind of stuff that, that I won't know what to do. That there will be a division, and fighting like over the paintings and things like that [Laughs]. I want her to write people's names on the backs of the paintings so I won't have to deal with it. (50-year-old daughter)

Concerns about End-of-Life Care

In addition to their worries about dying, elders and family caregivers articulated their concerns and care preferences regarding the care the elders would receive from healthcare team members in their last days. Specifically, they reported four major preferences.

Receiving Competent, Consistent and Responsive Care

Elders and family caregivers felt that quality care required the involvement of skilled healthcare professionals who were competent, "consistent and responsive" to the elders' needs. For elders, it was of critical importance to feel they could depend on reliable caregivers that met their basic needs:

Well [hospice] volunteers means that no one person would come every week, instead you would probably get a stream of people coming in, none of whom you knew and I don't like that idea at all . . . . Just that whoever takes care of me shows me respect . . . taking good care of me. You know, keeping me clean and fed and whatever. If I can't eat—well that's another thing but . . . I just think to take good care of me, see that my needs were taken care of. (82-year-old female elder)

For family members, these concerns seemed to be associated with their anxieties about meeting the elders' escalating needs as death approached (see above). Their descriptions of adequate care often emphasized the medical and concrete aspects of care (e.g., keeping the elder safe and clean, and ensuring their adherence to medication regimens):

I think hygiene is way up on the scale as far as her, granny's is. Her body is so fragile and her skin is so, you know, tender, so I mean for them making sure she's gets the proper hygiene. And medical, um, well granny won't take a lot of medical, but I mean, but they're there for any medical needs. But, I think, just trying to make her comfortable as possible. (48-year-old grandson)

Managing Pain

Elders and family caregivers were concerned that the elders receive good pain control and prompt alleviation of physical discomfort at the end of their lives. For several participants, this was a primary reason for choosing hospice or palliative care services:

Well that, the hospitals, they never used to give you enough painkiller to make enough difference because they said you were going to become addicted. Well what difference does it make at that point? And so I would want someone managing that and I . . . I think I would want to go to hospice and let them handle it. (86-year-old female elder)

I happen to be a big proponent of hospice-type transitions from life to death. And, I'm a big believer in you make the person comfortable. At that point, I don't care if he gets hooked on a particular drug. It's irrelevant. But if he could have his needs tended to, the pain alleviated, and the transition as smooth as possible, I'd rather see that—except to go quickly. (48-year-old daughter-in-law)

Being Treated with Dignity and Respect

Elders and family caregivers also agreed that respectful treatment was of paramount concern in end-of-life care. For elders, this meant appreciating their need for autonomy and control, and being cared for in a courteous, compassionate manner. Family members also articulated the importance of having providers who treated the elders with dignity and valued each patient as a unique, "whole person":

Just that, that whole, you know, just having respect and beauty and concern around. . . . But a nursing home staff in all fairness is totally overloaded, I mean so it's not like totally all their fault. It's our system's fault, it's like, we don't value that so much. (50-year-old daughter)

To try to meet the person on their own level. In my mother's case, in other words, to try and find out what is important to that person and take an interest in those things with them. Share with them those things. If someone thinks clipping coupons is important, than the social worker who's coming says look at all these coupons I found, we can go get such and such at so and so or if the person is a musician and the social worker would come and say well I have a new recording of so and so's orchestra doing such and such. (52-year-old daughter)

Living While Dying

Many of the elders thought it was important to continue living as they had their entire lives. "Focusing on living" instead of dying included eating the foods they loved, participating in activities they enjoyed (e.g., walking, sewing, card-playing, and socializing) with friends and family.

Just comradeship. . . . [Having] people that are around that I will talk with, or will talk with me, and you would miss them if you don't see them at least once a week, or more than that. (84-year-old male elder)

This concern was associated with the desire to be treated with dignity and respect, and to die at home in the context of intimate surroundings, people, and routines! Elders emphasized the critical importance of having a measure of control over their lives and choice in their care during the dying process.

Well, if I could eat—to get some decent food—and they wouldn't cut me off my martinis or beer. That's about all. (80-year-old male elder)

Although not often a primary concern, most family caregivers expressed an understanding of how important it was for the elder to continue "living while dying," and sought to provide them with opportunities to enjoy their cherished activities.

Well, I think she wants to maintain a sense of normalcy, that things are still the way they used to be as much as possible. So even if life is slipping away, she still can enjoy it. She can still feel at home. So little things, like being able to watch her favorite television shows. . . . Being able to get out—she likes to get out and drive around. You know, just anything that would make her feel normal. So eating the types of things that she's enjoyed in the past, being able to go to a movie with us, go for a drive with the relatives. All the types of things like that. (48-year-old son)

A "Good Death"

In response to a being asked to describe a good death, participants expressed their fundamental end-of-life preferences for the elders' final days.

Dying at Home

Almost all participants expressed a preference for the elder to die at home. Dying at home was viewed as a more "natural death," where elders could more easily be surrounded by friends and family, and their final wishes could be best met. Several family caregivers worried that the patient's needs might outstrip the supports and resources necessary to keep the elder at home until death, but preferred that the death take place at home if at all possible.

Dying Quickly, Without Suffering

For elders and family members, the ideal death was seen as one where the elder dies swiftly, "peacefully, and without pain." One patient summed this perspective up memorably:

Just let me die. Quickly. Fast. And painlessly. . . . Stand out there and have lightening strike me, or anything that would do me in like that! (84-year-old male elder)

Many imagined a "natural" death, spending their last moments comfortably ensconced in a favorite chair or sitting in a garden surrounded by natural beauty. Some hoped they would simply be able to "go to sleep and not wake up":

Good death would be able to roll out in a wheelchair onto a garden patio and be surrounded by beautiful flowers, you know, I mean that would be all right. Just that . . . having respect and beauty and concern around you. (50-year-old daughter)

He would sit down in his chair and he wouldn't wake up. That would be ideal. (48-year-old daughter-in-law)

Avoiding High-tech Life Support

For most elders, the desire to die naturally meant not having to accept unwanted intervention, and not taking advantage of feeding or breathing "tubes," or other medical technologies meant to prolong their lives.

Well, I don't want this—I don't want to be resuscitated. If I'm going I want to go, and that's supposed to prevent them from putting me on any machines. I don't want to wake up a lunatic or something, you know, be alive—breathing but not knowing what's going on. I don't want that. . . . I want to go—no life saving treatments for me. It might be a terrible thing to say. . . . It's my life. (80-year-old male elder)

For the most part, family caregivers reported that they respected these concerns and believed it important to follow their elders' preferences, even if they did not share them:

Um yes, we, we talked, we talked about it and she just basically wants to be at home, not hooked up to any machines um, you know, just to die naturally, you know, just go. She don't want to go to a revival or resuscitory thing, you know, she dies, she just wants to die, you know. (47-year-old grandson)

Being Prepared

The elders expressed a preference to be made aware of their impending death so that they could "get things in order." Many worked to develop a sense of completion in their lives, had arranged their financial and other affairs, and felt to some extent prepared to die. Those who did not feel a sense of completion or closure reported that having time for preparation was quite important to them.

Well, I wouldn't want to go in my sleep. I'd want to prepare better. I'd want some doctor to say "[Name], you only have two days, three days, six days," whatever and then I can prepare myself better—get things straightened out with the kids, get my will set, and just have a priest with me and that's all. I don't want to die in my sleep. (80-year-old male elder)

Family caregivers were not aware of and did not share the elders' desire to be prepared for death, although some shared regrets that they had not talked enough or spent enough time with elders when they were still "able to do things."

Addressing Spiritual Needs

Many family members hoped their loved ones would achieve "peace of mind" at the end of their lives, and felt this was an important component of a good death. This sense of peace was most often expressed in spiritual or religious terms; several family members hoped that elders would achieve "spiritual closure" through faith and prayer, and wanted them to have access to clergy to talk with about their spiritual concerns.

> I guess it's um, being taken care of spiritually . . . contacting the people at the church. And have somebody come talk to him, and um, give him a peace of mind. (56-year-old son)

Although we asked questions about faith, spirituality, and religion, there was a great deal of variability in the extent to which faith was important to the elders. Most denied that having their spiritual or faith needs addressed were essential to a "good death" in the way they were to family caregivers.

Communication about End-of-Life Care Preferences

As part of our analysis, the researchers examined the ways in which families talked about death and dying, and how family communication influenced the congruence between participants in expressed challenges, concerns, and preferences. When asked about the extent to which they had discussed dying or their care preferences with family members, the majority of elders and family members—six of the ten dyads—indicated they had not done so. Three elders believed the lack of communication was due to their own lack of desire to talk about dying or end-of-life care with family members. Two others reported that it was difficult to talk about these subjects with family, either due to their own or their family members' discomfort.

> It doesn't make me feel uncomfortable but I can't think of anything that I could, that I can add to it that I haven't already thought about. . . . No, I think I'd like to talk to them about that. They don't seem to want to talk about it—'cause it's an unpleasant thing and they don't always go for it—kind of push it back. But I want to talk a little more about this. (82-year-old male elder)

Four families indicated that they had talked about dying and discussed the elders' care preferences. Even though she had talked with her husband, one caregiver indicated that she found these conversations about dying and his care preferences extremely uncomfortable.

In order to examine the relationship, if any, between participants' communication patterns and congruence in end-of-life care preferences, we compared the responses of families who reported communication constraints with those who reported open communication. As illustrated in Table 3, the level of congruence was much higher among families reporting open communication regarding dying and end-of-life care. None of the four families with open communication and half of the six families with communication constraints shared end-of-life concerns or preferences that were not congruent. Examples of the latter include: the 84-year-old male elder who stated a preference to be alone at the time of death, and his 47-year-old daughter who reported he wished to be surrounded by family; the 101-year-old female elder who expressed a strong desire to be kept informed of her evolving health status whose 67-year-old son preferred her not to be informed of these changes; and the 64-year-old male elder who expressed a strong desire to die at home without the use of life-sustaining machines, contrasting his 55-year-old wife's preference for him to die at the hospital, with full access to medical and technological resources.

Discussion

The findings of this study were generally consistent with the empirical literature on congruence between patients and surrogate decision-makers, which suggests that agreement about dying and end-of-life care ranges from poor to moderate (Engelberg et al., 2005; Moorman & Carr, 2008; Mularski et al., 2004). Elder participants acknowledged their need for support and care as their illnesses progressed, but—in contrast to family caregivers—most strongly valued their independence, and wanted to maintain control over their lives and continue to participate in activities they enjoyed. This parallels the finding that family members often underestimate the patient's need for autonomy and control over their own care (Farber et al., 2003; McSkimming et al., 1999; Singer, et al., 1999; Vig & Pearlman, 2004). Elders were greatly concerned about becoming a burden on their families, echoing another well-documented finding, particularly with older patients (McPherson et al., 2007; Vig & Pearlman, 2004).

Table 3 Communication Patterns and Congruence in End-of-Life Care Preferences

Communication Pattern	Congruence	Incongruence
Communication Constraints	3	3
Open Communication	4	0

The lack of apparent spiritual or religious needs on the part of the elders may be due, in part, to the lack of minority elder participants; a wealth of prior research suggests spirituality is of primary importance to African Americans and Latinos at the end of life (Born, Greiner, Sylvia, & Ahluwalia, 2004; Waters, 2001). One African-American elder shared that she spent all of her waking hours in prayer, but she too denied a desire to talk with others about her faith. This may reflect a perception that spiritual needs are felt to be intrinsic, and not as something that requires intervention from others.

Family caregivers felt most challenged by the responsibilities of managing and providing adequate care, and were concerned about their capacity to meet their loved ones' physical and spiritual needs as the illness progressed. The preeminence of these concerns is consistent with the literature (Terry et al., 2006) and reflects the high level of cognitive, emotional, and physical investment made by family caregivers at the end of life (Waldrop et al., 2005). Although other researchers have found strong congruence around the importance of preparation and a sense of completion in determining a good death (Engelberg et al., 2005; Steinhauser et al., 2000), in this study only elder participants identified this as a significant preference. Unlike the elders, family caregivers were concerned about elders' spiritual wellbeing, and felt that achieving "peace of mind" was essential to experiencing a good death.

Despite these differences, elders and family caregivers reported many congruent concerns and preferences. Consistent with the literature on quality of life at the end of life, most elders and family caregivers preferred that the elder die at home (Tang & McCorkle, 2003; Steinhauser et al., 2000), and for death to come swiftly, without pain or suffering (Heyland et al., 2006; Vig & Pearlman, 2004). Experiencing loss related to the elders' physical, functional, and cognitive decline, and managing advanced illness in the face of an uncertain and unpredictable future were among the most difficult challenges reported by the elders and their care-givers. Accepting the inherent uncertainty and ambiguity of the dying process may indeed be one of the more significant challenges for terminally ill patients and their families (Bern-Klug, 2004; Gardner, 2008; McKechnie, Macleod & Keeling, 2007). Elders and family caregivers also shared concerns about the wellbeing of survivors following the patient's eventual death.

There was particularly consistent agreement regarding end-of-life care preferences, specifically around the importance of reliable, high-quality care, and the avoidance of life-sustaining treatment. Another shared concern was that elders be treated with dignity and respect by formal caregivers, and would be allowed to continue living until death, a finding echoed in the literature (Chochinov et al., 2002). A finding not compatible with prior literature was the shared preference of elders and family caregivers to avoid using life-sustaining treatment. Many studies suggest that family members are less likely than older patients to prefer life-support, and that surrogates often underestimate elders' preference for aggressive measures at the end of life (Hamel, Lynn, Teno, Covinsky, Wu, Galanos et al., 2000; Pruchno, Lemay, Field, & Levinsky, 2005). The present finding may be another artifact of a sample that includes few minority elders, who are more likely than white patients to prefer life-sustaining medical treatment (Phipps, True, Harris, Chong, Tester, Chavin et al., 2003; Steinhauser et al., 2000). Nonetheless, the findings suggest the need for further exploration of patients and family preferences for life-sustaining treatment.

Replicating findings from prior research (Parker, Clayton, Hancock, Walder, Butow, Carrick et al., 2007; Teno, Lynn, Wenger, Phillips, Murphy, Connors et al., 1997), a minority of families had communicated with each other about end-of-life concerns and preferences. Despite the advantages of open family communication (Metzger & Gray, 2008), the literature on advance care planning and family communication suggests that less than 20% actually talk about dying and their preferences for care (Bradley & Rizzo, 1999; Rosnick & Reynolds, 2003; Teno et al., 1997). Lack of communication can contribute to family conflict between the elder and family surrogates, difficulties in decision-making and advance care planning, and ultimately to poorer quality end-of-life care (Kramer, Boelk, & Auer, 2006). This corroborates our finding that a lack of communication was associated with greater incongruence, and suggests the importance of future research on the impact of family conflict on end-of-life experiences and outcomes.

Conclusions & Implications

While many of these findings were consistent with the literature on congruence in patient and caregiver perceptions, the current study is unusual in that it compared the subjective experiences of older chronically and terminally ill patients with those of their matched family caregivers. This study confirms that end-of-life concerns and care preferences found with broader populations also apply to frail elders and their caregivers. The findings further suggest that there may be more family congruence around preferences for end-of-life care than around challenges, concerns, and wishes related to dying. Open family communication was associated with greater congruence in patient and family preferences, which supports prior findings that open communication is associated with better adjustment in family caregivers after the death of their loved ones (Kramer, 1997; Metzger & Gray, 2008). These results have important implications for intervention and research, as they highlight potential sources of unmet needs and conflict among dying elders and their family members.

Although there were more areas of congruence than incongruence among family members, the findings of this study suggest that healthcare professionals providing end-of-life care would be prudent to view family reports as imperfect proxies for elder's concerns, challenges, and preferences. Principle domains of incongruence included the elders' difficulties in accepting dependence, their fears of becoming a burden, and desire to be prepared for death. Unlike the elders, family caregivers were primarily concerned with providing adequate care to meet the elders' physical and spiritual care needs. The study highlights the need for more focused and comprehensive assessment of terminally ill elders and their family caregivers, and for sensitivity to potential differences in preferences and concerns.

It is perhaps not surprising that elders and family caregivers viewed the end-of-life experience somewhat differently, given their different ages, roles, and perspectives. Incongruence presents difficulties only when patients and caregivers with different views are unable to communicate openly and resolve differences with each other (de Haes & Teunissen, 2005). Family conflict and communication constraints can present significant barriers to the provision of quality care, the completion of advance directives, and the attainment of a "good death" (Covinsky, Fuller, Yaffe, Johnston, Hamel, Lynn et al., 2000; Kramer et al., 2006). Terminally ill elders and their families may therefore derive particular benefit from interventions that address congruent and incongruent experiences, and teach communication and family problem-solving skills around the end-of-life and end-of-life care. Working to enhance families' efforts to talk about and resolve differences, and to make informed decisions about care is fundamental to facilitating advance care planning, and reducing inappropriate procedures and hospitalizations.

There were some limitations to this study, which involved a small, non-representative sample of primarily white, low-income elders, recruited purposively from a unique comprehensive health and long-term care program in the Midwest. Casual generalizations should not, therefore, be made to other populations of terminally ill elders and family caregivers. The sample lacked heterogeneity in terms of race/ethnicity, and cultural factors have been shown to be important variables in end-of-life preferences (Phipps et al., 2003). There was also a good deal of variability in medical diagnosis, elders' living situations, and family caregivers' relationships to the elder, all of which may have influenced the findings.

Despite these limitations, this qualitative study identifies subjective concerns and care preferences of terminally ill elders and their family caregivers at the end of life. The findings highlight the need for more focused and comprehensive assessment of terminally ill elders and their family caregivers, and attention to potential differences in patient and family preferences and concerns. Further research into this population's unique needs and perceptions, including the dynamics of family communication and decision making at the end of life, is necessary to further healthcare efforts to better meet elders' psychosocial needs, enhance their well-being, and facilitate a "good death." Understanding elders'

experiences and preferences, identifying areas of congruence and incongruence, and improving communication in families are essential to providing quality end-of-life care to all dying patients and their families.

References

Bern-Klug, M. (2004). The Ambiguous Dying Syndrome. *Health and Social Work, 29*(1), 55–65.

Born, W., Greiner, K., Sylvia, E., & Ahluwalia, J. (2004). Knowledge, attitudes, and beliefs about end-of-life care among inner-city African Americans and Latinos. *Journal of Palliative Medicine, 7*(2), 247–256.

Bradley, E., & Rizzo, J. (1999). Public information and private search: Evaluating the Patient Self-Determination Act. *Journal of Health Politics, Policy and Law, 24*(2), 239–273.

Chochinov, H., Hack, T., Hassard, L., Kristjianson, S., McClement, S., & Harlos, M. (2002). Dignity in the terminally ill: A cross-sectional, cohort study. *The Lancet, 360*(9350), 2026–2030.

Cohen, S. R., & Leis, A. (2002). What determines the quality of life of terminally ill cancer patients from their own perspective? *Journal of Palliative Care, 18*(1), 48–58.

Covinsky, K., Fuller, J., Yaffe, K., Johnston, C., Hamel, M., Lynn, J., et al. (2000). Communication and decision-making in seriously ill patients: Findings of the SUPPORT project. *Journal of the American Geriatrics Society, 48*(5), S187–S193.

Crabtree, B., & Miller, W. (1999). Using codes and code manuals: A template organizing style of interpretation. In B. F. Crabtree & W.L. Miller (Eds.), *Doing qualitative research* (2nd ed., pp. 163–178). Thousand Oaks, CA: Sage.

de Haes, H., & Teunissen, S. (2005). Communication in palliative care: A review of recent literature. *Current Opinion in Oncology, 17*(4), 345–350.

Desbiens, N., & Mueller-Rizner, N. (2000). How well do surrogates assess the pain of seriously ill patients? *Critical Care Medicine, 28*, 1347–1352.

Emanuel, L., von Gunten, C., & Ferris, F. (2000). Gaps in end-of-life care. *Archives of Family Medicine, 9*, 1176–1180.

Engelberg, R., Patrick, D., & Curtis, J. (2005). Correspondence between patients' preferences and surrogates' understandings for dying and death. *Journal of Pain and Symptom Management, 30*(6), 498–509.

Farber, S., Egnew, T., Herman-Bertch, J., Taylor, T., & Guldin, G. (2003). Issues in end-of-life care: Patient, caregiver, and clinician perceptions. *Journal of Palliative Medicine, 6*(1), 19–31.

Field, M. J., & Cassel, C. K. (Eds.). (1997). *Approaching death: Improving care at the end of Life*. Institute of Medicine. Washington, DC: National Academy Press.

Gallo, W., Baker, M., & Bradley, E. (2001). Factors associated with home versus institutional death among cancer patients in Connecticut. *Journal of the American Geriatrics Society, 49*, 771–777.

Gardner, D. (2008). Cancer in a dyadic context: Older couples' negotiation of ambiguity and meaning in end-of-life. *Journal of Social Work in End-of-life and Palliative Care, 4*(2), 1–25.

Hamel, M., Lynn, J., Teno, J., Covinsky, K., Wu, A., Galanos, A., et al. (2000). Age-related differences in care preferences, treatment decisions, and clinical outcomes of seriously ill, hospitalized adults: Lessons from SUPPORT. *Journal of the American Geriatrics Society, 48*(5/Supplement), S176–S182.

Heyland, D., Dodek, P., Rocker, G., Groll, D., Garni, A., Pichora, D., et al. (2006). What matters most in end-of-life care: perceptions of seriously ill patients and their family members. *Canadian Medical Association Journal, 174*(5), 627–633.

Higginson, I., & Sen-Gupta, G. (2000). Place of care in advanced cancer: a qualitative systematic literature review of patient preferences. *Journal of Palliative Medicine, 3*(3), 287–300.

Kramer, B. J., & Auer, C. (2005). Challenges to providing end-of-life care to low-income elders with advanced chronic disease: Lessons learned from a model program. *The Gerontologist, 45,* 651–660.

Kramer, B. J., Boelk, A., & Auer, C. (2006). Family conflict at the end of life: Lessons learned in a model program for vulnerable older adults. *Journal of Palliative Care 9*(3), 791–801.

Kramer, B. J., Christ, G., Bern-Klug, M., & Francoeur, R. (2005). A national agenda for social work research in palliative and end-of-life care. *Journal of Palliative Medicine 8,* 418–431.

Kramer, D. (1997). How women relate to terminally ill husbands and their subsequent adjustment to bereavement. *Omega: Journal of Death and Dying, 34*(2), 93–106.

Laakkonen, M., Pitkala, K., & Strandberg, T. (2004). Terminally ill elderly patients' experiences, attitudes, and needs: A qualitative study. *Omega: Journal of Death and Dying, 49*(2), 117–129.

McCormick, T., & Conley, B. (1995). Patients' perspectives on dying and on the care of dying patients. *Western Journal of Medicine, 163*(3), 236–243.

McKechnie, R., Macleod, R., & Keeling, S. (2007). Facing uncertainty: The lived experience of palliative care. *Palliative and Supportive Care, 5,* 367–376.

McPherson, C., & Addington-Hall, (2003). Judging the quality of care at the end of life: Can proxies provide reliable information? *Social Science and Medicine, 56,* 95–109.

McPherson, C., Wilson, K., & Murray, M. (2007). Feeling like a burden: Exploring the perspectives of patients at the end of life. *Social Science & Medicine, 64*(2), 417–427.

McPherson, C., Wilson, K., Lobchuk, M., & Brajtman, S. (2008). Family caregivers' assessment of symptoms in patients with advanced cancer: Concordance with patients and factors affecting accuracy. *Journal of Pain Symptom Management, 35*(1), 70–82.

McSkimming, S., Hodges, M., Super, A., Driever, M., Schoessler, M., Franey, S. G., et al. (1999). The experience of life-threatening illness: Patients' and their loved ones' perspectives. *Journal of Palliative Medicine, 2*(2), 173–184.

Metzger, P., & Gray, M. (2008). End-of-life communication and adjustment: Pre-loss communication as a predictor of bereavement-related outcomes. *Death Studies, 32*(4), 301–325.

Moorman, S., & Carr, D. (2008). Spouses' effectiveness as end-of-life surrogates: Accuracy, uncertainty, and errors of overtreatment or undertreatment. *Gerontologist, 48*(6), 811–819.

Morrison, S. (2005). Health care system factors affecting end-of-life care. *Journal of Palliative Medicine, 8*(Supplement 1), S79–S87.

Mularski, R., Curtis, R., Osborne, M., Engelberg, R., & Ganzini, L. (2004). Agreement among family members and their assessment of the quality of dying and death. *Journal of Pain and Symptom Management, 28*(4), 306–315.

National Consensus Project (2004). *Clinical practice guidelines for quality palliative care.* Brooklyn, NY.

National Institutes of Health (NIH). (2004). *State-of-the-science conference on improving end-of-life care: Conference statement.* Bethesda, MD: National Institutes of Health.

Padgett, D. K. (2008). *Qualitative methods in social work research: Challenges and rewards* (2nd ed.). Thousands Oaks, CA: Sage Publications, Inc.

Parker, S., Clayton, J., Hancock, K., Walder, S., Butow, P., & Carrick, S. et al. (2007). A systematic review of prognostic/end-of-life communication with adults in the advanced stages of a life-limiting illness: Patient/care-giver preferences for the content, style, and timing of information. *Journal of Pain and Symptom Management, 34*(1), 81–93.

Patton, M. (2002). *Qualitative research and evaluation methods* (3rd ed.). Thousands Oaks, CA: Sage Publications, Inc.

Phipps, E., True, G., Harris, D., Chong, U., Tester, W., Chavin, S., et al. (2003). Approaching the end of life: Attitudes, preferences, and behaviors of African-American and white patients and their family caregivers. *Journal of Clinical Oncology, 21*(3), 549–554.

Pritchard, R., Fisher, E., Teno, J., Sharp, S. Reding, D., Knaus, W., et al. (1998). Influence of patient preferences and local health system characteristics on the place of death. (SUPPORT Investigators: Study to Understand Prognoses and Preferences for Risks and Outcomes of Treatment). *Journal of the American Geriatrics Society, 46*(10), 1242–1250.

Pruchno, R., Lemay, E., Field, L., & Levinsky, N. (2005). Spouse as health care proxy for dialysis patients: Whose preferences matter? *Gerontologist, 45*(6), 812–819.

Rosnick, C., & Reynolds, S. (2003). Thinking ahead: Factors associated with executing advance directives. *Journal of Aging & Health, 15*(2), 409–429.

Scholz, R. and Tietje, R. (2002). *Embedded case study methods: Integrating quantitative and qualitative knowledge.* Thousand Oaks, CA: Sage Publications.

Shalowitz, D., Garrett-Meyer, E., & Wendler, D. (2006). The accuracy of surrogate decision makers: A systematic review. *Archives of Internal Medicine, 166,* 493–497.

Singer P., Martin D., & Kellner M. (1999). Quality end-of-life care: patients' perspectives. *Journal of the American Medical Association, 281,* 163–168.

Sneeuw, K., Sprangers, M., & Aaronson, N. (2002). The role of health care providers and significant others in evaluating the quality of life of patients with chronic disease. *Journal of Clinical Epidemiology, 55*(11), 1130–1143.

Steinhauser A., Christakis N., Clipp E., McNeilly M., McIntyre L., & Tulsky J. (2000). Factors considered important at the end of life by patients, family, physicians, and other care providers. *Journal of the American Medical Association, 284*(19), 2476–2482.

Sulmasy, D., Terry, P., Weisman, C., Miller, D., Stallings, R., Vettese, M., et al. (1998). The accuracy of substituted judgments in patients with terminal disease. *Annals of Internal Medicine, 128*(8), 621–629.

SUPPORT Principal Investigators (1995). A controlled trial to improve care for seriously ill hospitalized patients: The study to understand prognosis and preferences for outcomes and risks for treatments (SUPPORT). *Journal of the American Medical Association, 274*(20), 1591–1598.

Tang, S., & McCorkle, R. (2003). Determinants of congruence between the preferred and actual place of death for terminally ill cancer patients. *Journal of Palliative Care 19*(4), 230–237.

Teno, J., Clarridge, B., Casey, V., Welch, L., Wetle, T., Shield, R., et al. (2004). Family perspectives on end-of-life care at the last place of care. *Journal of the American Medical Association, 291*(1), 88–93.

Teno, J., Lynn, J., Wenger, N., Phillips, R., Murphy, D., Connors, A., et al. (1997). Advance directives for seriously ill hospitalized patients: Effectiveness with the patient self-determination act and the SUPPORT intervention. SUPPORT Investigators. *Journal of the American Geriatric Society, 45*(4), 500–507.

Terry, W., Olson, L., Wilss, L., & Boulton-Lewis, G. (2006). Experience of dying: Concerns of dying patients and of carers. *Internal Medicine Journal, 36*(6), 338–346.

Thomas, C., Morris, S., & Clark, D. (2004). Place of death: Preferences among cancer patients and their carers. *Social Science & Medicine, 58,* 2431–2444.

Vig, E., Davenport, N., & Pearlman, R. (2002). Good deaths, bad deaths, and preferences for the end of life: A qualitative study of geriatric outpatients. *Journal of the American Geriatric Society, 50*(9), 1541–1548.

Waldrop, D., Kramer, B.J., Skretny, J., Milch, R., & Finn, W. (2005). Final transitions: Family caregiving at the end of life. *Journal of Palliative Medicine, 8*(3), 623–638.

Waters, C. (2001). Understanding and supporting African Americans' perspectives of end-of-life care planning and decision making. *Qualitative Health Research, 11,* 385–398.

Vig, E., & Pearlman, R. (2004). Good and bad dying from the perspective of terminally ill men. *Archives of Internal Medicine, 164*(9), 977–981.

Yin, R. (2003). *Case study research: Design and methods* (3rd ed.). Thousand Oaks, CA: Sage Publications.

Zettel-Watson, L., Ditto, P., Danks, J., & Smucker, W. (2008). Actual and perceived gender differences in the accuracy of surrogate decisions about life-sustaining medical treatment among older spouses. *Death Studies, 32*(3), 273–290.

Critical Thinking

1. What are the barriers to quality end-of-life care?
2. What were the major worries and fears about dying expressed by the elders and their family caregivers?
3. What were the end-of-life preferences for the elders in their final days?

Acknowledgements—The authors' extend their appreciation to Elder Care Partnerships staff and administration, and to End-of-Life committee members who provided ongoing support and consultation. Special thanks to the elders and their family members who offered their valuable insights.

The Myriad Strategies for Seeking Control in the Dying Process

TRACY A. SCHROEPFER, HYUNJIN NOH, AND MELINDA KAVANAUGH

Research on end-of-life care has produced evidence that achieving a sense of control is viewed by terminally ill individuals (Singer, Martin, & Kelner, 1999; Volker, Kahn, & Penticuff, 2004b; Wilson et al., 2007) and those who care for them (Teno, Casey, Welch, & Edgman-Levitan, 2001) as playing an important role in the quality of their dying process. Terminally ill individuals have been found to consider the ability to exercise control as a desirable psychosocial outcome (Singer et al.) and a psychological comfort (Ganzini, Johnston, McFarland, Tolle, & Lee, 1998). Furthermore, the inability to achieve a sense of control has been associated with moderate to extreme suffering for some terminally ill individuals (Wilson et al., 2007) and a desire to hasten death for others (Back, Wallace, Starks, & Pearlman, 1996; Chin, Hedberg, Higginson, & Fleming, 1999; Coyle & Sculco, 2004; Oregon Department of Human Services [ODHS], 2000). Although sense of control evidently plays a key role in the psychological wellbeing of terminally ill individuals, less clear are the aspects of the dying process over which terminally ill individuals want to exercise control and the strategies they use for doing so.

In this article, we seek to advance our understanding of the role control plays in the dying process of terminally ill elders by investigating the aspects of the dying process over which terminally ill elders seek to exercise control, the strategies they use to do so, and whether they desire to exercise more control. By gaining a deeper understanding of the role control plays in the dying process of elders, health care and service providers and informal caregivers can work toward ensuring that elders exercise control in their dying process, thereby working toward the goal of improving the quality of end-of-life care.

Current Knowledge of Control's Role in the Dying Process

The literature on the role of control in the dying process is continually expanding. Some information is available regarding the aspects of the dying process over which individuals,

not necessarily elders, desire to exercise control, as well as the way in which they want to do so.

Aspects to Control

The factors motivating the consideration of a hastened death have been studied both retrospectively and prospectively. In retrospective studies, health care professionals or survivors of the deceased are asked to write case studies or respond to surveys concerning the factors cited by now deceased patients, who had considered or requested a hastened death. In prospective studies, individuals with a terminal illness (an illness likely to result in death), or who have been defined as terminally ill (less than 6 months to live), are directly asked about their consideration to hasten death and their reasons for doing so. Both retrospective and prospective studies provide insight into aspects of the dying process over which terminally ill individuals would like to exercise control.

Retrospective studies have found that loss of control over bodily functions (Back et al., 1996; Chin et al., 1999; ODHS, 2007) and physical symptoms (Volker, 2001) have served as factors motivating the consideration of a hastened death. A desire for control over the manner of death was found in both retrospective (Back et al.; Ganzini et al., 2002; ODHS, 2000; Volker) and prospective studies. In prospective studies, respondents who feared dying might become intolerable felt that having control over the manner of their death provided them with a sense of control (Ganzini et al., 1998; Schroepfer, 2006), as it did for those who feared a loss of control more generally (Chapple, Ziebland, McPherson, & Herxheimer, 2006). Respondents also noted that exercising control over the manner of death served to enhance their feelings of control over the disease itself (Albert et al., 2005), provided psychological comfort (Ganzini et al., 1998), and afforded a way to exercise control in an "untenable situation" (Coyle & Sculco, 2004, p. 703).

Other studies have sought to gain understanding about the aspects of dying over which terminally ill elders seek control by posing the question directly to bereaved caregivers, terminally ill individuals, and individuals living with a terminal illness. In one retrospective study, bereaved family members included in their definition of quality end-of-life care the ability for their deceased loved ones to have exercised control over their own health care decisions and daily routine (Teno et al., 2001). In another retrospective study (Volker, Kahn, & Penticuff, 2004a), advance practice nurses reported that patients sought control over decisions related to treatment, transitioning to dying, and end-of-life care, as well as over their comfort and dignity. In prospective studies, terminally ill individuals reported seeking to exercise control in end-of-life decisions (Singer et al., 1999; Volker et al., 2004b), over their dignity and physical comfort, the place of their death, and in preparing family for their pending death (Volker et al., 2004b). Although not all of the respondents in the aforementioned studies were elders, the information provides insight into aspects of the dying process over which terminally ill elders may desire to exercise control. To determine the control strategies used for doing so, an understanding must first be gained regarding the conceptualization of control.

Perceived Control Theories and Evidence

Numerous studies have been conducted on sense of control or, as it is often referred to in the literature, perceived control, which has to do with the *expectation* or *perception* of "engaging in actions" either to attain desirable outcomes or to evade those seen as undesirable (Rodin, 1986, p. 141). Perceived control is often presented as a "one-process construct," but Rothbaum, Weisz, and Snyder (1982) have advanced the argument that it may actually be a "two-process construct" consisting of primary and secondary control (p. 8). These researchers define primary control as the perception that the individual has the ability to *directly* influence a desired outcome or avoid an undesirable one. Such beliefs develop when individuals endeavor to change *directly* the external environment to fit their own needs and are successful. Secondary control, in contrast, is the perception that the individual has the ability to influence more *indirectly* a desired outcome (Rothbaum et al.). This perception is formed when individuals endeavor to *fit* into their external environment and are able to do so. Thus, primary control attempts are focused on the external world and secondary control attempts on the individual's internal self.

The life-span model of successful aging proposed by Schulz and Heckhausen (1996), which incorporates their life-span theory of control (Heckhausen & Schulz, 1995), builds on the notion of a two-process construct and argues that humans seek to exert control over the environment throughout their life span to attain goals. They propose three control strategies for doing so: selective primary control, compensatory primary control, and compensatory secondary control. Selective primary control involves individuals' "investment of resources" such as their time, abilities, or efforts to attain a particular goal (Schulz & Heckhausen,

1996, p. 710). When individuals' own resources are no longer sufficient to attain a particular goal, then compensatory primary control strategies become necessary, which require the assistance of others. Finally, compensatory secondary control involves the use of cognitive strategies on the part of individuals, which can include comparing their situation to someone whose situation is worse, disengaging from prior goals, augmenting the value of a new goal, or diminishing the value of an old goal (Heckhausen & Schulz). The use of compensatory secondary control strategies can work to maintain or lessen the losses that an individual is experiencing in his or her life.

Control Strategies Used

We are unaware of any research that has focused on control strategies used by elders in their dying process; however, evidence is available regarding the use of primary and secondary control strategies by elders with acute and chronic health conditions. In general, elders with chronic conditions have been found to use primary and secondary control strategies (Wrosch & Schulz, 2008). Due to age-related declines in late life, however, the tendency has been for elders to move toward using more compensatory secondary control strategies (Heckhausen, 1997). For elders experiencing a high number of health problems, Wrosch, Heckhausen, and Lachman (2000) found that the secondary control strategies of positive reappraisal and lowered aspirations were more strongly associated with their subjective well-being compared with elders who persisted in using primary control strategies.

Whether the findings regarding the control strategies used by elders with acute and chronic conditions hold true for terminally ill elders remains unclear at this time, as do the aspects over which terminally ill elders desire to exercise control. This study seeks to provide such insight by interviewing terminally ill elders about the aspects of their dying process over which they exercise control, the ways in which they exercise such control, and whether they would want more control.

Design and Methods
Participants

A purposive sample of 102 respondents was obtained at hospices throughout southern Wisconsin. Eligible respondents had to be at least 50 years of age, been told by a physician that they had 6 months or less to live, and deemed mentally competent by their nurse or social worker. Although age 50 would not normally be considered the lower age limit for elders, prior research experience with hospice populations (Schroepfer, 2006, 2007, 2008) has shown that to have enough male respondents, the age of inclusion needs to be lowered.

Procedure

A single-session face-to-face interview was conducted with each of 102 elders utilizing a mixed-method survey instrument. Interviews were audiotaped so that the qualitative portion could be captured verbatim, and the quantitative portion checked against what the interviewer recorded in the survey booklet. Interviews ranged in length from 23 to 178 min, with a mean of 63 min. Of the 102 respondents who completed the interview process, 18 respondents were dropped from the analysis because they declined to answer the control questions of interest. We have no way of knowing whether declining to answer these questions was systematically related to the level of control they exercised in their dying process. We do know, however, that a comparison between these 18 respondents and the 84 who completed the control questions revealed no differences in regard to age, gender, marital status, education, primary hospice diagnosis, or quality of life. Therefore, the final sample size used for analysis was 84.

Data Collection

Respondents were asked a series of questions regarding the control they were experiencing in their lives to determine the type of control strategies they were using. To learn about the aspects of the dying process over which they exercised control, respondents were asked if there were parts of their life over which they *felt* they had control. If respondents answered yes, they were asked to specify the parts. To determine the type of control strategy they used, they were next asked a series of questions regarding each part of their life over which they felt they had control. First, respondents were asked if *they* did things to directly control or be in charge of that part of their life. If they said yes, they were asked to talk about what they did and how satisfied they were with it. Next, respondents were asked if there were other people whom they believed helped them control that part of their life. If yes, they were asked to talk about how these individuals helped them exert control. Finally, all respondents were asked if there were other parts of their life over which they would like to exercise control. If they said yes, they were asked to specify the parts and what they felt prevented them from having control. If they said no, they were asked why they did not want more control.

Quantitative data were gathered on respondents' demographic information to explore whether the control strategies utilized by respondents differed based on their age, education, gender, marital status, or primary hospice diagnosis. Age was coded as a continuous variable, as was education, which was based on the number of years of schooling that respondents had completed. The respondents' gender was coded as a dummy variable (0 = female and 1 = male), as was their marital status (0 = not married and 1 = married/partner). Respondents' primary hospice diagnosis was grouped into four categories: cancer and, respiratory, heart, and muscular diseases.

To determine whether the use of control strategies was associated with respondents' quality of life, quantitative data were gathered via a quality-of-life measure. Based on

a previous study (Schroepfer, 2006) that sought to determine the factors that led terminally ill elders to consider or not consider a hastened death, nine factors were reported by elders as important to experiencing a quality dying process. These factors included having a reason for living, being able to maintain dignity, not feeling like a burden, living a life full of meaning and full of enjoyment, and feeling a sense of purpose, independent, useful, and hopeful. A thorough review of related literature produced several surveys containing one or more of the items but none that encompassed all nine items or that were designed for elders.

To address this problem, we used items from three survey instruments. The first is the Functional Assessment of Chronic Illness Therapy (FACIT)—spiritual well-being, a 12-item scale that has been designed to measure the spiritual domain of quality of life. Three items were borrowed from the eight-item subscale: a reason for living, a sense of purpose, and life has meaning. Tested in cancer populations (Peterman, Fitchett, Brady, Hernandez, & Cella, 2002), this survey has been found to have internal consistency, high test–retest correlations, concurrent validity, discriminant validity, and a positive association with measures of quality of life. Four items were borrowed from the FACIT—palliative care: burden, dependence, usefulness, and hope. This scale is newer and currently undergoing psychometric testing. The third survey, the Structured Interview for Symptoms and Concerns (SISC), is a 13-item instrument designed specifically for patients receiving palliative care for advanced cancer. This instrument has been found to have high interrater reliability, good test–retest correlations, and concurrent validity. The two items taken from this survey measuring dignity and enjoyment of life were reworded, as was the response set. The reason for rewording the items is that they are worded as questions in the SISC, a format that does not fit with the statement format of the other items. Rewording of the response set occurred because it appears complicated and could prove burdensome to terminally ill elders. These items were measured on a 5-point ordinal scale ranging from 0 = *not at all* to 4 = *very much*. All nine items were summed, resulting in a possible score range of 0–36 wherein a higher score represented a higher quality of life.

Quantitative Analytic Approach

Bivariate analyses were conducted to determine if the control strategies used by respondents differed based on age, education, gender, marital status, and primary hospice diagnosis, as well as respondents' quality-of-life scores. One-way analysis of variance (ANOVA) statistics were run to test the association between the control strategies used by respondents and their age, education, and quality-of-life scores. Cross-tabulations using the Pearson chi-square association test were conducted to test differences based on gender, marital status, and primary hospice diagnosis.

Qualitative Analytic Approaches

Using Schulz and Heckhausen's (1996) theoretical framework, we conducted a directed content analysis (Hsieh & Shannon, 2005) of the information concerning what respondents or others did to control the various parts of their dying process over which they felt they exercised control. Directed content analysis uses theory to predetermine the categories that will be used in exploring the qualitative data. For this study, the first author read each interview transcript multiple times and grouped responses into the following control strategy categories: selective primary control, compensatory primary control, and compensatory secondary control. Responses coded into selective primary control were those in which respondents described externally investing their efforts alone into attaining a particular goal. Respondents' descriptions of exercising control externally with assistance from others were coded into compensatory primary control. Finally, responses that described the use of cognitive strategies to exercise control internally were coded into one of three types of compensatory secondary control strategies: adjustment of goals by lowering aspirations, self-protective positive reappraisal (Wrosch et al., 2000), and self-protective social comparisons (Chipperfield & Perry, 2006). As a reliability check, two members of the research team independently coded the responses based on the strategies identified. Initially, the team members were 76 % in agreement and, after a discussion of the differing categorizations, arrived at a consensus on the remaining 24 %.

Once the directed content analysis of the control strategies had been concluded, the two team members independently coded (a) the aspects of the dying process over which elders reported exercising control and (b) the aspects over which they desired to exercise control. This analysis did not employ a theoretical framework and so the team members utilized conventional content analysis (Hsieh & Shannon, 2005). Using an inductive method, themes were identified from repeated readings of the transcripts (Patton, 1990) and preliminary codes generated to represent the themes. Separately, the team members repeatedly read through and categorized the responses to the question regarding the parts of life over which respondents felt they had control. This same approach was used with responses to the questions regarding whether respondents felt there were other parts of their life they would like to control. If respondents answered yes, then team members categorized the parts that respondents wanted to control and what they felt prevented them from exercising that control. If respondents answered no, then responses regarding why they did not want more control were categorized. As with the directed content analysis, a reliability check was conducted between the two members of the research team, with an 82 % initial agreement and full consensus reached upon discussion.

Results

The demographic characteristics of the 84 respondents were varied. Respondents ranged in age from 51 to 96 years, with a mean age of 76 years. The vast majority of respondents ($n = 82$; 98 %) were White and 2 (2 %) Black. Regarding gender and marital status, a little over half were female (55 %; $n = 46$) and 42 % ($n = 35$) married/partnered, 33 % ($n = 28$) widowed, and 25 % ($n = 21$) single/separated/divorced. Respondents were fairly well educated, with a range of 7–25 years of school completed and a mean of 13 years. The vast majority of respondents had some form of cancer (88 %; $n = 74$), and others were diagnosed with respiratory (5 %; $n = 4$), heart (4 %; $n = 3$), neurological (2 %; $n = 2$), and renal (1 %; $n = 1$) diseases.

Control Strategies Exercised

All 84 respondents described the way in which they exercised control (see Table 1). Of these respondents, 83 reported using a primary control strategy in combination with another primary or compensatory secondary control strategy; only one reported exercising a single primary control strategy. This 84-year-old never-married woman described using selective primary control. Although she had cancer, her focus was not on the illness itself but on the goal of strengthening her legs so she could be more mobile. When asked if other people helped her exercise control, she said no. Thus, although it was likely that others were assisting because her mobility was limited, she did not feel their doing so helped in her exercise of control.

Nineteen (23 %) of the 84 respondents reported they could no longer completely rely on their own resources to attain their goals and so asked for assistance (compensatory primary control). Respondents viewed asking others for assistance in a positive light noting that the assistance enabled them to maintain some control:

> I feel like I'm probably . . . see, I'm not a quitter and I may have to ask for help but I do . . . and that way I can stay on a schedule and maintain a life that I feel that I'm still contributing something to my family. (62-year-old married woman)

Awareness of the need for assistance to exercise control did not necessarily mean that respondents would not like to exercise control on their own (selective primary control). For example, a 62-year-old married woman was used to having full control of her own home and stated, "Oh yeah, I would definitely like to go back to the way it was before all of this happened and be able to maintain my complete house and not have to ask for help in anything."

Forty-two (50 %) of the 84 respondents used a combination of selective and compensatory primary control. These respondents were able to use their own personal skills and resources to attain some goals but required assistance to attain others. For example, one 70-year-old divorced man

Table 1 Qualitative Themes Regarding Control Exercised in the Dying Process (*N* = 84)

Theme	n (%)
Control strategies exercised	
Selective primary control	1 (1)
Compensatory primary control	19 (23)
Selective and compensatory primary control	42 (50)
Compensatory primary and secondary control	8 (9)
Selective primary control, and compensatory	14 (17)
Primary and secondary control	
Aspects of life over which control was exercised	
Decision making	50 (59)
Independence	18 (21)
Mental attitude	18 (21)
Instrumental activities of daily living	18 (21)
Activities of daily living	14 (17)
Personal relationships	9 (11)
Desire for more control	
Yes (*n* = 43; 51 %)	
Independence	14 (33)
Body functioning	13 (30)
Illness	10 (23)
Generativity	6 (14)
No (*n* = 41; 49 %)	
Satisfied with current level of control	31 (76)
Physical condition prevents exercising more control	7 (17)
God's in control	1 (2)
No explanation provided by respondent	2 (5)

exercised selective primary control in regard to attaining his goal of setting a daily schedule for eating, bedtime, and leisure activities; however, to attain his goal of bathing himself, he required assistance (compensatory primary control).

Compensatory secondary control was used in combination with compensatory primary control by 8 (9 %) respondents and in combination with selective and compensatory primary control by 14 (17 %) respondents. For respondents who exercised compensatory secondary control, at least one of the following three strategies was used: lowering aspirations, positive reappraisal, and social comparison. The eight respondents, who used a combination of compensatory

primary and secondary control, used one of each type of control strategies. The 14 respondents who used a combination of selective primary control, and compensatory primary and secondary control, each reported one selective and one compensatory primary control strategy and one or two secondary control strategies. For those using compensatory secondary control, lowering aspirations was the most common strategy used: 16 (73 %) of the 22 respondents spoke about adjusting their goals (lowering their aspirations) concerning exercising control. For example, an 88-year-old divorced woman sought to reframe her own inability to write checks any longer such that it was something her daughter needed to experience: "I think she [daughter] just offered [to write her checks] and I said sure . . . I said that's fine. I felt it would be a good experience for her."

Quantitative analyses were conducted to determine whether respondents' demographic characteristics differed by these control strategy groups (CPC; SPC and CPC; CPC and CSC; and SPC, CPC, and CSC; Table 2). By necessity, the sole respondent who reported using only selective primary control was dropped from these analyses given the absence of variation. One-way ANOVA and chi-square tests revealed no significant differences in respondents' age, gender, marital status, education, or primary hospice diagnosis by the control strategy grouping reported (see Table 2).

A one-way ANOVA test was also conducted on the control strategy groups and respondents' quality-of-life score (see Table 2). The overall mean for quality of life was 22.6, with a range of 6–35: higher scores represent higher quality of life. Based on the finding of a significant *F* ratio, $F(3, 79) = 5.15; p < .01$, Tukey's honestly significant difference post hoc test was run to determine, through pairwise multiple comparisons, the control strategies that did and did not differ in regard to quality of life. The post hoc tests results revealed that respondents who used a combination of selective and compensatory primary control ($p < .05$) or a combination of selective primary control, compensatory primary control, and compensatory secondary control ($p < .05$) reported a significantly higher quality of life than respondents who used only compensatory primary control. No significant difference was found between respondents who used compensatory primary and compensatory secondary control and those who used only compensatory primary control. Although this group does not significantly differ, the result is likely due to the small sample size ($n = 8$). Thus, the overall finding from these tests suggests that exercising more than one control strategy was associated with higher quality of life than exercising only one control strategy.

Aspects of Life Over Which Control Was Exercised

Respondents were asked to name and discuss the parts of their lives over which they exercised control, and they named anywhere from one ($n = 27$; 32 %), to two ($n = 34$; 40 %),

Table 2 Demographics and Quality of Life of Elders Adopting Control Strategies (*N* = 84)

Demographic	SPC (1 %; *n* = 1)	CPC (23 %; *n* = 19)	SPC & CPC (50 %; *n* = 42)	CPC & CSC (9 %; *n* = 8)	SPC, CPC, & CSC (17 %; *n* = 14)
Age (in years), *M*	80.0	77.5	76.1	74.8	72.8
Education (in years), *M*	15.0	12.8	13.2	12.8	15.1
Gender, %					
Female (*n* = 46)	100.0	63.2	54.8	37.5	50.0
Male (*n* = 38)	0.0	36.8	45.2	62.5	50.0
Marital status, %					
Not married (*n* = 49)	100.0	57.9	64.3	50.0	42.9
Married (*n* = 35)	0.0	42.1	35.7	50.0	57.1
Primary diagnosis, %					
Cancer (*n* = 74)	100.0	84.2	95.2	75.0	78.6
Respiratory (*n* = 4)	0.0	5.3	2.4	12.5	7.1
Heart disease (*n* = 3)	0.0	5.3	0.0	12.5	7.1
Neurological (*n* = 2)	0.0	5.3	0.0	0.0	7.1
Renal failure (*n* = 1)	0.0	0.0	2.4	0.0	0.0
Quality of life, *M*		18.5 [a]	23.2 [b]	24.1 [a,b]	24.7 [b,*]

Notes: The levels of significance for continuous variables are based on one-way analysis of variance tests. Means in the same row that have different superscripts differ at $p \le .05$. SPC = selective primary control; CPC = compensatory primary control; CSC = compensatory secondary control.

[*] $p < .05$.

to three (*n* = 14; 17 %) to four parts (*n* = 9; 11 %). Content analysis of these discussions revealed six thematic areas regarding the parts of their lives over which respondents felt they exercised control: decision making, independence, mental attitude, instrumental activities of daily living (IADLs), activities of daily living (ADLs), and personal relationships.

Decision Making

Exercising control through decision making was reported by 50 (59 %) of the 84 respondents, one of whom exercised control by herself and the others who did so with assistance. These respondents talked about making decisions or participating in the decision-making process with others regarding where to live, their finances, plans for death, how people provided their care, treatments they chose to receive, and their daily schedule and activities. Respondents noted that making a decision and having it supported by others provided them with a sense of control. A 72-year-old married woman stated, "I could tell her [daughter] this is what I want to do and we do it together. I feel like I'm a little bit more in control." Several respondents noted that it was not the size of the decision or what was being decided; rather, it was having a decision to make that made them feel more in control. An 86-year-old widower made this point when he said, "It's really small things like the choice of where you want to eat. It's nice if somebody gives you a choice."

Independence

Eighteen (21 %) of the 84 respondents reported that being independent was a part of their life over which they exercised control. Independence was expressed by respondents as the ability to "go where I want and do what I want," "live my own life," and "don't have to ask for help from others." These 18 respondents spoke in adamant tones when talking about having control over their independence, as illustrated by a 73-year-old married man's, "I can do what I damn well please!" and a 79-year-old widow's, "I don't *have* to ask for help from others." Control over independence was clearly very important.

Mental Attitude

Exercising control internally over their own mental attitude was discussed by 18 (21 %) of the 84 respondents. Using this compensatory secondary control strategy, a 77-year-old married man noted, "Well, I have control over my feelings; I have control over my mind." . . . An 81-year-old married man reported, "Well, I can control my mental attitude toward the disease, knowing that its terminal and I can't do much about that." . . . This ability to exercise control internally was viewed in a positive light, as expressed by one 72-year-old divorced woman who said, "Well, my viewpoint . . . is you cannot always control certain things you find yourself in but you (can) always choose your attitude."

Instrumental Activities of Daily Living

The ability to exercise control over one's IADLs was reported by 18 (21 %) respondents. Respondents spoke about being able to control their finances, order groceries over the telephone, and perform basic household chores. For example, a 67-year-old divorced woman reported exercising control over household chores: "Yesterday, my grandsons were here and they came to do the lawn and stuff like that, so I can still direct them and take care of the outdoors without being outdoors."

Activities of Daily Living

Fourteen (17 %) respondents reported exercising control over ADLs. The importance of doing so is evident in the following statement by a 73-year-old married man:

> . . . I uh, you know, I wash myself up every morning and uh, brush my teeth and all of those little tasks—don't need any help other than my wife will—we usually do it in this room and she'll bring in the equipment, you know. But if I had to, I could go into that bathroom next door and take care of it. It's just a little simpler this way so, but I could do it, and I know I could.

Although still needing assistance with her bath, a 76-year-old divorced woman made a point to let the interviewer know that she still exercises some control over her bath: "Yeah, they [hospice certified nursing assistant] insist I should be helped with a bath, but I can still lift myself up out of the tub." Concerning ADLs, the 14 respondents were all quick to point out that they exercised control, even if they were receiving assistance.

Personal Relationships

Nine (11 %) of 84 respondents talked about having control over how they relate with their family and friends. They talked about the value those relationships held for them and how they felt they had control over making sure they were positive relationships. An 81-year-old married man talked about how concerned he was by the impact his illness had on his loved ones and how he wanted to make certain the impact was positive.

> I try to influence my family's feelings toward my situation. I get the impression that . . . I'm concerned that they are also concerned about my situation—that it's affecting them now. They're calling everyday, they try to come everyday. So I'm sure it's had a direct effect on their lives.

In addition to making sure their impact on loved ones was positive, respondents also talked about ensuring that those relationships were as normal as possible. One 86-year-old widower talked about how he made sure that he and his girlfriend "date just like anybody else."

Desire for More Control

Although all 84 respondents reported experiencing a sense of control in their dying process, the question remained whether they felt it was enough. All 84 respondents were asked whether there were other parts of their life that they would like to control and 43 (51 %) answered yes. When asked to identify those parts, four thematic areas surfaced: independence, body functioning, illness, and generativity. Having identified the part of their life they wanted to control, they were then asked to talk about what prevented them from doing so.

Fourteen (33 %) respondents noted that they would like to exercise more control over their ability to be independent such as being able to stay in their house alone sometimes or being able to get in their car and drive wherever they wanted by themselves. It is interesting to note that when describing how they would exercise control in regard to their independence, all 14 respondents discussed the importance of being alone sometimes, a desire that may have resulted from the constant presence of caregivers. One 76-year-old divorced woman stated, "I would like to be independent again. . . . do what I want and go where I want . . . navigate by myself." When asked what prevented them from exercising such control, all 14 noted that it was their illness, which left them fatigued, nauseous, dizzy, or in pain.

Exercising control over their own bodies was the desire of 13 (30 %) of the 43 respondents. The functions that respondents wanted more control over were incontinence, sexual performance, muscle and leg movement, appetite, physical strength, and memory. Lacking control over functions that people normally can control was very upsetting, as evidenced by one 90-year-old married man who was struggling with incontinence: "Well, accidents happen without any warning a lot of times." Again, when asked what prevented their exercising control, all 13 people stated that it was their illness.

The third most common theme to emerge was the desire to control their illness: 10 (23 %) respondents spoke about wanting to control the impact their illness had on their ability to function physically in their daily lives. They also spoke of wanting to control their illness such that it would not be terminal. A 76-year-old divorced woman who was terminally ill with lung cancer said wistfully, "Just maybe—the only thing, oh, that's more or less a desire . . . that they x-ray me once, and see that the spots are gone . . . controlling these spots on my lungs." Although the desire was strong to exercise such control and fight their illness, respondents stated that what prevented them from doing so was that it was "not realistic."

The fourth theme that arose was the desire expressed by six respondents (14 %) to exercise control now and after their death on behalf of the next generation, a stage of development referred to by Erik Erikson as generativity

(Erikson, Erikson, & Kivnick, 1986). Erikson's seventh stage of his developmental theory, generativity versus stagnation, proposes that as part of their own development, adults assist the younger generation in leading meaningful lives. Although Erikson proposes this as a midlife stage of development, terminally ill elders who reported seeking to be instrumental in their children and grandchildren's future lives ranged in age from 62 to 84 years. For example, a 62-year-old divorced woman longed to assist financially loved ones in difficult circumstances. A 73-year-old married man talked about his need for ensuring his grandchildren's future education, and an 81-year-old married man who had lung cancer wanted to talk with young people about the dangers of smoking. Perhaps knowing that time was limited, these respondents felt the need to make a lasting impact on the next generation. When asked what prevented them from doing so, they talked about their children's resentment and need for independence. One 71-year-old widow stated:

> He's a 21 year old man . . . I guess I would like him to have ways of being helped physically, medically, healthcare-wise. I can't do any of that. . . . [I]f I were healthy, I couldn't do those things. People have to do for themselves what they have to do. I'd like to make his life easier because there are things that I've seen because I'm older.

For the 41 (49 %) respondents who answered no to the question regarding whether there were other parts of their life that they would like to control, all but 2 (5 %) provided an explanation. The vast majority (76 %; n = 31) reported they were satisfied with their current level of control. Some of these individuals reported their satisfaction was due to their still exercising the same amount of control as before their illness: "I'm still kind of fully in charge of what I've done before." Others spoke of feeling happy or peaceful with life in its current state: "I'm satisfied—life is where it should be." The other eight respondents provided different explanations. Seven (17 %) respondents stated that their physical condition left them unable to control other parts of their lives. An 84-year-old widow noted, "I'm not capable of doing the thing I would want to control." The eighth respondent, a 55-year-old divorced woman, remarked she did not want control because "God's in control."

Discussion

The results from this study offer an understanding of the role control plays in the dying process of terminally ill elders and the potential association it has with quality of life in the dying process. The 84 elders interviewed provided information about the strategies they used to exercise control in their dying process, the aspects over which they exercised control, and whether they desired to exercise more control.

Control Strategies

Either on their own (selective primary control) or with the assistance of another (compensatory primary control), all 84 elders were exercising a form of primary control to attain a particular goal. The fact that these elders sought to exercise primary control, although they were very ill and their time was limited, is evidence of its importance.

Another important finding concerned the mix of control strategies that terminally ill elders used to exercise control. Although about a fifth of respondents exercised only one primary control strategy, the majority used two to four primary and secondary control strategies. Respondents had goals they wanted to attain and appeared to choose a control strategy that fit with the abilities they possessed related to that goal. It is also significant that although the exercise of primary control is visible to others, the exercise of secondary control may not be; yet, changing the internal self to fit with the external world did provide these respondents with a sense of control. For example, one 63-year-old married woman, who was chair bound during the day, spent her days alone. A hospice worker came by each day and the woman always asked the worker to turn on the radio before she left. She loved to listen to the radio and felt that by asking the worker, she had control over being able to do so. One day, however, she forgot to have the worker turn on the radio. Unable to do so herself (selective primary control) or ask others to do it for her (compensatory secondary control), she turned to a compensatory secondary control strategy: "I didn't have any of them to turn on my radio. My God, I thought, well all right, no sound but I could (still) hear the birds." The use of multiple strategies is not only evidence of these elders' desire to exercise control but their adaptability in doing so.

Findings from the study also reveal that the use of multiple strategies appears to be associated with quality of life in the dying process. Although the sole use of selective primary control could not be tested due to only one elder reporting its use, comparisons were made between the use of only compensatory primary control and the use of other combinations of control strategies. The one-way ANOVA test revealed that exercising more than one control strategy (compensatory primary control) was associated with a higher reported quality of life in the dying process, which has important implications for practitioners.

Aspects Controlled

The aspects respondents reported exercising control over provided insight into the world of terminally ill elders, which, due to being home or facility bound for the most part, was a smaller world than when they were healthy. As their world grew smaller, the areas in which they could exercise control became more limited. The six thematic areas that respondents spoke of concerning the exercise of control were decision making, independence, mental attitude,

IADLs, ADLs, and personal relationships. Being able to make decisions that influenced their world and future death, to come and go and be alone, to choose their attitude, to perform IADLs or ADLs, and to ensure their relationships were positive, were the key aspects of the dying process over which respondents sought to exercise control. Realizing at some level that their world and often their ability to exercise control were constrained in ways they had not been before, respondents appeared to adapt by focusing on areas inside their world, being flexible in how they exercised control, as well as how much control they exercised.

More Control?

Study results revealed that over half of the respondents wanted to exercise more control in their dying process. Just as independence was an aspect of the dying process that many respondents reported exercising control over, 14 respondents who were not currently exercising such control desired to do so. The severity of their illness prevented exercising this control, just as it did in two other areas: their illness and bodily functions. Although they desired control in these areas, terminally ill elders were realistic regarding their inability to do so.

Perhaps the most surprising finding was that respondents wanted to exercise more control over the future success of their children and grandchildren. Erickson proposed generativity as a stage of development that takes place at midlife. Although these elders were not in midlife, perhaps in the final stage of life, the need to ensure the success of the next generation presented itself yet again. An alternative explanation may simply be that in providing for the next generation, these elders were able to leave behind a legacy of love.

Study Limitations and Future Implications

Although this qualitative study employed a large sample size, and new understandings were gained on the role of control in the dying process of terminally ill elders, limitations were present. First, 98 % of the sample were Caucasian elders. Future research should be conducted with other racial/ethnic elders to determine the extent to which culture influences the role of control in an elder's dying process. The role of the individual and the exercise of control tend to be Western values and so not all groups may view control in the same manner as the current study participants. Second, the lives of terminally ill elders are not stagnant; rather, they can shift very quickly due to advancing illness. The 84 respondents who volunteered to participate in the study may have done so because they were less ill than others who were not recruited. They may still have been at a point in their illness where they could exercise primary control more readily and rely less on secondary control strategies. The current study was cross-sectional in nature and so the results are based on one time point in

the respondents' dying process. A longitudinal study following elders throughout their dying process would provide greater insight into whether they continue to be adaptive in the use of control strategies and what they seek to control changes. Third, the respondents participating in the current study were all receiving hospice care either at home or in a hospice inpatient facility. Future studies should look at elders who are dying in other environments and not receiving hospice care, such as a hospital or nursing home. It is not clear from the current study whether the environment itself and the type of end-of-life care being provided influenced respondents' control strategies or the aspects of the dying process over which they desired control. Fourth, the respondents in this sample were terminally ill (less than 6 months to live), but it is feasible that elders with terminal or chronic conditions may experience similar physical limitations that impact their exercise of control. Certainly, the findings for this study's terminally ill respondents bear similarities to the research findings discussed in the literature review on elders with chronic conditions in that they, too, have been shown to use a mix of primary and secondary control strategies (Wrosch & Schulz, 2008) and to use compensatory secondary control strategies, including positive reappraisal and lowering aspirations (Heckhausen, 1997). Future research should look more closely at the exercise of control for elders with acute, chronic, and terminal conditions to determine the similarities and differences in regard to how control is exercised and its relationship to quality of life. Fifth, in order for terminally ill elders to exercise control in their dying process, particularly when the control strategy is compensatory and necessitates the assistance of others, family members must be supportive of their doing so. A recent study (Schroepfer, 2008) found that the relational content of social relationships defined as the "functional nature or quality of social relationships" (House, Umberson, & Landis, 1988, p. 302) was related to the consideration of a hastened death. Quantitatively, poor or conflictual support was found to be a highly significant predictor of the consideration to hasten death, and, qualitatively, if an elder felt his or her own suffering or the suffering his or her care placed on loved ones was burdensome, he or she was likely to consider a hastened death. The current study did not include measures of the relational content of those who indirectly or directly supported the elders in their exercise of control in the dying process, or the impact of relational content on their quality of life. Future studies on exercising control in the dying process should quantitatively include relational content measures and qualitatively include questions on not only how others assist an elder in the exercise of control but also the elder's experience with their doing so. Sixth, the finding regarding the association of control strategies with quality of life was limited to a bivariate analysis. Future research on this finding should employ the use of multivariate analyses to control for relevant control and predictor variables.

Practice Implications

The knowledge gained from these interviews has important implications for practitioners and family members providing care to elders during their dying process. Being cognizant of the life an elder had prior to his or her dying process and how that life has changed since the illness is important knowledge for family members to remember and practitioners to garner. As the health that once allowed an elder to be very much a part of the world outside his or her home or facility declines, so does the size of his or her world. Understanding this, family members and practitioner can seek to support the elder's exercise of control within that smaller world, as well as the strategies he or she chooses to use. If family members and the practitioner are assisting the elder with a task, then supporting the elder's need to exercise control as much as possible is key for the elder in exercising compensatory primary control. If an elder is physically limited to such a point that exercising primary control alone or with the assistance of another is not practical, then it is important that family members and the practitioner be aware that the elder may seek to exercise control internally over his or her mental attitude. Based on the expression of an elder's attitude, it may appear that he or she is giving up; however, it may actually be that he or she is taking a realistic approach to the situation and using the compensatory secondary control strategy of lowering his or her aspirations. Based on the elder's situation, the family and the practitioner must then determine whether the elder is lowering his or her aspirations unnecessarily or simply being realistic. Family members or the practitioner can then work with the elder to either reframe his or her situation in a way that allows for raising aspirations or, in the case of a realistic viewpoint, support the elder's use of the control strategy. Because the exercise of more than one control strategy appears to be associated with a reportedly higher quality of life in an elder's dying process, then family members and practitioners can work to ensure that elders have the opportunity to do so whenever possible.

Decision-making, independence, mental attitude, IADLs, ADLs, and relationships were aspects of the dying process over which the respondents sought to exercise control. Providing the support and the opportunities for such control to be possible is an important role for family and the practitioner. For example, elders who talk about the importance of their always having been independent may necessitate their family members and practitioners locating such opportunities. The elders in the current study tended to equate independence with time alone; thus, family members and the practitioner can work to ensure that the elder has a period of privacy each day. Another example is the role decision making plays in the dying process. The study's respondents were not focused on the size of a decision or the need to make one alone: They primarily wanted to be a part of the process and have the support of others in doing so. These interventions and others based on familial knowledge and a thorough assessment of an elder's pre- and post-terminal illness life will assist family members and practitioners in ensuring that elders' control preferences are supported in their final stage of life.

Funding

Support for this study was provided by the John A. Hartford Foundation Faculty Scholars Program in Geriatric Social Work.

References

Albert, S. M., Rabkin, J. G., Del Bene, M. L., Tider, T., O' Sullivan, I., Rowland, L. P., et al. (2005). Wish to die in end-stage ALS. *Neurology, 65,* 68–74.

Back, A., Wallace, J., Starks, H., & Pearlman, R. (1996). Physician-assisted suicide and euthanasia in Washington state: Patient requests and physician responses. *Journal of the American Medical Association, 275,* 919–925.

Chapple, A., Ziebland, S., McPherson, A., & Herxheimer, A. (2006). What people close to death say about euthanasia and assisted suicide: A qualitative study. *Journal of Medical Ethics, 32,* 706–710.

Chin, A., Hedberg, K., Higginson, G., & Fleming, D. (1999). Legalized physician-assisted suicide in Oregon—The first year's experience. *New England Journal of Medicine, 340,* 577–583.

Chipperfield, J. G., & Perry, R. P. (2006). Primary- and secondary-control strategies in later life: Predicting hospital outcomes in men and women. *Health Psychology, 25,* 226–236.

Coyle, N., & Sculco, L. (2004). Expressed desire for hastened death in seven patients living with advanced cancer: A phenomenologic inquire. *Oncology Nursing Forum, 31,* 699–706.

Erikson, E. H., Erikson, J. M., & Kivnick, H. Q. (1986). *Vital involvement in old age.* New York: W. W. Norton.

Ganzini, L., Harvath, T., Jackson, A., Goy, E., Miller, L., & Delorit, M. (2002). Experiences of Oregon nurses and social workers with hospice patients who requested assistance with suicide. *New England Journal of Medicine, 347,* 582–588.

Ganzini, L., Johnston, W. S., McFarland, B. H., Tolle, S. W., & Lee, M. A. (1998). Attitudes of patients with amyotrophic lateral sclerosis and their care givers toward assisted suicide. *New England Journal of Medicine, 339,* 967–973.

Heckhausen, J. (1997). Developmental regulation across adulthood: Primary and secondary control of age-related challenges. *Developmental Psychology, 33,* 176–187.

Heckhausen, J., & Schulz, R. (1995). A life-span theory of control. *Psychological Review, 102,* 284–304.

House, J. S., Umberson, D., & Landis, K. R. (1988). Structures and processes of social support. *Annual Review of Sociology, 14,* 293–318.

Hsieh, H., & Shannon, S. E. (2005). Three approaches to qualitative content analysis. *Qualitative Health Research, 15,* 1277–1288.

Oregon Department of Human Services. (2000). *Oregon's Death with Dignity Act: The second year's experience.* Portland: Oregon Health Division.

Oregon Department of Human Services. (2007). *Ninth annual report on Oregon's Death with Dignity Act.* Portland: Oregon Health Division.

Patton, M. (1990). *Qualitative evaluation and research methods* (2nd ed.). Newbury Park, CA: Sage.

Peterman, R. H., Fitchett, G., Brady, M., Hernandez, L., & Cella, D. (2002). Measuring spiritual well-being in people with cancer: The Functional Assessment of Chronic Illness Therapy–Spiritual Well-Being Scale (FACIT–Sp). *Annals of Behavioral Medicine, 24,* 49–58.

Rodin, J. (1986). Health, control and aging. In M. M. Baltes & P. B. Baltes (Eds.), *The psychology of control and aging* (pp. 139–165). Hillsdale, NJ: Lawrence Erlbaum.

Rothbaum, F., Weisz, J. R., & Snyder, S. S. (1982). Changing the world and changing the self: A two-process model of perceived control. *Journal of Personality and Social Psychology, 42,* 5–37.

Schroepfer, T. A. (2006). Mind frames towards dying and factors motivating their adoption by terminally ill elders. *Journal of Gerontology: Social Sciences, 61,* S129–S139.

Schroepfer, T. A. (2007). Critical events in the dying process: The potential for physical and psychosocial suffering. *Journal of Palliative Medicine, 10,* 136–147.

Schroepfer, T. A. (2008). Social relationships and their role in the consideration to hasten death. *The Gerontologist, 48,* 612–621.

Schulz, R., & Heckhausen, J. (1996). A life span model of successful aging. *American Psychologist, 31,* 702–714.

Singer, P. A., Martin, D. K., & Kelner, M. (1999). Quality end-of-life care: Patients' perspectives. *Journal of the American Medical Association, 281,* 163–168.

Teno, J. M., Casey, V. A., Welch, L. C., & Edgman-Levitan, S. (2001). Patient-focused, family-centered end-of-life medical care: Views of the guidelines and bereaved family members. *Journal of Pain and Symptom Management, 22,* 738–751.

Volker, D. (2001). Oncology nurses' experiences with requests for assisted dying from terminally ill patients with cancer. *Oncology Nursing Forum, 28,* 39–49.

Volker, D. L., Kahn, D., & Penticuff, J. H. (2004a). Patient control and end-of-life care. Part I: The advanced practice nurse perspective. *Oncology Nursing Forum, 31,* 945–953.

Volker, D. L., Kahn, D., & Penticuff, J. H. (2004b). Patient control and end-of-life care. Part II: The patient perspective. *Oncology Nursing Forum, 31,* 954–960.

Wilson, K. G., Chochinov, H. M., McPherson, C. J., LeMay, K., Allard, P., Chary, S., et al. (2007). Suffering with advanced cancer. *Journal of Clinical Oncology, 25,* 1691–1697.

Wrosch, D., Heckhausen, J., & Lachman, M. W. (2000). Primary and secondary control strategies for managing health and financial stress across adulthood. *Psychology and Aging, 15,* 387–399.

Wrosch, C., & Schulz, R. (2008). Health-engagement control strategies and 2-year changes in older adults' physical health. *Psychological Science, 19,* 537–541.

Critical Thinking

1. What were given as examples of the person's control over the "instrumental activities of daily living"?

2. What were given as examples of the person's control over the "activities of daily living"?

3. What were given as examples of the elderly person's control over decision making?

UNIT 7

Living Environment in Later Life

Unit Selections

Learning Outcomes

After reading this Unit, you will be able to:

- Identify the services that residents in Verona, New Jersey, receive that assist them in remaining in their current homes as they age.

- Identify the goal of educational initiatives in Verona for older people who are attempting to age in place.

- Describe the variety of niche communities that exist for older adults today.

- Identify the fastest-growing niche communities in the country at the present time.

- Cite what is the most effective strategy to get cities to adopt innovations that benefit older adults.

- Discuss what should be included in the successful advocacy to the local government for changes that would benefit older adults.

- Discuss the various services people living in a village can receive from other village members or as part of their village services provided routinely and paid for by service fees.

- Explain how Keystone's health services are better able to coordinate the services for their village patients.

Student Website
www.mhhe.com/cls

Internet References

American Association of Homes and Services for the Aging
www.aahsa.org
Center for Demographic Studies
http://cds.duke.edu
Guide to Retirement Living Online
www.retirement-living.com
The United States Department of Housing and Urban Development
www.hud.gov

Unit 4 noted that old age is often a period of shrinking life space. This concept is crucial to an understanding of the living environments of older Americans. When older people retire, they may find that they travel less frequently and over shorter distances because they no longer work and many neighborhoods have stores, gas stations, and churches in close proximity. As the retirement years roll by, older people may feel less in control of their environment due to a decline in their hearing and vision as well as other health problems. As the aging process continues, elderly people are likely to restrict their mobility to the areas where they feel most secure. This usually means that an increasing amount of time is spent at home. Estimates show that individuals aged 65 and above spend 80 to 90 percent of their lives in their home environments. Of all other age groups, only small children are as neighborhood- and housebound. The house, neighborhood, and community environments are, therefore, more crucial to elderly individuals than to any other adult age group. The interaction with others that they experience within their homes and neighborhoods can either be stimulating or foreboding, pleasant or threatening. Across the country, older Americans live in a variety of circumstances, ranging from desirable to undesirable.

Approximately 70 percent of people who are elderly live in a family setting, usually a husband-wife household; 20 percent live alone or with nonrelatives; and the remaining number live in institutions such as nursing homes. Although only about 5 percent of elderly people live in nursing homes at any one time, 25 percent of people aged 65 and above will spend some time in a nursing home setting. The longer one lives, the more likely he or she is to eventually live in a total-care institution. Because most older Americans would prefer to live independently in their own homes for as long as possible, their relocation—to other houses, apartments, or nursing homes—is often accompanied by a considerable amount of trauma and unrest. The fact that aged individuals tend to be less mobile and more neighborhood-bound than any other age group makes member's living environment

© Ariel Skelley/Blend Images LLC

crucial to their sense of well-being. Articles in this section focus on some alternatives available to aged people, from family care, to assisted living to nursing homes. In "A Little Help Can Go a Long way," David Crary identifies services that are necessary for an older person to be able to age in place and remain in his or her current home. In "Happy Together," Sally Abrahms notes that as the baby boomers age, they do not want to move into assisted living or nursing home facilities. Amanda Lehning discusses the various types of neighborhoods and communities that are emerging for senior residents. In "City Governments and Aging in Place: Community Design, Transportation and Housing Innovation Adoption," she explains how community changes could benefit older adults. Martha Thomas describes the advantage of moving to one of the emerging neighborhood concepts called *villages* for seniors in "The Real Social Network."

A Little Help Can Go a Long Way

"Aging in Place" Requires Good Luck, Support Network

DAVID CRARY

Retirement communities may have their perks, but Beryl O'Connor says it would be tough to match the birthday surprise she got in her own backyard when she turned 80 this year.

She was tending her garden when two little girls from next door–"my buddies," she calls them–brought her a strawberry shortcake. It underscored why she wants to stay put in the house that she and her husband, who died 18 years ago, purchased in the late 1970s.

"I couldn't just be around old people–that's not my life-style," she said. "I'd go out of my mind."

Physically spry and socially active, O'Connor in many respects is the embodiment of "aging in place," growing old in one's own longtime home and remaining engaged in the community rather than moving to a retirement facility.

According to surveys, aging in place is the overwhelming preference of Americans over 50. But doing it successfully requires both good fortune and support services—things that O'Connor's pleasant hometown of Verona has become increasingly capable of providing.

About 10 miles northwest of Newark, Verona has roughly 13,300 residents nestled into less than 3 square miles. There's a transportation network that takes older people on shopping trips and to medical appointments, and the town is benefiting from a $100,000 federal grant to put in place an aging-in-place program called Verona LIVE.

Administered by United Jewish Communities of MetroWest New Jersey, the program strives to educate older people about available services to help them address problems and stay active in the community. Its partners include the health and police departments, the rescue squad, the public and public schools, and religious groups.

Among the support services are a home maintenance program with free safety checks and minor home repairs, access to a social worker and job counselor, a walking club and other social activities. In one program, a group of middle-school girls provided one-on-one computer training to about 20 older adults.

Social worker Connie Pifher, Verona's health coordinator, said a crucial part of the overall initiative is educating older people to plan ahead realistically and constantly reassess their prospects for successfully aging in place.

"There are some people who just can do it, especially if they have family support," said Pifher, "And then you run into people who think they can do it, yet really can't. You need to start educating people before a crisis hits."

There's no question that aging in place has broad appeal. According to an Associated Press-LifeGoesStrong.com poll conducted in October 2011, 52 percent of baby boomers said they were unlikely to move someplace new in retirement. In a 2005 survey by AARP, 89 percent of people age 50 and older said they would prefer to remain in their home indefinitely as they age.

That yearning, coupled with a widespread dread of going to a nursing home, has led to a nationwide surge of programs aimed at helping people stay in their neighborhoods longer.

Critical Thinking

1. What support is probably the most critical for families that want to age in place?

2. What percent of the population over 50 would prefer to age in place in a 2005 poll that was taken?

3. What do older people dread most about their living arrangements?

Happy Together

Villages: Helping People Age in Place.

SALLY ABRAHMS

For years, boomers have denied they are going to get old. Now, with knees that need scoping and birthday cakes with way too many candles, the defiant generation is finally thinking about the future—especially where and how to live.

Visits to their parents in sterile, regimented assisted living or nursing homes are leaving boomers dismayed. They want better choices for Mom—and for themselves. While they may be a decade or more away from needing care, they're overhauling or honing traditional models and inventing new ones.

In choosing how they want to age, and where, boomers are helping shape the future of housing. "They have changed expectations every decade they've gone through; I don't think it will stop now," says John McIlwain, senior fellow for housing at the Urban Land Institute. Down the road, he says, "there won't be one single trend. People will be doing a lot of different things." They already are. The common denominator in existing and still-to-be-created models, say experts, is the desire to be part of a community that shares common interests, values or resources. People want to live where neighbors know and care about one another and will help one another as they age. That doesn't mean they'll become primary caretakers; if it gets to that point, outside professionals may need to help.

They also won't necessarily retire from their jobs if they live in a "retirement" community. Today's housing options reflect the attitude of older Americans: Stay active, keep learning, develop relationships and have fun for as long as possible.

Niche Communities

The concept: Live with others who share similar lifestyles, backgrounds or interests.

The numbers: Around 100 across the country. **The price:** Depends on community type.

Prices can range from $800 a month for a rental at an RV park or $1,700 at an artists' community, up to several hundred thousand dollars to buy a unit at a university community, with monthly addons of $2,000 or more that include some meals, housekeeping, social activities and medical care.

"With 78 million baby boomers, housing options are virtually unlimited," says Andrew Carle, founding director of the Program in Assisted Living/Senior Housing Administration at George Mason University in Virginia. In the next 20 years, he says, name an interest group and there'll be a community for it. "Will there be assisted living for vegetarians or a community for Grateful Dead fans? Residential cruise ships with long-term care? Absolutely."

Today's niche communities are already varied. They're geared to healthy adults but often have an assisted care component. They include places like Rainbow's End RV Park in Livingston, Texas, which offers assisted living, Alzheimer's day care, respite for caregivers and short-term care for the sick or frail. The Charter House in Rochester, Minn., provides a home for former Mayo Clinic staffers, among others. The Burbank Senior Arts Colony in Los Angeles attracts retired or aspiring artists, musicians, actors and writers. Aegis Gardens in Fremont, Calif., caters to older Asians.

The swanky Rainbow Vision in Santa Fe, N.M., is primarily—but not exclusively—for gay, lesbian, bisexual and transgender (GLBT) clients. While it has assisted living, there's also a cabaret, an award-winning restaurant and a top-notch spa. With 3 million GLBT older Americans—a figure projected to nearly double by 2030—and typically no adult children to care for them, such communities are expected to multiply.

Hands down, the fastest-growing niche community sector is university-based retirement communities (UBRCs). So far there are 50 or more on or near such college campuses as Dartmouth, Cornell, Penn State and Denison University. While residents are usually in their 70s, 80s and up—besides independent living, there is assisted living and nursing care—UBRCs will appeal to boomers, the most highly educated demographic, when they grow older, says Carle. Residents can take classes and attend athletic or cultural events at the nearby college campus, professors lecture at the UBRC, and young students can complete internships.

Five years ago, Harvey Culbert, 75, a former medical physicist from Chicago, and his wife moved to Kendal at Oberlin, which is affiliated with the Ohio college. He has audited, for free, a course in neuroscience, sings in a college group, and is taking voice lessons from a retired Kendal music teacher. "I'm always interested in improving what I do," he says.

Cohousing

The concept: A group, usually composed of strangers at the start, creates a communal-type housing arrangement that is intergenerational or all older people, with separate units but some shared common space. The group may buy the property, help design it, make all rules by consensus and manage it independently. Residents eat some dinners together and often form deep relationships. **The numbers:** 112 intergenerational cohousing communities, with another 40 to 50 planned; four elder cohousing projects, with 20 or so in the works. More than half are in California. **The price:** $100,000 to $750,000, monthly fees $100 to $300; 10 percent of projects offer rentals for $600 to $2,000 a month.

Intergenerational cohousing is geared to families with younger children but also draws boomer couples and singles. The youngest elder cohousing residents are in their 60s. Members live in separate, fully equipped attached or clustered units, and share outdoor space and a common house where communal meals take place. The common house also contains a living room and guest (or caretaker's) quarters. What's in the rest of the space depends on the members; it could be a media or crafts room, or a studio for exercise and meditation.

"I think cohousing is a marvelous way to live," says Bernice Turoff, an 85-year-old widow and member of the intergenerational Nevada City Co-housing community in California. "It's a close community where people really care about one another. If you get sick, 14 people say, 'How can I help you?'"

Charles Durrett, her neighbor and an architect who, along with his wife, Kathryn McCamant, brought the concept of cohousing to the United States from Denmark in the 1980s, says older members act as surrogate grandparents. Last year, when one of the older residents was dying, all ages pitched in to help or visit.

Today, older boomers live in both intergenerational and elder cohousing. "I'd be surprised if cohousing doesn't double every couple of years in the next 20 years," says Durrett. Getting popular: cohousing in cities.

Green House

The concept: A new style of nursing home created by gerontologist William Thomas that looks, feels and operates more like a cozy house than an institution. Ten or so residents live together and get ultra-individualized care from nursing staff that knows them well and cooks their meals in an open country-style kitchen. **The numbers:** 87 Green House projects serving 1,000 residents; 120 projects in development. **The price:** The same Medicaid and Medicare coverage offered to traditional nursing homes; the minority paying out of pocket are charged the going rate in the area for a more conventional nursing home.

Residents' private bedrooms and bathrooms surround a living and dining room that looks like it could be in a single-family

home; a screened-in porch or a backyard offers outdoor access. As much as possible, residents make their own decisions, such as when they'll wake up.

Proponents point to studies showing a Green House can improve an older person's quality of life, provide at least comparable, if not better, care than a traditional nursing home, and reduce staff turnover. "The good news and the bad news is that you get to spend the rest of your life with 10 people," says Victor Regnier, a professor of architecture and gerontology at the University of Southern California.

Stanley Radzyminski, 90, might not be able to communicate with a few dementia residents in his Green House at Eddy Village Green in Cohoes, N.Y., but says, "I really like it here. I have my own room and privacy, and if I need help, the staff is outstanding. We all want to think we can take care of ourselves, but it's not always possible."

The Village Model

The concept: Live in your own home or apartment and receive discounted, vetted services and social engagement opportunities. **The numbers:** 56, with 17 in the Washington, D.C., area alone, and 120 in development around the country.

The price: $100- to $1,000-a-year membership fee, with an average of $500 for a single member, $650 or so for a household.

Growing quickly in popularity, this model will become even more popular in the coming years, say housing experts. That's because studies show most older people want to age in place. The first village was established in 2002 at Beacon Hill Village in Boston; in the last four years alone, 90 percent of the villages have formed.

Village members call a central number for help of any kind. That might be transportation to the grocery store or the doctor, or the name of a plumber, acupuncturist, computer tutor, caregiving agency, home modifications specialist, babysitter for visiting grandkids, dog walker or home delivery company. Because the village may have up to 400 members (although new groups may have fewer than 100), vendors find it an attractive market. The group buys theater tickets in bulk, for example, or contracts with a service provider; consolidated services save everyone money.

Villages offer plenty of opportunities to socialize, whether it's taking yoga down the street with neighbors, attending outings to museums or movies, or participating in a book club, walking group or supper gathering.

Rita Kostiuk, national coordinator for the Village to Village Network, which helps communities establish and manage their own villages, has noticed something about the new people calling for information: "The majority are boomers."

On the horizon: Already, demographers are seeing more older Americans moving, or contemplating moving, into cities and suburban town centers. Rather than being saddled with a house requiring nonstop upkeep or feeling isolated in the burbs, they're within walking distance of shops, entertainment and public transportation. So their ability or desire to drive is not a big deal.

Another trend: divorced, widowed or never-married older women living together. Some who don't know one another are keeping such agencies as nonprofit Golden Girls Housing in Minneapolis busy. Golden Girls offers networking events for women who want to live together, lists requests for women looking, and steers them to services that can help. They don't match women, though; women do that themselves. Others opting for this setup are already friends.

David Levy, a gerontologist and lawyer by training, runs seven groups a week for caregivers. Inevitably, the conversation turns from the parents they care for to themselves. "These boomer women may be estranged from, or never had, kids, have diminished funds, and not a significant other on the horizon. They want to know, 'What's going to happen to me? Who will be there for me?' " he says.

It looks like they'll have choices.

Critical Thinking

1. What will the effect of the Green House concept be on nursing homes in the future?

2. What is the advantage that the villages offer to older people in terms of their preferred living choices?

3. What attracts older persons to moving to downtown cities and suburban town centers?

SALLY ABRAHMS writes about aging, boomer, health and workplace issues. She lives in Boston.

City Governments and Aging in Place: Community Design, Transportation and Housing Innovation Adoption

Amanda J. Lehning

The physical environment of many cities in the United States presents barriers to elder health, well-being, and the ability to age in place. These include community design that separates residential and commercial areas (Handy, 2005), the absence of adequate alternative transportation services (Rosenbloom & Herbel, 2009), and limited accessible housing (Maisel, Smith, & Steinfeld, 2008). Recent studies (e.g., AARP Public Policy Institute, 2005) suggest an emerging consensus regarding the innovative policies and programs needed to address these physical barriers, including the following: (a) zoning and infrastructure changes that could allow older adults to remain connected to their community, (b) developing a range of transportation services and mobility options, and (c) creating a wide variety of housing supports and choices. City governments often provide services that may help older adults age in place, including senior centers, recreation programs, and social services. However, there are no previous studies that have explored city government adoption of policies that address the impact of the physical environment on older adults. Informed by an internal determinants and diffusion framework, there are two aims of this mixed-methods study. The first is to examine the characteristics associated with city government adoption of community design, housing, and transportation innovations that affect older adults. The second is to use qualitative interviews to explain the quantitative findings and provide additional findings around the process of adopting these innovations.

A growing interest in adapting the physical environment of communities to better meet the needs of older adults is a reaction to a confluence of factors, including the aging of the U.S. population, a projected increase in disability and chronic disease in future cohorts of older adults, and an inadequate long-term care system. Due to the aging of the Baby Boomer generation and increased longevity, by the middle of the 21st century, a projected 88.5 million Americans will be aged 65 and older (U.S. Census Bureau, 2009). Although the percentage of older adults with a disability decreased in recent years (Crimmins, 2004), the 85 and older population, whose members experience a greater incidence of functional and cognitive impairment, is expected to triple over the next 40 years (U.S. Census Bureau, 2008). In addition, research indicates an increase in chronic illness among Baby Boomers compared with the previous cohort (Martin, Freedman, Schoeni, & Andreski, 2009), suggesting that improvements in morbidity and disability rates will reverse in the near future. The growing number of older adults who require assistance with functioning will rely on a U.S. long-term care system characterized by high costs (Komisar & Thompson, 2007), unmet need (Zarit, Shea, Berg, & Sundstrom, 1998), and poor quality (U.S. Government Accountability Office, 2005). Further, even as 93% of older adults want to remain in their own homes (Feldman, Oberlink, Simantov, & Gursen, 2004) and governments attempt to reduce long-term care costs and increase the supply of community-based services, public reimbursement continues to favor institutional care (Harrington, Ng, Kaye, & Newcomer, 2009).

Physical Environments and Elder Health and Well-being

Community Design

In recent decades, the percentage of older adults living outside of cities has steadily increased, and a majority of elders today are suburbanites (Frey, 1999). Thus, many older adults live in communities characterized by the separation of commercial and residential areas, creating a situation in which access is severely restricted for those who no longer operate their own vehicle. The distances between residential and commercial areas, combined with the absence of sidewalks in many suburban neighborhoods, discourages walking as a mode of transportation or physical activity.

Research suggests that zoning and infrastructure changes can positively affect the health and well-being of community residents. First, mixed-use and walkable neighborhoods can help individuals maintain or increase their life space (Beard, Blaney, Cerda, Frye, Lovasi, Ompad, Rundle, & Vlahov, 2009), thereby improving access to goods and services. Second, residents of neighborhoods with a variety of walking destinations score higher on measures of social capital (Leyden, 2003). Third, mixed-use and walkable neighborhoods are related to increased physical activity (Berke, Koepsell, Moudon, Hoskins, & Larson, 2007) and decreased limitations of instrumental activities of daily living (IADL; Freedman, Grafova, Schoeni, & Rogowski, 2008).

Transportation

The majority of older adults get around their communities in a car, with 75% as the driver and 18% as a passenger (Feldman et al., 2004). Impairments such as reduced cognitive functioning, however, hamper the ability of many older adults to drive safely (Lynott et al., 2009). Older nondrivers make 15% fewer trips for medical appointments and 65% fewer trips for religious, social, or community activities compared with their driving counterparts (U.S. Government Accountability Office, 2004). Policies and programs that help older adults continue to safely operate their own vehicle, such as improving the visibility of street signs and simplifying intersections, could positively affect elder health and well-being. Approximately 33% of older adults do not have public transportation in their communities (Rosenbloom & Herbel, 2009), and many that do experience inadequate service that is viewed as unsafe, unresponsive, and inconvenient (Adler & Rottunda, 2006). Complementary paratransit services mandated by the Americans with Disabilities Act of 1990 address the mobility needs of some elders (Koffman, Raphael, & Weiner, 2004), although eligibility criteria mean that approximately 40% of older adults with a disability do not qualify for these services (Rosenbloom, 2009). A recent study found that the negative impact of driving cessation on elder well-being can be avoided if transportation needs are met through other modes of travel (Cvitkovich & Wister, 2003), suggesting that alternative transportation services, such as senior vans, can benefit elders.

Housing

The cost of maintaining a home presents a significant barrier to aging in place, and in a recent survey more than 50% of older respondents reported spending more than 30% of their income on housing (Feldman et al., 2004). Further, the majority of housing in the United States includes design features that make it inaccessible to individuals with disabilities (Maisel et al., 2008). Federal laws such as the Fair Housing Amendments of 1988 mandate the inclusion of accessible features (i.e., wide entrances and interior doors, accessible light switches) in new multifamily housing (Kochera, 2002), but do not address accessibility in single-family homes or small multifamily buildings (American Planning Association, 2006). In addition, regulatory barriers such as restrictions for converting a garage into a dwelling unit not only keep densities low but also limit the housing options of older adults (Rosenthal, 2009). For example, in many communities zoning ordinances prevent the development of accessory dwelling units (ADUs; Pollack, 1994), an attached or detached permanent structure located on the same lot as a single-family home that includes a private kitchen and bathroom. For older adults who need to downsize because of financial or physical functioning reasons (e.g., difficulty climbing stairs), ADUs serve as an alternative form of housing, whereas for older adults who can remain in their own home but require some financial or personal care support, adding their own ADU creates a rental unit or a living space for a caregiver (Pynoos, Nishita, Cicero, & Caraviello, 2008).

Changing the home environment is associated with improved outcomes for individuals with a disability (Wahl, Fange, Oswald, Gitlin, & Iwarsson, 2009). Incorporating accessibility features is associated with a lower risk of health problems (Liu & Lapane, 2009), slower decline in IADL independence (Gitlin, Corcoran, Winter, Boyce, & Hauck, 2001), and reduced health care expenses (Stearns et al., 2000).

Purpose of the Study

As described earlier, there is growing evidence that community design, transportation, and housing innovations can have a positive impact on elder health, well-being, and the ability to age in place. However, there is little evidence as to why city governments may institute these policies and programs. To begin to address this gap in the literature, this study examined city government adoption of 11 innovations by testing 3 hypotheses informed by an internal determinants and diffusion framework. In addition, this study used qualitative interviews to explain the quantitative findings and provide additional findings around the process of adopting these innovations.

A combined internal determinants and diffusion framework is often used to guide investigations into the process of adopting an innovation, defined as a program or policy that is new to the adopting unit (Berry & Berry, 1999; Walker, 1969). Diffusion models propose that governments adopt innovations because they are influenced by other governments; policymakers often must devise solutions to problems quickly within the context of limited resources and therefore look to others as they determine the appropriate policy response (Colvin, 2006). Internal determinants models propose that factors within a government jurisdiction, such as community characteristics, determine whether the government will adopt innovations (Berry & Berry). The author selected this framework because it has been applied to previous investigations of the adoption of policy agendas rather than only one specific policy (e.g., Walker), has been used in research on local government innovations (e.g., Shipan & Volden, 2005), and allows flexibility in terms of the specific internal characteristics influencing policy adoption.

This study tested three hypotheses informed by previous studies using an internal determinants and diffusion framework. The first hypothesis, based on the ideas of Berry and Berry (1999), is three diffusion factors will be positively associated with the adoption of these innovations. First, because uncertainty regarding the potential impact of an innovation can be overcome by observing its effects in nearby jurisdictions, governments will adopt innovations that are perceived as being beneficial elsewhere. Second, governments want to gain a competitive advantage to, for example, attract high-income households to increase their tax base, and therefore adopt policies that have popular support in other jurisdictions. Third, governments are more likely to adopt innovations when citizens advocate for these changes.

The second hypothesis is five community characteristics will be positively associated with the adoption of these innovations. In previous studies, larger total population and higher socioeconomic status of the population have positively influenced innovation adoption (Shipan & Volden, 2005; Walker, 1969). In the United States, recognition of older adults as a distinct social group that deserves special consideration in matters of public policy dates back to the passage of the Social Security Act of 1935 (Elder & Cobb, 1984). Therefore, the percent of older adults living in the community could be associated with the adoption of these innovations. Further, many of these innovations are designed for those who have a physical disability, suggesting the inclusion of the percent of the adult population with a disability.

The third hypothesis is two government characteristics will be positively associated with innovation adoption. First, higher per capita government spending may be a proxy for fiscal health, and local governments that are in poor fiscal health may be more conservative than innovative, particularly in terms of innovations that require a commitment of financial resources (Wolman, 1986). Second, policy entrepreneurs, or those who work within government to promote and advocate for policy innovations (e.g., elected officials), may be particularly influential in terms of increasing awareness and consideration of innovations (Mintrom, 1997).

Methods

This study used a sequential explanatory mixed-methods design, which involves a larger quantitative study followed by a smaller qualitative study (Creswell & Plano Clark, 2007). As this is the first study to examine the factors that influence the adoption of these specific innovations, the use of both quantitative and qualitative methods provided a more in-depth understanding of this topic. Qualitative interviews also allowed the author to expand beyond the quantitative findings to collect information that would be difficult to capture using a more structured online survey, including the process of innovation adoption.

The University of California Berkeley Committee for the Protection of Human Subjects classified this study as exempt from Institutional Review Board approval.

Quantitative Phase
Sample and Data Collection Procedures

The sample for this study included all 101 cities located in the San Francisco Bay Area. City governments were selected because they have jurisdiction over the use of land, including aspects of community design, housing, and transportation (Feldstein, 2007). Primary data were collected via online surveys developed by the author. Following a small pilot of the survey, the author sent an invitation to participate via electronic mail to the director of city planning in each city. Survey data collection took place between March and August of 2009. A total of 62 of 101 (61.4%) city planners returned completed surveys, and these data were combined with secondary data from the 2000 U.S. Census and the California 2000 *Cities Annual Report*.

Measures

Table 1 describes the measures and distribution of the dependent and independent variables. For the dependent variables, the survey asked respondents if their city had adopted the 11 community design, transportation, and housing innovations shown in the table. Due to the distribution of frequencies, the community design outcome was dichotomized to compare cities with both innovations to those with one or none. Transportation, housing, and total number of innovations were measured as count variables.

For the independent variables, the survey asked respondents whether they had knowledge of benefits of these innovations

Table 1 Description of Measures and Sample ($N = 62$)

Variables	Description	Frequency (%)
Dependent variables		
Community design	0: zero or one innovation adopted	22 (35.5)
• Incentives to encourage mixed-use neighborhoods	1: Both innovations adopted	40 (64.5)
• Changes in infrastructure to improve walkability		
Transportation (range: 0–5)	0	13 (21.0)
• Education programs for older drivers	1	18 (29.0)
• Assessment programs for older drivers	2	25 (40.3)
• Infrastructure changes to improve older driver safety	3	5 (8.1)
• Alternative transportation	4	1 (1.6)
• Slower-moving vehicle ordinance	5	0

(continued)

Table 1 Description of Measures and Sample (*N* = 62)

Variables		Description	Frequency (%)
Housing (range: 0–4)	0		0
• Accessory dwelling unit ordinance	1		15 (24.2)
• Developer incentives to guarantee housing units for seniors	2		19 (30.6)
• Incentives to make housing accessible	3		15 (24.2)
• Home modification assistance	4		13 (21.0)
Total number of innovations (range: 0–11)	0		0
	1		2 (3.2)
	2		4 (6.5)
	3		4 (6.5)
	4		5 (8.0)
	5		17 (27.4)
	6		12 (19.4)
	7		11 (17.7)
	8		5 (8.1)
	9		2 (3.2)
	10		0
	11		0
Independent variables			
Diffusion factors			
Benefits		0: No knowledge of benefits in other jurisdictions	7 (11.3)
		1: Knowledge of benefits in other jurisdictions	55 (88.7)
Advantage		0: Does not believe other cities gained an advantage by adopting innovations	15 (24.2)
		1: Does believe other cities gained an advantage by adopting innovations	47 (75.8)
Public advocacy		0: Has not experienced public advocacy from residents to adopt innovations	18 (29.0)
		1: Has experienced public advocacy from residents to adopt innovations	44 (71.0)
Community characteristics			
Size (range: 2,125–776,733)		0: Population size < 50,000	42 (67.7)
		1: Population size ≥ 50,000	20 (32.3)
Education (range: 48.2%–98.8%)		0: Percent of the population with a high school diploma ≤ 89	31 (50.0)
		1: Percent of the population with a high school diploma >89	31 (50.0)
Income (range: 37,184–200,001)		0: Household median income ≤ 67,352	31 (50.0)
		1: Household median income >67,352	31 (50.0)
65 + (range: 5.1%–45.1%)		0: Percent of the population aged 65 and older ≤ 11.1	31 (50.0)
		1: Percent of the population aged 65 and older >11.1	31 (50.0)
Disability (range: 8.5%–25.5%)		0: Percent of the adult population with a disability ≤ 15.2	31 (50.0)
		1: Percent of the adult population with a disability >15.2	31 (50.0)
Government characteristics			
Spending (range: 294–6,550)		0: City per capita government spending ≤ 1,013	31 (50.0)
		1: City per capita government spending >1,013	31 (50.0)
Policy entrepreneur		0: No individual within government has advocated for innovation adoption	28 (45.2)
		1: An individual within government has advocated for innovation adoption	34 (54.8)

in other jurisdictions, believed other cities gained an advantage by adopting these innovations, experienced public advocacy to adopt these innovations, and if there was an individual within government advocating for adoption. Data on community characteristics were obtained from the 2000 U.S. Census (the most recent year that included all necessary data for cities in the sample), and the California 2000 *Cities Annual Report* provided information on per capita government spending. Population size was coded into categories of less than 50,000 versus 50,000 or more, a demarcation of small and large cities used by federal agencies (e.g., the Office of Management and Budget) and professional organizations (e.g., National League of Cities). Due to problems with functional form, the author transformed continuous variables for community characteristics into dichotomous variables using median splits.

Statistical Analysis

The author calculated four different regression equations to examine the association between internal determinants and diffusion factors and innovation adoption. Tolerance and variance inflation factor results indicated that multicollinearity is not a concern with independent variables. Logistic regression was used to estimate odds ratios for the dichotomous outcome variable of community design innovations. Poisson regression was used to analyze the other three outcome variables (i.e., transportation, housing, and total number of innovations) as these measured counts of the number of innovations adopted. As recommended by Cameron and Trivedi (2009), robust standard errors for the parameter estimates were obtained to adjust for minor underdispersion.

Qualitative Phase
Sample and Data Collection Procedures

After completing the survey, 28 city planners indicated their willingness to participate in a follow-up interview. Ten interview participants were selected using maximum variation sampling, which allows the researcher to explore phenomena using cases that vary by characteristics (Sandelowski, 2000). The author selected interview participants representative of community characteristics (e.g., high and low education, high and low income, high and low percent of the population 65 and older, high and low percent of the population with a disability) and a range in the total number of innovations adopted. The researcher conducted, recorded, and transcribed the interviews in November and December of 2009. Interviewees were asked about the decision process involved in adopting innovations, including how the idea developed and facilitators of and barriers to adoption.

Data Analysis

Following the recommendation of Miles and Huberman (1984), qualitative data analysis consisted of three concurrent activities: data reduction, data display, and conclusion drawing/verification. Analysis of interview data was informed by previous research but was also inductive in nature, with data reduction starting at the basic level of line-by-line coding (Padgett, 1998). Following the first review of all interview transcripts, the researcher developed initial codes, which were refined after multiple iterations through the data. During data display, the researcher created spreadsheets for each code that included direct quotes as well as data from the online surveys (i.e., community characteristics and specific innovations adopted by the local government of the interview participant). This visual display allowed the researcher to further refine codes, establish a set of themes expressed by multiple interview participants, and draw conclusions about the data. The researcher then verified conclusions by a final review of the interview transcripts, a procedure that has been used by other qualitative researchers to determine the validity of qualitative data analysis (Miles & Huberman).

Results
Quantitative

Table 2 presents the results of the regression of internal determinants and diffusion factors on innovation adoption. Model 1 presents the logistic regression for the adoption of community design innovations. Cities that experienced public advocacy or had a higher percent of the population with a disability had an increased odds of adopting both community design innovations. However, these results should be interpreted with caution as wide confidence intervals indicate problems with the precision of the model.

Model 2 presents the regression of the number of transportation innovations, and public advocacy was significantly associated with innovation adoption. As shown in Model 3, cities with a higher percent of the population aged 65 and older adopted fewer housing innovations and those with a higher percent of the population with a disability adopted more housing innovations. In Model 4, which presents the regression of the total number of innovations, the relationship between percent of the population with a disability and innovation adoption was also significant. In addition, higher per capita government spending was negatively associated with innovation adoption, whereas the existence of a policy entrepreneur was positively associated with innovation adoption.

Qualitative

Qualitative interviews uncovered potential explanations for the quantitative findings and also additional findings. Three concepts were identified through analysis of the qualitative interviews: advocacy and public resistance, disability and age, and city and resident economic resources.

Advocacy and Public Resistance

Advocacy by city residents was described as a facilitator of the adoption process. According to one city planner, "Every large project had its genesis with some sort of citizens' group that came to the city with a concept and got that to move forward." Another said, "We respond to things we're pushed to do." A third city government respondent reported that "Activists come to public meetings and they share info about their needs. It is clear what they want: they call me and they definitely call their council people."

Table 2 Regression Results for the Adoption of Community Design, Transportation, and Housing Innovations (*N* = 62)

Internal determinants and diffusion variable	Model 1[a]: community design, OR (95% CI)	Model 2[b]: transportation, *B* (95% CI)	Model 3[b]: housing, *B* (95% CI)	Model 4[b]: total number of innovations, *B* (95% CI)
Diffusion factors				
Benefits	1.46 (0.29–7.40)	.09 (−.29 to .46)	.02 (−.19 to .23)	−.01 (−.34 to .33)
Advantage	2.26 (0.40–12.81)	−.03 (−.43 to .37)	−.07 (−.29 to .16)	.08 (−.16 to .31)
Public advocacy	4.28* (0.88–20.73)	.35** (.02 to .68)	.11 (−.13 to .35)	.17 (−.04 to .38)
Community characteristics				
Size	3.39 (0.55–20.70)	−.03 (−.41 to .34)	.12 (−.07 to .32)	.11 (−.06 to .27)
Education	1.34 (0.23–7.77)	−.02 (−.39 to .35)	−.10 (−.34 to .14)	−.06 (−.22 to .10)
Income	2.00 (0.17–22.81)	−.15 (−.62 to .33)	.17 (−.058 to .39)	.05 (−.10 to .20)
65+	0.70 (0.16–3.08)	.04 (−.33 to .42)	−.26** (−.51 to .02)	−.11 (−.26 to .03)
Disability	8.79* (0.69–112.14)	.19 (−.33 to .72)	.28** (.03 to .54)	.22** (.05 to .40)
Government characteristics				
Spending	0.28 (0.06–1.28)	−.15 (−.49 to .18)	−.08 (−.267 to .11)	−.12* (−.26 to .01)
Policy entrepreneur	0.85 (0.18–3.91)	.21 (−.12 to .53)	.07 (−.16 to .30)	.15* (−.02 to .32)

Note: OR = odds ratio; CI = confidence interval.
[a] Logistic regression.
[b] Poisson regression.
*$p < .10$. **$p < .05$.

Public resistance, often discussed as concerns about mixed-use neighborhoods and higher-density development, is perceived by city planners as a barrier to adopting these innovations. One city planner referred to "the traditional NIMBY [not in my backyard] people." Another interviewee noted "There are parts of town where people don't want more dense neighborhoods . . . People prefer single-family homeownership." Another planner recalled resistance to an accessible apartment building: "The concerns raised were about how it would affect parking in the neighborhood and wanting to make sure it would be well managed and well designed."

Disability and Age

Several interviewees mentioned advocacy by and on behalf of younger individuals with disabilities. One planner explained, "When we built more accessible housing, it wasn't seniors per se, but a disability group pushed the city. The basic idea was 'why are you spending all this money to keep people in institutions when you could keep people in their homes?'." Another interview participant noted the increased visibility of individuals with disabilities in this region compared with other parts of the United States: "There are probably not more people here with disabilities, but they are more out in the community." A third interviewee said, "I think, anecdotally, this area is a magnet for people with disabilities because we have such great services."

City and Resident Economic Resources

Interviewees indicated that they viewed some of these innovations as a way to improve the fiscal health of their city. The following quote is from a city with relatively low spending that adopted a high number of innovations: "We see all these policies and provisions coming into place to make downtown more vital, more interesting, and more economically competitive. The thought process is getting more people into downtown." Similarly, another city planner explained that a recent push by a city to create more walkable mixed-use neighborhoods was motivated in part because "people want more lively places, more lively streets, and they want more of a 24-hr presence."

In terms of resident economic resources, some cities do not see any need for public supports for their more economically advantaged aging residents. For example, as one city planner explained: "This is an affluent community, so it doesn't require as much public assistance. I think the seniors do need household assistance and sometimes medical assistance . . . We are going to promote increased density near the commercial district, and also second units so you can have your nurse living nearby, but most of these services are private in this community." According to another, "there is a sense that we have addressed a good chunk of part of the need, and I mean by income levels. I tend to focus on below market housing, but there are other niches outside of my scope. There could be a need for empty nester housing but that is not part of our focus."

Discussion

This mixed-methods study is the first attempt to explore local government adoption of community design, transportation, and housing innovations that could improve elder health, well-being, and the ability to age in place. The quantitative phase tested three hypotheses informed by an internal determinants and diffusion framework using data collected via online surveys with city planners. The qualitative phase used data collected through telephone interviews designed to explain and supplement the quantitative results.

The first hypothesis proposed that three diffusion factors would be positively associated with the adoption of community design, transportation, and housing innovations that could benefit older adults: knowledge of benefits in other jurisdictions, a belief that cities gain an advantage from adopting innovations, and public advocacy. Only public advocacy was significant, and only for community design and transportation innovations. In qualitative interviews, a number of participants reported that resident advocacy influences policy decisions. However, interviews also suggest that public resistance can present a barrier to innovation adoption. Similar to a recent study examining barriers to the adoption of ADU ordinances (Liebig et al., 2006), public resistance came up in discussions about mixed-use and higher-density development, ranging from NIMBY sentiments to residential concerns about parking problems.

The second hypothesis proposed that five community characteristics would be positively associated with innovation adoption: population size, population education, household median income, percentage of the population aged 65 and older, and percent of the adult population with a disability. This hypothesis was partially supported as the percent of the population with a disability was associated with the adoption of community design, housing, and total number of innovations. The percent of the population aged 65 and older was not significant in three of the models and was negatively associated with the adoption of housing innovations. Interview participants mentioned disability advocates more often than older adults or groups representing their interests. Historically, due to their high voter turnout and the organizational power of groups such as AARP, older adults have successfully pushed policymakers at the federal level to adopt policies (e.g., Medicare) targeted to meet their needs (Elder & Cobb, 1984). At the local level, however, interviews suggest that public advocacy for changes to the physical environment comes from residents with disabilities rather than older adults. Previous research has found that advocacy can lead to the adoption of innovations that are particularly salient to residents, such as those around sex education and gambling (Mooney & Lee, 2000), but plays a smaller role in innovations more removed from people's everyday lives, such as hazardous waste policies (Daley & Garand, 2005). Some of the innovations examined in this study (e.g., incentives to develop accessible housing) address difficulties associated with functional status rather than age. Disability groups may be more active because individuals who have a disability are more aware of the physical barriers in their communities than older adults who face the possibility of disability in the future. Alternatively, younger individuals with disabilities may be more effective advocates for the adoption of these innovations because the general response to disability varies across age populations. It has been suggested that for younger individuals, disability is more often viewed as a result of problems in the social and physical environment, whereas for older adults disability is more typically attributed to disease (Kane, Priester, & Neumann, 2007). City governments may therefore perceive these innovations as more appropriate for younger adults with disabilities.

The implication is that service providers and advocates should facilitate the involvement of older adults through education and community-building activities. This has proved a successful strategy by the Elder Friendly Communities Project in Calgary, Canada, which has successfully brought about changes, including infrastructure improvements, by training and supporting older adults to plan and carry out actions to change their community (Austin, Des Camp, Flux, McClelland, & Sieppert, 2005). In addition, aging service providers and advocates may also need education about the ways in which the physical environment can affect older adults. Councils on Aging, for example, could broaden their service and advocacy efforts to address community design, transportation, and housing.

Contrary to the second hypothesis and previous research (Berry & Berry, 1999; Shipan & Volden, 2005), there was no significant association with population education or income in any of the four regression models. As discussed in interviews, city government perceptions of the need for many of these innovations may depend on the residents' private economic resources, and city planners in wealthier communities may assume that older residents are wealthy and do not require public assistance. It is possible that older adults with higher education and incomes are less likely to require the public provision of environmental adaptations because of their reduced risk for physical limitations (Freedman & Martin, 1999), lower rates of impairments, and slower deterioration of physical functioning (Mirowsky & Ross, 2000). Higher levels of education have been linked with improved access to care, higher quality of care, and better health behaviors (Goldman & Smith, 2002), and these elders may be able to delay or avoid disability because they can obtain personal care, assistive devices, medical care, healthy foods, and exercise equipment (Schoeni, Freedman, & Martin, 2008). Cities whose residents have a lower socioeconomic status, and are therefore more vulnerable to disease and disability, may be more receptive to advocacy efforts to put these innovations in place.

For the third hypothesis, the positive significant association between the existence of a policy entrepreneur and the total number of innovations indicates that enlisting the support of individuals with a formal role in city government may be an effective strategy to innovation adoption. This is consistent with the proposition of Walker (1973) that "the presence of a single aide on a legislative staff who is enthusiastic about a new program, or the chance reading of an article by a political leader can cause [governments] to adopt new programs more rapidly" (p. 1190). Per capita government spending had an inverse relationship with the total number of innovations. Similar to previous studies (e.g., Boyne & Gould-Williams, 2005), this finding combined with qualitative data suggests that the need for economic revitalization could inspire innovation adoption because it creates a greater need for innovative solutions. For example, because city governments receive much of their revenue from sales taxes, property taxes, and user fees (Warner, 2010), incentives for mixed-use development and the construction of residential buildings that dedicate units for seniors could improve city finances. Another implication of this research is that advocates and residents pushing for these innovations should emphasize the potential economic benefits associated with some of these changes.

Findings from the current study should be interpreted in light of its limitations, and future research should examine whether the results are applicable to other cities. First, this study achieved fairly good response rates but may still have some nonresponse error. Second, future research should address the limitation of self-report data by, for example, soliciting participation from multiple employees in each city. Third, because the nonlinear relationship between the continuous variables and outcome variables indicated problems with functional form, the author used median splits, which in turn affects model precision and could lead to overestimation or underestimation of significant statistical relationships (Maxwell & Delaney, 1993). The small sample size also affects the validity of the quantitative results. For example, the logistic regression model for community design innovations may be overestimating the odds ratios (Nemes, Jonasson, Genell, & Steineck, 2009). Fifth, results may not be generalizable outside of the San Francisco Bay Area because of its unique characteristics, including higher population income and education and rapid population growth at the end of the 20th century (Kawabata & Shen, 2007). Furthermore, the region has a reputation for embracing innovative land use and transportation policies and is often the subject of case studies of these types of innovations (e.g., Bhatia, 2007; Kawabata & Shen).

Additionally, the use of cross-sectional data does not allow for an understanding of the diffusion of innovations over time (Berry & Berry, 1990). Future research should employ techniques such as event history analysis to ascertain which innovations have been in place for years and which have been only recently adopted, uncover if there are particularly influential cities affecting the diffusion process, and further clarify the factors associated with the adoption of these innovations. Other policy researchers (e.g., Downs & Mohr, 1976) have criticized an internal determinants and diffusion framework for the variation in results reported across studies. It is not unusual for factors that are positively associated with one type of policy innovation to be negatively associated, or not associated at all, with other innovations (Downs & Mohr). The researcher selected this framework in part because of its flexibility in the specific characteristics associated with policy adoption, and therefore it is not surprising that results differed from previous research on, for example, local antismoking policies (see Shipan & Volden, 2005).

The findings and limitations of this study suggest the need for additional research into local government adoption of community design, transportation, and housing innovations that could benefit older adults. Future research should explore modifications to an internal determinants and diffusion framework as it relates to these policies and programs. For example, although per capita government spending has been used as a proxy measure for government resources in earlier research on local government policy adoption (e.g., Shipan & Volden, 2005), other measures (e.g., city revenues) could be used in future studies. Future studies should also explore whether younger individuals with disabilities are more active in advocating for these innovations than older adults. It is possible that this finding reflects the Bay Area, which, as mentioned by interview participants, has a history of supporting disability rights and the independent living movement. It is also possible that older adults are not as engaged in public policy at the local level, and therefore more research is needed to understand how to promote their community involvement. Third, although there is emerging evidence that these innovations can improve elder health, well-being, and ability to age in place, more research is needed to explore the impact of the environment on older adults. Establishing an empirical evidence base for aging in place will ensure that local governments devote their often scarce resources toward effective policies, programs, and infrastructure changes.

Conclusion

This mixed-methods study explored city-level adoption of community design, transportation, and housing innovations that have the potential to improve elder health, well-being, and the ability to age in community. Quantitative and qualitative results indicate that advocacy is an effective strategy to encourage city adoption of innovations that affect the mobility and quality of life of older adults. Successful advocacy efforts should facilitate the involvement of older residents, target key decision makers within government, emphasize potential financial benefits to the city, and focus on cities whose aging residents are particularly vulnerable to disease and disability.

References

AARP Public Policy Institute. (2005). Livable communities: An evaluation guide. Washington, DC: AARP. Retrieved July 8, 2009, from http://assets.aarp.org/rgcenter/il/d18311_communities.pdf

Adler, G., & Rottunda, S. (2006). Older adults' perspectives on driving cessation. *Journal of Aging Studies, 20,* 227–235. doi: 10.1016/j.jaging. 2005.09.003

American Planning Association. (2006). Policy guide on housing. Policy adopted by American Planning Association (APA) Board of Directors. Retrieved January 4, 2010, from http://www.planning.org/policy/guides/pdf/housing.pdf

Austin, C. D., Des Camp, E., Flux, D., McClelland, R. W., & Sieppert, J. (2005). Community development with older adults in their neighborhoods: The Elder Friendly Communities Program. *Families in Society, 86,* 401–409.

Beard, J. R., Cerda, M., Blaney, S., Ahern, J., Vlahov, D., & Galea, S. (2009). Neighborhood characteristics and change in depressive symptoms among older residents of New York City. *American Journal of Public Health, 99,* 1308–1314. doi:10.2105/AJPH.2007. 125104.

Berke, E. M., Koepsell, T. D., Moudon, A. V., Hoskins, R. E., & Larson, E. B. (2007). Association of the built environment with physical activity and obesity in older persons. *American Journal of Public Health, 97,* 486–492. doi: 10.2105/AJPH.2006.085837

Berry, F. S., & Berry, W. (1999). Innovation and diffusion models in policy research. In P. A. Sabatier (Ed.), *Theories of the policy process* (pp. 169–200). Boulder, CO: Westview Press.

Berry, F. S., & Berry, W. D. (1990). State lottery adoptions as policy innovations: An event history analysis. *The American Political Science Review, 84,* 395–415.

Bhatia, R. (2007). Protecting health using an environmental impact assessment: A case study of San Francisco land use decisionmaking. *American Journal of Public Health, 97,* 406–413. doi:l0.2105/AJPH.2005. 073817

Boyne, G. A., & Gould-Williams, J. S. (2005). Explaining the adoption of innovation: An empirical analysis of public management reform. *Environment and Planning* C: *Government and Policy, 23,* 419–435. doi:10.1068./c40m

Cameron, A. C, & Trivedi, P. K. (2009). *Microeconometrics using Stata.* College Station, TX: Stata Press.

Colvin, R. A. (2006). Innovation of state-level gay rights laws: The role of Fortune 500 corporations. *Business and Society Review, 111,* 363–386. doi:10.1111/j. 1467–8594.2006.00277.x

Creswell, J. W., & Piano Clark, V. L. (2007). Designing and conducting mixed methods research Thousand Oaks, CA: Sage Publications.

Crimmins, E. M. (2004). Trends in the health of the elderly. *Annual Review Public Health, 25,* 79–98. doi: 10.1146/annurev.publhealth. 25.102802.124401

Cvitkovich, Y., & Wister, A. (2003). Bringing in the life course: A modification to Lawton's ecological model of aging. *Hallym International Journal of Aging, 4,* 15–29.

Daley, D. M., & Garand, J. C. (2005). Horizontal diffusion, vertical diffusion, and internal pressure in state environmental policymaking, 1989–1998. *American Politics Research, 33,* 615–644. doi.l 177/1 532673X04273416

Downs, G.W., & Mohr, L.B. (1976). Conceptual issues in the study of innovation. *Administrative Science Quarterly, 21,* 700–714.

Elder, C. D., & Cobb, R. W. (1984). Agenda-building and the politics of aging. *Policy Studies Journal, 13,* 115–129.

Feldman, P. H., Oberlink, M. R., Simantov, E., & Gursen, M. D. (2004). A tale of two older Americas: Community opportunities and challenges. New York: Center for Home Care Policy and Research.

Feldstein, L.M. (2007). General Plans and Zoning: A Toolkit on Land Use and Health. Sacramento, CA: California Department of Health Services. Retrieved February 26, 2010, from http://www.phlpnet.org/ healthy-planning/products/general-plans-and-zoning

Freedman, V., & Martin, L. (1999). The role of education in explaining and forecasting trends in functional limitations among older Americans. *Demography, 36,* 461–173. doi: 10.2307/2648084

Freedman, V. A., Grafova, I. B., Schoeni, R. F., & Rogowski, J. (2008). Neighborhoods and disability in later life. *Social Science & Medicine, 66,* 2253–2267. doi:10.1016/j.socscimed.2008.01.013

Frey, W. H. (1999). Beyond social security: The local aspects of an aging America Washington, DC: The Brookings Institution.

Gitlin, L. N., Corcoran, M. A., Winter, L., Boyce, A., & Hauck, W. W. (2001). A randomized controlled trial of a home environmental intervention to enhance self-efficacy and reduce upset in family caregivers of persons with dementia. *The Gerontologist, 41,* 15–30. doi:10.1093/geront/41.1.4

Goldman, D., & Smith, J. P. (2002). Can patient self-management help explain the SES health gradient? *Proceedings of the National Academy of Sciences, 99,* 10929–10934. doi:10.1073/pnas.l62086599

Handy, S. (2005). Smart growth and the transportation-land use connection: What does the research tell us? *International Regional Science Review, 28,* 146–167. doi:10.1177/0160017604273626

Harrington, C., Ng, T., Kaye, S. H., & Newcomer, R. (2009). Home and community-based services: Public policies to improve access, costs and quality. San Francisco: UCSF Center for Personal Assistance Services.

Kane, R. L., Priester, R., & Neumann, D. (2007). Does disparity in the way disabled older adults are treated imply ageism? *The Gerontologist, 47,* 271–279. doi:10.1093/geront/47.3.271.

Kawabata, M., & Shen, Q. (2007). Commuting inequality between cars and public transit: The case of the San Francisco Bay Area, 1990—2000. *Urban Studies, 44,* 1759–1780.

Kochera, A. (2002). Accessibility and visitability features in single-family homes: A review of state and local activity. Washington, DC: AARP Public Policy Institute.

Koffman, D., Raphael, D., & Weiner, R. (2004). The impact of federal programs in transportation for older adults. Washington, DC: AARP Public Policy Institute.

Komisar, H. L., & Thompson, L. S. (2007). National spending for long-term care. Washington, DC: Georgetown University. Retrieved July 7, 2009, from http://ltc.georgetown.edu/pdfs/whopays2006.pdf

Leyden, K. M. (2003). Social capital and the built environment: The importance of walkable neighborhoods. *American Journal of Public Health, 93,* 1546–1551.

Liebig, P. S., Koenig, T., & Pynoos, J. (2006). Zoning, accessory dwelling units, and family caregiving: Issues, trends, and recommendations.

Liu, S. Y., & Lapane, K. L. (2009). Residential modifications and decline in physical function among community-dwelling older adults. *The Gerontologist, 49,* 344–354. doi:10.1093/geront/gnp033

Lynott, J., Haase, J., Nelson, K., Taylor, A., Twaddell, H., Ulmer, J., et al. (2009). Planning complete streets for an aging America. Washington, DC: AARP Public Policy Institute.

Maisel, J. L., Smith, E., & Steinfeld, E. (2008). Increasing home access: Designing for visitability. Washington, DC: AARP Public Policy Institute.

Martin, L. G., Freedman, V. A., Schoeni, R. F., & Andreski, P. M. (2009). Health and functioning among Baby Boomers approaching 60. *The journal of Gerontology, 64B,* 369–377. doi: 10.1093/geronb/gbn040

Maxwell, S. E., & Delaney, H. D. (1993). Bivariate median splits and spurious statistical significance. *Psychological Bulletin, 113,* 181–190. doi:10.1037/0033-2909.113.1.181

Miles, M. B., & Huberman, M. A. (1984). Qualitative data analysis: An expanded sourcebook. Thousand Oaks, CA: Sage.

Mintrom, M. (1997). Policy entrepreneurs and the diffusion of innovation. *American Journal of Political Science, 41,* 738–770.

Mirowsky, J., & Ross, C. (2000). Socioeconomic status and subjective life expectancy. *Social Psychology Quarterly, 63,* 133–151.

Mooney, C, & Lee, M. H. (2000). The influence of values on consensus and contentious morality policy: US death penalty reform, 1956–82. *The Journal of Politics, 62,* 223–239.

Nemes, S., Jonasson, J. M., Genell, A., &: Steineck, G. (2009). Bias in odds ratios by logistic regression modeling and sample size. *BMC Medical Research Methodology, 9,* 56–60. doi: 10.1186/1471-2288-9-56

Padgett, D. K. (1998). Qualitative methods in social work research: Challenges and rewards. Thousand Oaks, CA: Sage Publications.

Pollack, P. B. (1994). Rethinking zoning to accommodate the elderly in single family housing. *Journal of the American Planning Association, 60,* 521–531. doi:10.1080/01944369408975608

Pynoos, J., Nishita, C., Cicero, C., & Caraviello, R. (2008). Aging in place, housing, and the law. *University of Illinois Elder Law Journal, 16,* 77–107.

Rosenbloom, S. (2009). Meeting transportation needs in an aging-friendly community. *Generations, 33,* 33–43.

Rosenbloom, S., & Herbel, S. (2009). The safety and mobility patterns of older women: Do current patterns foretell the future? *Public Works Management & Policy, 13,* 338–353. doi:10.1177/1087724X09334496

Rosenthal, L. A. (2009). The role of local government: Land use controls and aging-friendliness. *Generations, 33,* 18–23.

Sandelowski, M. (2000). Whatever happened to qualitative description? *Research in Nursing & Health, 23,* 334–340.

Schoeni, R. F., Fteedman, V. A., & Martin, L. G. (2008). Why is late-life disability declining? *The Milbank Quarterly, 86,* 47–89. doi:10.1111/j.1468-0009.2007.00513.x

Shipan, C.R., & Volden, C. (2005). The diffusion of local antismoking policies. Retrieved August 12, 2011, from: http://psweb.sbs.ohio-state.edu/intranet/rap/volden.pdf.

Stearns, S. C., Bernard, S. L., Fasick, S. B., Schwartz, R., Konrad, R., Ory, M. G., et al. (2000). The economic implications of self-care: The effect of lifestyle, functional adaptations, and medical self-care among a national sample of Medicare beneficiaries. *American Journal of Public Health, 90,* 1608–1612.

U.S. Census Bureau. (2008). An older and more diverse nation by midcentury. Retrieved June 19, 2009, from http://www.census.gov/Press-Release/www/releases/archives/population/012496.html

U.S. Census Bureau. (2009). Facts for features: Older Americans month: 2009. Retrieved June 1, 2009, from http://www.census.gov/Press-Release/www/releases/archives/facts_for_features_special_editions/013384.html

U.S. Government Accountability Office. (2004). Transportation-disadvantaged seniors: Efforts to enhance senior mobility could benefit from additional guidance and information. Washington, DC: GAO.

U.S. Government Accountability Office. (2005). Nursing homes: Despite increased oversight, challenges remain in ensuring high-quality care and resident safety. Retrieved June 2, 2009, from http://www.gao.gov/new.items/d06117.pdf

Wahl, H., Fange, A., Oswald, F., Gitlin, L. N., & Iwarsson, S. (2009). The home environment and disability-related outcomes in aging individuals: What is the empirical evidence? *The Gerontologist, 49,* 355–367. doi: 10.1093/geront/gnp056

Walker, J. L. (1969). The diffusion of innovations among the American states. *The American Political Science Revieiv, 63,* 880–899.

Walker, J. L. (1973). Comment: Problems in research on the diffusion of policy innovations. *The American Political Science Review, 67,* 1186–1191.

Warner, M. E. (2010). The future of local government: Twenty-first century challenges. *Public Administration Review,* s1, s145–s147.

Wolman, H. (1986). Innovation in local government and fiscal austerity. *Journal of Public Policy, 6,* 159–180.

Zarit, S. H., Shea, D. G., Berg, S., & Sundstrom, G. (1998). Patterns of formal and informal long term care in the United States and Sweden. AARP Andrus Foundation Final Report. State College, PA: Pennsylvania State University.

Critical Thinking

1. What effect did the percent of the population aged 65 and older have on city government's willingness to make beneficial community changes for older persons?

2. What effect did the percent of a community's population with disabilities have on city government's willingness to make beneficial changes for older persons?

3. The growing interest in adapting the physical environment of communities to better meet the needs of older adults is a reaction to what factors?

Acknowledgments—The author would like to thank Andrew Scharlach, Michael Austin, Fred Collignon, Ruth Dunkle, Letha Chadiha, and two anonymous reviewers for valuable feedback on earlier drafts of this article.

Funding—U.S. Department of Housing and Urban Development's Doctoral Dissertation Research Grant; Society for Social Work Research; Hartford Doctoral Fellows Program; National Institute on Aging (T32-AG000117).

The Real Social Network

Villages: Helping People Age in Place.

More than a neighborhood, a village gives older people a better chance to stay in their own home longer.

MARTHA THOMAS

On a bitterly cold morning a few years ago, Eleanor McQueen awoke to what sounded like artillery fire: the ice-covered branches of trees cracking in the wind. A winter storm had knocked out the power in the rural New Hampshire home that Eleanor shared with her husband, Jim. "No heat, no water. Nada," Eleanor recalls.

The outage lasted for nine days; the couple, both 82 at the time, weathered the ordeal in isolation with the help of a camp stove. Their three grown kids were spread out in three different states, and the McQueens weren't very close to their immediate neighbors. "We needed someone to see if we were dead or alive," Eleanor says.

But the McQueens were alone, and it scared them. Maybe, they admitted, it was time to think about leaving their home of 40 years.

Luckily, last year the McQueens found a way to stay. They joined Monadnock at Home, a membership organization for older residents of several small towns near Mount Monadnock, New Hampshire. The group is part of the so-called village movement, which links neighbors together to help one another remain in the homes they love as they grow older.

The concept began in Boston's Beacon Hill neighborhood in 2001, when a group of residents founded a nonprofit called Beacon Hill Village to ease access to the services that often force older Americans to give up their homes and move to a retirement community. More than 56 villages now exist in the United States, with another 120 or so in development, according to the Village to Village (VtV) Network, a group launched in 2010 that provides assistance to new villages and tracks their growth nationwide.

It works like this: Members pay an annual fee (the average is about $600) in return for services such as transportation, yard work, and bookkeeping. The village itself usually has only one or two paid employees, and most do not provide services directly. Instead, the village serves as a liaison—some even use the word concierge. The help comes from other able-bodied village members, younger neighbors, or youth groups doing community service. Villages also provide lists of approved home-maintenance contractors, many of whom offer discounts to members. By relying on this mix of paid and volunteer help, members hope to cobble together a menu of assistance similar to what they would receive at a retirement community, but without uprooting their household.

The earliest villages, like Beacon Hill, were founded in relatively affluent urban areas, though new villages are now sprouting in suburbs and smaller rural communities, and organizers are adapting Beacon Hill's model to fit economically and ethnically diverse communities. Each is united by a common goal: a determination to age in place. A recent AARP survey found 86 percent of respondents 45 and older plan to stay in their current residence as long as possible. "And as people get older, that percentage increases," says Elinor Ginzler, AARP expert on livable communities.

In its own quiet way, the village movement represents a radical rejection of the postwar American ideal of aging, in which retirees discard homes and careers for lives of leisure amid people their own age. That's the life Eleanor and Jim McQueen turned their backs on when they joined Monadnock at Home.

What a Village Takes

Want to organize a village of your own? The Village to Village (VtV) Network offers information on helping villages get started. Membership benefits include tools and resources developed by other villages, a peer-to-peer mentoring program, and monthly webinars and discussion forums.

- To find out if a village exists in your region, the VtV website has a searchable online map of all U.S. villages now open or in development.
- The creators of Boston's Beacon Hill Village have written a book on starting a village: *The Village Concept: A Founders' Manual* is a how-to guide that provides tips on fund-raising, marketing, and organizational strategies.
- Existing resources can make your neighborhood more "villagelike," says Candace Baldwin, codirector of the VtV Network. The best place to start is your local agency on aging. The U.S. Department of Health and Human Services offers a searchable index of these services.—M.T.

"To dump 40 years of building a home to move into a condominium doesn't appeal to me at all," Jim says. "The idea of Monadnock at Home is, I won't have to."

You could call it the lightbulb moment—literally: A bulb burns out in that hard-to-reach spot at the top of the stairs, and that's when you realize you're dependent on others for the simplest of household chores. "It's horrible," says Candace Baldwin, codirector of the VtV Network. "I've heard so many stories from people who say they can't get on a ladder and change a lightbulb, so they have to move to a nursing home. A lightbulb can be a disaster."

Especially when the homeowner won't ask for help. Joining a village can ease the resistance, says Christabel Cheung, director of the San Francisco Village. Many members are drawn by the opportunity to give aid as well as receive it. "A lot of people initially get involved because they're active and want to do something," she says. "Then they feel better about asking for help when they need it."

Last winter Blanche and Rudy Hirsch needed that help. The couple, 80 and 82, live in a three-story brick town house in Washington, D.C.; they pay $800 per year

in dues to Capitol Hill Village (CHV). During the blizzard-filled February of 2010, Rudy was in the hospital for hip surgery and Blanche stayed with nearby friends as the snow piled up. On the day Rudy came home, Blanche recalls, the driver warned that if their walkways weren't clear "he'd turn around and go back to the hospital." She called CHV executive director Gail Kohn, who summoned the village's volunteer snow brigade. A pair of young architects who lived nearby were quickly dispatched with shovels.

The Hirsches have discussed moving; they've postponed the decision by installing lifts so Rudy can get up and down the stairs. Remembering her visits to a family member who lived in a retirement home, Blanche shudders: "Everyone was so old. It's depressing."

Avoiding "old-age ghettos," says Kohn, is a major draw for villagers. She touts the intergenerational quality of Capitol Hill, full of "people in their 20s and people in their 80s," and CHV organizes a handful of events geared toward people of different ages. One program brings high school freshmen and village members together in the neighborhood's public library, where the kids offer informal computer tutoring to the older folks.

Such social-network building is a natural outgrowth of village life. Indeed, Beacon Hill Village was founded on the idea of forging stronger bonds among members. "There was a program committee in existence before the village even opened its doors," says Stephen Roop, president of the Beacon Hill Village board. "Most of my friends on Beacon Hill I know through the village."

One fall evening in Chicago, Lincoln Park Village members gathered at a neighborhood church for a potluck supper. A group of about 80—village members and college students who volunteer as community service—nibbled sushi and sipped Malbec wine as they chatted with Robert Falls, artistic director of Chicago's Goodman Theatre.

Lincoln Park Village's executive director, Dianne Campbell, 61, doesn't have a background in social work or gerontology; her experience is in fund-raising for charter schools and museums, and she lives in Lincoln Park. To village member Warner Saunders, 76, that's a big plus. "She doesn't see us as elderly clients who need her help," says Saunders, a longtime news anchor for Chicago's NBC affiliate, WMAQ-TV. "I see Dianne as a friend. If she were a social worker, and I viewed my relationship with her as that of a patient, I would probably resent that."

For Saunders, Lincoln Park Village makes his quality of life a lot better. He recently had knee and hip surgeries, and his family—he lives with his wife and sister-in-law—relies on the village for transportation and help in finding contractors. "I'd call the village the best bargain in town," he says.

Others, however, might balk at annual dues that can approach $1,000 for services that might not be needed yet. To expand membership, many villages offer discounts for low-income households.

At 93, Elvina Moen is Lincoln Park Village's oldest, as well as its first "member-plus," or subsidized, resident. She lives in a one-room apartment in an 11-story Chicago Housing Authority building within Lincoln Park. The handful of member-plus residents pay annual dues of $100 and in return receive $200 in credit each year for discounted services from the village's list of vetted providers. Since joining, Moen has enlisted the village to help paint her apartment and install ceiling fans.

But beyond home improvements, Moen doesn't ask a lot from the village yet—she's already created her own village, of a sort. When she cracked her pelvis three years ago, members of her church brought her meals until she got back on her feet; she pays a neighbor to help clean her apartment. Her community-aided self-reliance proves that intergenerational ties and strong social networks help everyone, not just the privileged, age with dignity.

Social scientists call this social capital, and many argue that we don't have enough of it. What the village movement offers is a new way to engineer an old-fashioned kind of connection. "As recently as 100 years ago most everyone lived in a village setting," says Jay Walljasper, author of *All That We Share: A Field Guide to the Commons*, a book about how cooperative movements foster a more livable society. "If you take a few steps back and ask what a village is, you'll realize it's a place where you have face-to-face encounters." He compares the village movement to the local-food movement, which also started with affluent urbanites. Think of a village as a kind of "artisanal retirement," a modern reinterpretation of an older, more enlightened way of life. And just as there's nothing quite like homegrown tomatoes, "there's no replacement for the direct connection with people who live near you," Walljasper says.

Strong, intergenerational communities—just like healthy meals—are good for everyone. Bernice Hutchinson is director of Dupont Circle Village in Washington, D.C., which serves a diverse neighborhood. Many members are well-off; some are getting by on Medicaid. "But at the end of the day," says Hutchinson, "what everyone wants is connectedness."

Connectedness alone, of course, can't ensure healthy aging. What happens next—when villagers' needs grow beyond help with grocery shopping or the name of a reliable plumber?

To meet the growing health demands of members, villages boast a range of wellness services, and many have affiliations with health care institutions. Capitol Hill Village, for example, has a partnership with Washington Hospital Center's Medical House Call Program, which provides at-home primary care visits for elderly patients.

A new village—Pennsylvania's Crozer-Keystone Village—flips the grassroots Beacon Hill model: It's the first village to originate in a health care institution. Barbara Alexis Looby, who oversees the village, works for Keystone, which has five hospitals in the southeastern part of the state. A monthly fee gives members access to a "village navigator," who schedules medical appointments and day-to-day logistics like errands. Members also get discounts on Keystone's health services. Because the village and the hospital system are aligned, says Looby, "the boundaries are flexible. You care for people when they come to the hospital, and you are in a position to coordinate their care when they leave." Keystone hopes this integration will lead to fewer ER visits and hospital readmissions.

How long can a village keep you safe at home? It depends. But Candace Baldwin, of VtV, says that the trust factor between members and the village can help family members and caregivers make choices and find services.

Michal Brown lives about 30 miles outside Chicago, where her 89-year-old mother, Mary Haughey, has lived in a Lincoln Park apartment for more than 20 years. She worries about her mom, who has symptoms of dementia. Brown saw a flyer about Lincoln Park Village in a pharmacy and immediately signed her mother up. Through the village, Brown enrolled her mom in tai chi classes and asked a village member to accompany her as a buddy.

Just before Christmas, Haughey became dizzy at her tai chi class. With her buddy's help, she made it to the hospital, where doctors discovered a blood clot in her lung. Without the village, Brown is convinced, her mother might not have survived.

Through the village, Brown has also learned about counseling services at a local hospital to help plan her mother's next steps. "We can add services bit by bit, whether it's medication management or home health care. The village knows how to get those services."

Nobody knows what Mary Haughey's future holds, but the village has given her options. And it has given her daughter hope that she can delay moving her mother to a nursing home. For now, it helps knowing that her mother is safe, and still in her own apartment, in her own neighborhood.

Critical Thinking

1. In terms of services needed by older persons, what are the advantages of joining and living in a village neighborhood?

2. How does the village movement hope to provide residents a menu of assistance similar to what they would receive in a retirement community?

3. What is the common goal of each village community?

MARTHA THOMAS is a Baltimore-based freelance writer.

UNIT 8

Social Policies, Programs, and Services for Older Americans

Unit Selections

Learning Outcomes

After reading this Unit, you will be able to:

- Cite the reasons the author of "Let's Restore the Middle Class" states were responsible for the middle class falling into poverty.

- Describe the steps the middle class has taken to cope with the challenge of a declining income.

- Describe the three myths that the author of "Social Security: Fears vs. Facts" believes exist regarding the future of the Social Security program.

- Identify one of those myths that you think has the greatest credibility and tell why you think that is so.

- Identify the reasons given for the Social Security program heading for insolvency.

- Cite the time when the Medicare and Social Security trust funds are expected to be insolvent.

- Identify the major benefits that the author of "Keep the Health Care Act" believes will result for the nation's new health care law.

- Enumerate the different groups that support keeping rather than repealing the Affordable Care Act.

- Explain the different positions of Republicans and Democrats regarding how to utilize future savings in the Medicare program.

- Identify the proposals that have been suggested for reducing the growth and costs of Medicare.

- Describe 3 of the 10 options for shoring up Social Security in the future that you think have the best chance of being adopted by Congress.

- Describe 3 of the 10 options for shoring up Social Security that you think are least likely to be adopted.

- Identify the different groups of people who depend on Social Security to provide a large part of their income.

- Explain why, at age 65 and older, Social Security provides a higher percentage of income for a woman than it does for a man.

- Describe the proposed changes in Medicare that Rep. Paul Ryan, a Wisconsin Republican, is proposing.

- Identify the specific changes in Medicare payments and benefits that Ryan's plan, known as "premium support" to its proponents, is proposing.

Student Website
www.mhhe.com/cls

Internet References

Administration on Aging
www.aoa.dhhs.gov

American Federation for Aging Research
www.afar.org

American Geriatrics Society
www.americangeriatrics.org

Community Transportation Association of America
www.ctaa.org

Community Reports State Inspection Surveys
www.ConsumerReports.org

Medicare Consumer Information from the Health Care Finance Association
cms.hhs.gov/default.asp?fromhcfadotgov_true

National Institutes of Health
www.nih.gov

The United States Senate: Special Committee on Aging
www.senate.gov/~aging

It is a political reality that older Americans will be able to obtain needed assistance from governmental programs only if they are perceived as politically powerful. Political involvement can range from holding and expressing political opinions, voting in elections, participating in voluntary associations to help elect a candidate or party, and holding political office.

Research indicates that older people are just as likely as any other age group to hold political opinions, are more likely than younger people to vote in an election, are about equally divided between Democrats and Republicans, and are more likely than young people to hold political office. Older people, however, have shown little inclination to vote as a bloc on issues affecting their welfare despite encouragement to do so by senior activists, such as Maggie Kuhn and the leaders of the Gray Panthers. Gerontologists have observed that a major factor contributing to the increased push for government services for elderly individuals has been the publicity about their plight generated by such groups as the National Council of Senior Citizens and the American Association of Retired Persons (AARP). The desire of adult children to shift the financial burden of aged parents from themselves onto the government has further contributed to the demand for services for people who are elderly. The resulting widespread support for such programs has almost guaranteed their passage in Congress.

Now, for the first time, groups that oppose increases in spending for services for older Americans are emerging. Requesting generational equity, some politically active groups argue that the federal government is spending so much on older Americans that it is depriving younger age groups of needed services.

The articles in this section raise a number of problems and issues that result from an ever-larger number and percentage of the population living to age 65 and older. In "Let's Restore the Middle Class," Barry Rand explains how the middle class has been pulled down for the last generation and what can be done to correct the problem. In "Social Security: Fears vs. Facts:

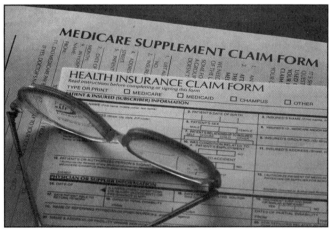

© Kent Knudson/Photolink/Getty Images

What Social Security Critics Keep Getting Wrong," Liz Weston attempts to dispel many of the fears that exist in the minds of the U.S. public regarding the future of the Social Security program. In "Social Security Heading for Insolvency Even Faster," the Associated Press article identifies the years when Social Security and Medicare hospital insurance will become insolvent.

Barry Rand outlines in "Keep the Health Care Act" what he believes are the major benefits for keeping the recently passed Health Care Act. In "Medicare May Soon Take New Shape," Robert Pear notes the different views of Republicans and Democrats that are presented regarding the best way to continue Medicare services and cut costs. Jonathan Peterson in "Time for a Tune-Up" outlines 10 options that are now on the policy table in Washington to avoid future shortfalls in Social Security funds. Barry Rand notes in "Protect Social Security" the current solvency of the Social Security program and what principles should be followed to guarantee its future financial stability. Patricia Barry identifies the proposed ways of saving Medicare that she found likely to be discussed during the 2012 election and beyond in "Retooling Medicare."

Let's Restore the Middle Class

A. BARRY RAND

As you read this column, a "super-committee" of the Congress—six Republicans and six Democrats—is hard at work in Washington. Its job is to find ways to reduce the federal deficit by an additional $1.2 trillion between 2012 and 2021.

This is a worthwhile goal. We need to address our nation's long-term fiscal problems. They affect all of us—Republicans, Democrats, independents and, most important, our children and grandchildren. How we address these problems will determine what their future will be.

That future will not be very bright if they are drowning in the red ink of budget deficits and a soaring national debt. But neither their future nor ours will be very bright if health care is unaffordable, or if there is no opportunity to attain long-term financial security.

That's why this is about much more than reducing the deficit. It's about what kind of country we want to be.

Our primary goal must be to restore prosperity to the middle class. A prosperous middle class has been the chief engine of growth in the economy for more than a century. While middle-class families prospered, low-income families were able to move up the economic ladder—to financial security and a better future.

But over the last generation, more and more of the middle class have fallen into poverty—pulled down by a lack of job opportunities, rising health care costs, inadequate savings and stagnant wages. Nor have incomes grown enough to offset increasing family burdens associated with child care and caring for aging parents.

Middle-class families cope by working longer, delaying retirement, relying on double incomes, reducing their standard of living, relying more on government programs to help them make ends meet and accumulating more debt.

This is taking a serious toll. Most Americans are reaching their 60s with so much debt that they can't afford to retire. In fact, working-age adults now make up 56.7 percent of the poor, defined by the Census Bureau as 2010 income under $22,113 for a family of four. In these challenging times, Social Security, Medicare and Medicaid have become increasingly important for middle-class families—especially for security in retirement.

Cutting these benefits—by increasing Medicare's eligibility age, for example, or forcing higher Medicare premiums—is exactly the wrong approach. Imposing these cuts, as many political leaders now propose, would force millions of older Americans out of the middle class and into poverty.

We are fighting—and we must all fight—to make sure that doesn't happen. To restore prosperity to the middle class, we need a four-part strategy:

1. Restore middle-class jobs.
2. Strengthen Social Security and increase retirement savings.
3. Slow the growth of health care costs and make Medicare sustainable.
4. Increase revenue for public investments to restore prosperity.

If we focus on restoring prosperity to the middle class, we will get our economy going again, put people back to work, increase the revenue needed to fund the government and reduce the deficit.

This will not happen overnight. It will take time and political courage. But it must be done. Failure to act will only put the American dream of a better life for ourselves, our children and grandchildren further out of reach.

Defining the Pressures

16%	Adults providing unpaid care to a family member or friend 50 +
53%	Families that don't think they have enough for comfortable retirement
34%	Head of a family, age 50–64, without retirement savings
75%	Families in 2010 living paycheck to paycheck

From 1989 to 2009

3%	Increase of full-time earnings for men
73%	Increase of average cost of one year of college
182%	Increase of health insurance premiums
292%	Increase of median debt of middle-class families

Sources: "Caregiving in the U.S.," National Alliance for Caregiving/AARP; Gallup: Harris Interactive: AARP Public Policy Institute

Critical Thinking

1. What current changes being considered by government would force the middle class out of their current standard of living and into poverty?

2. What four steps were proposed to restore prosperity to the middle class?

3. What were presented as the advantages of restoring prosperity to the middle class?

Social Security: Fears vs. Facts

What Social Security Critics Keep Getting Wrong

LIZ WESTON

I've been writing about Social Security for nearly two decades. But even I still have trouble wrapping my brain around some of the system's complexities—from how benefits are calculated to how the trust fund works. So it's not surprising that myths about Social Security persist, often fed by the program's critics. With the debate about Social Security's future once again heating up, these three myths need to be put to rest—so we can focus on the real issues.

Myth #1: By the Time I Retire, Social Security Will Be Broke

If you believe this, you are not alone. More and more Americans have become convinced that the Social Security system won't be there when they need it. In an AARP survey released last year, only 35 percent of adults said they were very or somewhat confident about Social Security's future.

It's true that Social Security's finances need work, because over the long term there will not be enough money to fully cover promised benefits. But radical changes aren't needed. In 2010 a number of different proposals were put forward that, taken in combination, would put the program back on firm financial ground for the future, including changes such as raising the amount of wages subject to the payroll tax (now capped at $106,800) and benefit changes based on longer life expectancy.

Myth #2: The Social Security Trust Fund Assets Are Worthless

Any surplus payroll taxes not used for current benefits are used to purchase special-issue, interest-paying Treasury bonds. In other words, the surplus in the Social Security trust fund has been loaned to the federal government for its general use—the reserve of $2.6 trillion is not a heap of cash sitting in a vault. These bonds are backed by the full faith and credit of the federal government, just as they are for other Treasury bondholders.

However, Treasury will soon need to pay back these bonds. This will put pressure on the federal budget, according to Social Security's board of trustees. Even without any changes, Social Security can continue paying full benefits through 2037. After that, the revenue from payroll taxes will still cover about 75 percent of promised benefits.

Myth #3: I Could Invest Better on My Own

Maybe you could, and maybe you couldn't. But the point of Social Security isn't to maximize the return on the payroll taxes you've contributed. Social Security is designed to be the one guaranteed part of your retirement income that can't be outlived or lost in the stock market. It's a secure base of income throughout your working life and retirement. And for many, it's a lifeline. Social Security provides the majority of income for at least half of Americans over age 65; it is 90 percent or more of income for 43 percent of singles and 22 percent of married couples. You can, and should, invest in a retirement fund like a 401(k) or an individual retirement account. Maybe you'll enjoy strong returns and avoid the market turmoil we have seen during the past decade. If not, you'll still have Social Security to fall back on.

Critical Thinking

1. Why do so many young people think Social Security will go broke before they can benefit from the program?

2. Where are Social Security's surplus funds invested to earn money for the program?

3. If the Social Security program went out of existence and people were to invest individually for their own retirement, do you think many of them would do so with adequate investments to assure they had a secure retirement income?

As *AARP The Magazine*'s personal finance columnist, LIZ WESTON offers advice on everything from car loans to home sales.

Social Security Heading for Insolvency Even Faster

Trust Funds Could Run Dry in about 2 Decades

Social Security is rushing even faster toward insolvency, driven by retiring baby boomers, a weak economy and politicians' reluctance to take painful action to fix the huge retirement and disability program.

The trust funds that support Social Security will run dry in 2033—three years earlier than previously projected—the government said Monday.

There was no change in the year that Medicare's hospital insurance fund is projected to run out of money. It's still 2024. The program's trustees, however, said the pace of Medicare spending continues to accelerate. Congress enacted a 2 percent cut for Medicare last year, and that is the main reason the trust fund exhaustion date did not advance.

The trustees who oversee both programs say high energy prices are suppressing workers' wages, a trend they see continuing. They also expect people to work fewer hours than previously projected, even after the economy recovers. Both trends would lead to lower payroll tax receipts, which support both programs.

Unless Congress acts—and forcefully—payments to millions of Americans could be cut.

If the Social Security and Medicare funds ever become exhausted, the nation's two biggest benefit programs would collect only enough money in payroll taxes to pay partial benefits. Social Security could cover about 75 percent of benefits, the trustees said in their annual report. Medicare's giant hospital fund could pay 87 percent of costs.

"Lawmakers should not delay addressing the long-run financial challenges facing Social Security and Medicare," the trustees wrote. "If they take action sooner rather than later, more options and more time will be available to phase in changes so that the public has adequate time to prepare."

The trustees project that Social Security benefits will increase next year, though the increase could be small. They project a cost-of-living-adjustment, or COLA, of 1.8 percent for 2013; the actual amount won't be known until October. Beneficiaries got a 3.6 percent increase this year, the first after two years without one.

More than 56 million retirees, disabled workers, spouses and children receive Social Security. The average retirement benefit is $1,232 a month; the average monthly benefit for disabled workers is $1,111.

About 50 million people are covered by Medicare, the medical insurance program for older Americans.

America's aging population—increased by millions of retiring baby boomers—is straining both Social Security and Medicare. Potential options to reduce Social Security costs include raising the full retirement age, which already is being gradually increased to 67, reducing annual benefit increases and limiting benefits for wealthier Americans.

Critical Thinking

1. What do the Social Security and Medicare trustees believe is causing the problems to ultimately run out of funds?

2. What would be the effect of the Social Security and Medicare programs running out of funds?

3. What is the current average retirement benefit coming from Social Security each month?

Keep the Health Care Act

It will strengthen Medicare and help Americans afford insurance coverage.

A. BARRY RAND

Recent attacks on the nation's new health care law underscore how divided and confused Americans are by the law and the impact it will have on them individually and on the country. We recognize there are serious arguments on both sides of this debate. We have analyzed them carefully and conclude that the Affordable Care Act will help millions of Americans afford insurance coverage, will strengthen Medicare and will add new benefits and protections that will help you and your family.

That's why AARP strongly opposes efforts to repeal the Affordable Care Act.

It includes many important benefits that are already improving health care for older Americans and their families:

- It strengthens Medicare by lowering drug costs for seniors in the Medicare Part D "doughnut hole" and by adding free preventive services. It also cracks down on waste and fraud while prohibiting any cuts to your guaranteed benefits.
- It improves insurance coverage, especially for those with preexisting conditions, who can no longer be denied coverage.
- It expands coverage by allowing parents to keep their children on their policies until age 26.
- It makes insurance more affordable by providing tax breaks and establishing state "exchanges" to provide greater choice and transparency for individuals and small businesses.
- It gives Americans a new option to plan and pay for the cost of long-term services through a voluntary insurance program known as the Community Living Assistance Services and Supports (CLASS) Act.

Repealing the Affordable Care Act would eliminate these important improvements and, according to the nonpartisan Congressional Budget Office, would add to our deficit and national debt, not decrease it. AARP is not alone. The American Heart Association, American Cancer Society, American Diabetes Association, as well as many women's health organizations, patient groups and others, object to repealing the law.

We have two goals at AARP: To ensure that the new law is implemented at the federal and state levels to garner maximum benefits for all Americans, and to ensure that they understand what the law means for them and how to make the best health care decisions.

These benefits vanish if the Affordable Care Act is repealed. Instead, doughnut hole charges soar. Those with preexisting conditions lose coverage. Preventive counseling and services disappear. Millions of young adults lose coverage. Insurance companies have free rein to deny coverage and raise rates against the ill and older people. And millions of small businesses will lose tax credits that are helping them provide their employees with health care coverage for the first time.

This is what's at stake in this debate. AARP will continue to fight to make sure that we do not regress to the health insurance practices of the past that ultimately drive up costs and do more harm than good.

Critical Thinking

1. What are the two goals the AARP want to pursue in support of the new Health Care Act?
2. What are the benefits lost if the Affordable Care Act is replaced?
3. Why does AARP think it would be a serious mistake to regress to health insurance practices of the past?

Medicare May Soon Take New Shape

Challenge: How to keep program solvent while providing good care.

Robert Pear

President Obama has deep disagreements with House Republicans about how to address Medicare's long-term problems. But in deciding to wade into the fight over entitlements, which he may address in a speech Wednesday afternoon, the president is signaling that he too believes Medicare must change to avert a potentially crippling fiscal crunch.

So the real issue now is not so much whether to re-engineer Medicare to deal with an aging population and rising medical costs, but how.

Even before they debate specific proposals, lawmakers across the ideological spectrum face several fundamental questions:

Will the federal government retain its dominant role in prescribing benefits and other details of the program, like how much doctors and hospitals are paid and which new treatments are covered? Will beneficiaries still have legally enforceable rights to all those services?

Will Medicare spending still increase automatically with health costs, the number of beneficiaries and the amount of care they receive? Or will the government try to limit the costs to taxpayers by paying a fixed amount each year to private health plans to subsidize coverage for older Americans and those who are disabled?

Public concern about the federal deficit and debt has revived interest in proposals to slow the growth of Medicare, including ideas from Mr. Obama's deficit reduction commission. Here are some leading proposals:

- Increase the age of eligibility for Medicare to 67, from 65.
- Charge co-payments for home health care services and laboratory tests.
- Require beneficiaries to pay higher premiums.
- Pay a lump sum to doctors and hospitals for all services in a course of treatment or an episode of care. The new health care law establishes a pilot program to test such "bundled payments," starting in 2013.
- Reduce Medicare payments to health care providers in parts of the country where spending per beneficiary is much higher than the national average. (Payments could be adjusted to reflect local prices and the "health status" of beneficiaries.)
- Require drug companies to provide additional discounts, or rebates, to Medicare for brand-name drugs bought by low-income beneficiaries.
- Reduce Medicare payments to teaching hospitals for the cost of training doctors.

In debate last year over Mr. Obama's health plan, Republicans said repeatedly that he was "raiding Medicare" to pay for a new entitlement providing insurance for people under 65. The Senate Republican leader, Mitch McConnell of Kentucky, said the Democrats were using Medicare as a piggy bank. Senator Jim Risch of Idaho said, "We are talking about a half-trillion dollars that is being stolen from Medicare." Senator Charles E. Grassley of Iowa said the cuts "threaten seniors' access to care."

Now it is Republicans, especially House Republicans, proposing to cut the growth of Medicare, with a difference.

"Any potential savings would be used to shore up Medicare, not to pay for new entitlements," said Representative Paul D. Ryan, Republican of Wisconsin and chairman of the House Budget Committee.

The House is expected to vote this week on his budget blueprint for the next 10 years.

Mr. Ryan points to Medicare's prescription drug coverage as a model. That benefit, added to Medicare under a 2003 law, is delivered entirely by private insurers competing for business, and competition has been intense. Premiums for beneficiaries and costs to the government have been much lower than projected.

Republicans rarely mention one secret to the success of Medicare's drug program. Under presidents of both parties, Medicare officials have regulated the prescription drug plans to protect consumers and to make sure the sickest patients have access to the drugs they need.

Many Democrats like Medicare as it is: an entitlement program in which three-fourths of the 47 million beneficiaries choose their doctors and other health care providers, and one-fourth have elected to enroll in managed-care plans. These Democrats acknowledge that care could be better coordinated, but say that could be done in the traditional fee-for-service Medicare program, without forcing beneficiaries into private health plans offered by insurance companies.

Marilyn Moon, a health economist and former Democratic trustee of the Medicare trust fund, said serious discussion of changes in Medicare was warranted, and she noted that the government spent more than a half-trillion dollars a year on the program. Still, Ms. Moon said, it would be preferable to shore up Medicare without "the philosophical sea change" sought by Republicans, who would give private insurers more latitude to decide what benefits are available and what services are covered.

Obama administration officials said Tuesday that Medicare could save $50 billion over 10 years by reducing medical errors, injuries, infections and complications that prolong hospital stays or require readmission of patients.

In any program as big as Medicare, which accounts for one-fifth of all health spending, even decisions about small, seemingly technical questions can have vast consequences for beneficiaries, the health care industry and the economy as a whole.

Gradually raising the eligibility age, for example, would save $125 billion over 10 years, the Congressional Budget Office says.

But it would increase costs for people who would otherwise have Medicare. Some of those 65- and 66-year-olds would obtain insurance from Medicaid or from employers, as active workers or retirees, thus increasing costs for Medicaid and for employer-sponsored health plans.

If Congress decided to make a fixed contribution to a private health plan on behalf of each Medicare beneficiary, lawmakers and lobbyists could spend years debating how to set payment rates and how to adjust them, based on increases in consumer prices or medical costs or the growth of the economy.

Those decisions would directly affect beneficiaries. Under the House Republican proposal, the Congressional Budget Office said, beneficiaries "would bear a much larger share of their health care costs," requiring them to "reduce their use of health care services, spend less on other goods and services, or save more in advance of retirement."

The history of Medicare is filled with unsuccessful efforts to rein in costs. Private health plans entered Medicare with a promise to shave 5 percent off costs, but ended up costing more than the traditional Medicare program. For two decades, Congress has tried to limit Medicare spending on doctors' services, but the limits have proved so unrealistic that Congress has repeatedly intervened to increase them.

Critical Thinking

1. How do the Republicans and Democrats differ in terms of possible new entitlements to the Medicare program?

2. How do the Republicans and Democrats differ in terms of whether the Medicare beneficiaries should be forced into private health plans offered by insurance companies?

3. Has the cost of current Medicare prescription drug coverage handled by private insurance companies been higher or lower than expected?

Time for a Tune-Up

JONATHAN PETERSON

Social Security faces challenges. Retirement for future generations is at stake. Here are 10 options on the table.

In just 21 years, Social Security will be able to pay only three-fourths of its promised benefits, an outlook that guarantees debate about the future of—and the meaning of—Social Security in American life. Yet the projected shortfall is not the only challenge facing the program and those who depend on it. Changes in lifestyle, demographics and the economy are bringing *insecurity* to many older Americans.

Experts have put forth a number of proposals that in some combination could sustain Social Security for the long haul, while making it more helpful and fair. Here are 10 options now on the policy table in Washington:

1. Increase the Cap

You make payroll tax contributions to Social Security on your earnings up to a limit ($110,100 in 2012). If you're like most workers, you earn less than the cap. Increasing the cap to $215,400—so that 90 percent of U.S. earnings are covered—would reduce Social Security's shortfall by about 36 percent. Eliminating it altogether would end almost all of the shortfall in one stroke. Supporters say that raising the cap would be fair and that the amount would not be onerous. The main argument against such a rise is that high earners already get less of a return on contributions than lower-income workers, because benefits are progressive by design. Also, raising the earnings base would amount to a big tax hike on high earners.

2. Raise the Payroll Tax Rate

In recent years, wage earners have paid a Social Security tax of 6.2 percent on earnings up to the income cap, as have their employers. (Congress temporarily cut the employee share to 4.2 percent in 2011 and 2012 as a way to boost the economy.)

Raising the tax rate to 6.45 percent for both employees and employers would eliminate 22 percent of the shortfall and could be phased in. Critics voice concerns about the economic impact and say employers might respond by cutting other payroll costs, such as jobs.

Other ways to raise revenues include increasing income taxes on benefits. Taxing the money that goes into "salary reduction plans," which let you divert pretax income to health care, transit and other uses, could reduce the shortfall by 10 percent. But such a move would hit consumers who may rely on such accounts.

3. Consider Women's Work Patterns

Women workers—single or married—tend to get lower benefits because they're paid less over the course of their careers and because they are more likely than men to take time off from paid employment for caregiving or child-rearing. One proposal would give workers credit for at least some of the time spent caregiving or child-rearing. At the same time, a non-married woman potentially gets a much smaller benefit (depending on her earnings history) than a nonworking wife because she can't rely on a higher-earning spouse for benefits. Measures addressing these issues would be gender-neutral, so they could also help some men. The cost of such a proposal would have to be offset, however, or it could increase the shortfall.

4. Adjust Benefits

Benefit cuts are nothing to cheer about, but they would save money. They could be structured in a way that doesn't hurt current or near-retirees and low-income individuals. Any changes could be phased in after a long lead time, giving younger workers years to adjust their financial plans.

Still, reducing benefits for modest-income people could affect their standard of living in retirement. Reducing benefits for higher earners could undermine the broad public support for Social Security as a program in which everyone pays in and everyone gets benefits.

5. Set a Minimum Benefit

People who had low incomes during their working lives—perhaps one in five earners—now may end up with benefits that are still below the poverty line. A minimum benefit might be set at 125 percent of the poverty line, indexed to wage increases to keep it adequate over time.

6. Modify the COLA Formula

Social Security benefits generally rise to keep up with the cost of living. This cost-of-living adjustment, known as the COLA, is currently based on the Consumer Price Index for Urban Wage Earners and Clerical Workers (known as CPI-W).

One proposal would switch to a different measure, the "chained CPI," which assumes consumers alter their buying patterns if a price goes up too much. Say the price of beef soars—people may switch to chicken. The chained CPI rises about 0.3 percentage point more slowly each year than the CPI-W, meaning benefits would grow more slowly, too—about 6 percent less over the course of 20 years. Adopting a chained CPI would reduce the shortfall by about 23 percent.

Another approach would substitute a formula known as CPI-E. It takes into special account the type of spending that is more common among people 62 and older, such as medical care, which continues to rise faster than other costs. This could increase benefits, expanding the shortfall by about 16 percent.

7. Raise the Full Retirement Age

The age at which you can get full Social Security benefits is gradually rising to 67 for people born in 1960 and later. Pushing it up even further would save money and provide an incentive for people to keep working.

A full retirement age of 68 could reduce the shortfall by about 18 percent. Raising it to 70 would close 44 percent. Such increases could be phased in, and proponents say this approach makes sense in an era of increased life expectancy. A healthy 65-year-old man, for example, is expected to live beyond 82. But not everyone has benefited equally from increases in longevity—lower-income, less educated workers have not gained as much as their more affluent, more educated counterparts. And a later full retirement age could be onerous for workers with health problems or physically demanding jobs. A related proposal—longevity indexing—would link benefits to increased life expectancy.

8. Give the Oldest a Boost

Americans are living longer, and the oldest often are the poorest. They may have little savings left; usually they no longer work and any pensions they have are likely eroded by inflation. A longevity bonus, for example, a 5 percent benefit increase for people above a certain age, say 85, could help them.

9. Establish Private Accounts

Free-market advocates have long pushed to make Social Security more of a private program, in which some of your payroll taxes would go into a personal account that would rise and fall with the financial markets. Supporters believe that stock market returns could make up for benefit cuts. You would own the assets in your personal account and could pass them on to your heirs. Personal accounts could be introduced gradually and become a choice for younger workers, while retirees and near retirees could remain in the current system. Opponents worry that they would replace a guaranteed, inflation-protected benefit for workers and, potentially, family members, with more limited protections. Private accounts only pay out the amount in the account. Also, diverting money to private accounts means additional funding could be needed to pay currently promised benefits.

10. Cover More Workers

Not all workers take part in Social Security. The largest uncovered group is about 25 percent of state and local government employees who rely on state pension systems. Bringing new hires into Social Security would raise enough new revenue to trim about 8 percent of the long-term shortfall (though down the road, when these people claim benefits, costs would rise). State and local governments may oppose such a measure because it would divert dollars from public pensions that are already underfunded.

Critical Thinking

1. Why do you think that at the present time the United States Congress has not discussed adopting any of the ten options that would help to shore up the Social Security funds?

2. Do you think that it is likely that Congress will establish private accounts in which some of a person's payroll taxes paid would go into an individual's account whose earnings would rise and fall with the financial markets?

3. What do you think is the probability that there will be a Social Security program when you reach retirement age and that you will receive a monthly check from the program?

From *AARP Bulletin*, a publication of AARP, June 2012, pp. 14, 16. Copyright © 2012 by AARP Bulletin. All rights reserved. Reprinted by permission of Jonathan Peterson and AARP.

Protect Social Security

A. BARRY RAND

In August, we celebrate the 75th anniversary of Social Security. Ever since Ida Mae Fuller received the first Social Security check in January 1940, Social Security has provided the foundation of retirement security and helped people to live their lives with independence and dignity.

At AARP, we are committed to protecting and fighting for Social Security so that people 75 years from now will still enjoy the peace of mind it provides today. We also know that Social Security needs to be strengthened for future generations, and we will work diligently toward that goal.

We understand that Social Security is much more than just a public policy. It is a guaranteed pension that, on average, replaces 40 percent of a retiree's wages. And because it is risk-free—the only part of the retirement system that is—it is the lifeline that many older Americans, their families, people with disabilities, widows and other survivors count on for their day-to-day lives.

Fighting for, protecting and strengthening Social Security won't be easy. The president's bipartisan fiscal commission—co-chaired by Alan Simpson and Erskine Bowles—and others in Washington are targeting Social Security to help close the growing federal budget deficit. More than most, we understand the importance of balanced budgets, but it's essential that the deficit not be closed by cutting benefits that today's seniors and future generations have earned over a lifetime of hard work.

If Washington wants to restore confidence in our nation's budget, lawmakers should deal with what's really caused our federal deficit. The fact is, Americans pay for Social Security, and it hasn't added one dime to the deficit. It's a sacred promise we make to seniors, our children and our grandchildren—one that must not be broken. We believe that.

As we look ahead, we are guided by some basic principles:

- Any changes to Social Security should be discussed as part of a broader conversation about how to help Americans prepare for a secure retirement, especially as other sources of retirement income—such as pensions, savings and home equity—have been crumbling over the past decade.
- If you pay into Social Security, you should receive the full benefits you've earned over a lifetime of hard work.
- Your Social Security benefits should keep up with inflation for as long as you live.

- You should continue to be covered in case you become disabled and can no longer work, and your family should continue to be protected if you die.
- We will provide educational support and advocate policies to help people save. And we will encourage better pensions and more private savings in addition to—not at the expense of—Social Security.

So as we celebrate Social Security's 75th anniversary in August, we need to protect and strengthen Social Security so future generations will continue to have a strong foundation of income they can count on in retirement for the next 75 years. You can count on AARP to lead this fight.

Critical Thinking

1. What percentage of a 65 or older person's income is provided by Social Security?

2. Why should a 65 or older person expect to be able to draw a Social Security check for the rest of their life?

2. What factor causes Social Security payments to be increased from time to time?

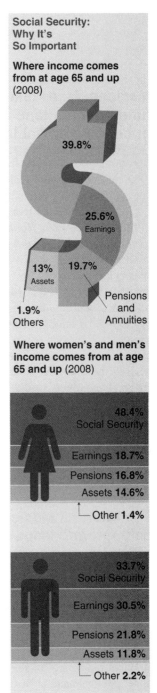

Social Security: Why It's So Important

Where income comes from at age 65 and up (2008)

- 39.8%
- 25.6% Earnings
- 19.7% Pensions and Annuities
- 13% Assets
- 1.9% Others

Where women's and men's income comes from at age 65 and up (2008)

Women:
- 48.4% Social Security
- Earnings 18.7%
- Pensions 16.8%
- Assets 14.6%
- Other 1.4%

Men:
- 33.7% Social Security
- Earnings 30.5%
- Pensions 21.8%
- Assets 11.8%
- Other 2.2%

Article 39

Retooling Medicare?

Patricia Barry

Medicare faces challenges. Retirement for future generations is at stake. Here are 7 options on the table.

Politicians are eyeing Medicare as a spending program ripe for cuts to help reduce the nation's deficit. And so it follows that the future of Medicare looms as a key battleground issue in the 2012 general election. But proposals to change the popular program tend to alarm older Americans, who see Medicare as part of their retirement security. And these same older Americans vote in large numbers. So stand by to hear all candidates claim that they want to "save" Medicare for future generations—but often in very different ways.

Proposed changes to the program include raising the eligibility age to 67, raising payroll taxes and requiring better-off beneficiaries to pay more. The most politically contentious plan, devised by Rep. Paul Ryan (R-Wis.), chairman of the House Budget Committee, would limit federal spending on Medicare and alter the way the government pays for benefits. Republicans say this plan is a fiscally responsible way of extending Medicare's viability as millions of boomers enter the program. Democrats call it "the end of Medicare as we know it" and a way to shift more costs to beneficiaries.

The future of Medicare looms as a key battleground issue in the 2012 election, and older Americans vote in large numbers

Polls show that most Americans prefer to keep Medicare as it is. "Ryan's plan is a fundamental change in the structure of the program," so it makes older voters more nervous than lesser proposals do, says Robert Blendon, professor of health policy at Harvard's School of Public Health. But whoever gains the upper political hand in November, he adds, will have to wrestle with the budget deficit—and some of those decisions will likely affect Medicare.

With that in mind, AARP asked policy experts from across the political spectrum—Henry Aaron, senior fellow of the economic studies program at the Brookings Institution; Stuart Butler, director of the Center for Policy Innovation at the Heritage Foundation; and experts at Avalere Health, a Washington health care policy and research company—to give arguments for and against some Medicare proposals. (Read these in full and contact the experts at earnedasay.org.) Here are summaries of their opposing positions on seven options that most directly affect beneficiaries:

Changing the Way Medicare Pays for Benefits

Medicare now offers two ways to receive benefits. If you're in traditional Medicare, the government pays directly for each covered medical service you use. If you're in a Medicare Advantage private plan, the government pays a set annual amount to the plan for your care. Under the Ryan plan—known as "premium support" to its proponents and as a "voucher system" to its critics—the government would allow you a certain sum of money to buy coverage from competing private plans or from a revised version of traditional Medicare.

For

This would put Medicare on a budget to hold down spending and reduce the tax burden on future generations. You'd receive a share of this budget to help you purchase your health care and have more flexibility to make choices. For example, if you wanted more generous coverage (such as seeing any doctor of your choice), you'd pay the premium difference out of your own pocket, and if the difference became too high, you could switch to a less expensive plan.

Against

The value of the voucher would be tied to some economic index—not to actual health costs, which generally rise faster than other costs. So there is a high risk that benefits would become increasingly inadequate and more out-of-pocket costs would be shifted to the consumer. Medicare already has competing private plans, through the Medicare Advantage and Part D drug programs, yet the hoped-for savings from them have not yet materialized.

Raising Medicare Eligibility Age to 67

Eligibility for Medicare has always been at age 65, except for younger people with disabilities. This proposal aims to gradually bring Medicare in line with Social Security, where full retirement age is now 66 and set to rise to 67 by 2027.

For

With more Americans living longer, and health spending on older people rising, we can't afford Medicare at age 65. Raising the eligibility age would reduce federal spending on Medicare by about 5 percent over the next 20 years.

Against

This proposal would increase other health care spending—especially costs for employer health plans and Medicaid—and uninsured people would pay full costs for a longer time. Medicare premiums would rise due to fewer people in the program to share costs.

Raising the Medicare Payroll Tax

This tax, which funds Medicare Part A hospital insurance, is currently 2.9 percent of all earnings (1.45 percent each for employers and employees; 2.9 percent for the self-employed). People who have paid this tax for a sufficient time do not pay monthly premiums for Part A.

For

Part A currently faces a small long-term deficit after 2024, when it's estimated that available funds will not fully pay for all services. Increasing the payroll tax by just 0.5 percent each for employers and employees would more than fix that problem, leaving a small surplus to act as a cushion against future shortfalls or fund extra benefits in Medicare.

Against

Raising the payroll tax would mean a higher rate of tax for each dollar earned by working Americans, slowing economic growth and increasing the tax burden on future generations. Even workers not earning enough to pay income taxes would pay this bigger tax.

Raising Medicare Premiums for Higher-Income People

Most people pay monthly premiums for Part B, which covers doctors' services and outpatient care, and for Part D prescription

drug coverage. The standard premiums pay for about 25 percent of the costs of these services, while Medicare pays the remaining 75 percent out of general tax revenues. People with incomes over a certain level—those whose tax returns show a modified adjusted gross income of $85,000 for a single person or $170,000 for a married couple—pay higher premiums.

For

The easiest way to bring in more money for Medicare would be to raise the premiums even more for higher income people—so that the wealthiest older people pay the full cost and receive no taxpayer-funded subsidy. Another option is to lower the income level at which the higher premium charge kicks in, so that more people have to pay it.

AARP asked policy experts from across the political spectrum to give arguments for and against some proposals to change Medicare. Join the discussion at earnedasay.org.

Against

Higher-income earners already have paid more into the Medicare program through higher payroll and income taxes, and now pay up to three times more for the same Part B and D coverage. If increased taxes make healthier and wealthier people drop out of the program, standard premiums would eventually become more expensive for everyone.

Changing Medigap Supplemental Insurance

About one in six people with Medicare buys private supplemental insurance, also known as medigap. It covers some of their out-of-pocket expenses under traditional Medicare, such as the 20 percent copayments typically required for Part B services. This option would limit medigap coverage, requiring people to bear more out-of-pocket costs.

For

People buy medigap to limit their out-of-pocket spending in Medicare. But because they pay less, they tend to use more Medicare services, increasing the burden for taxpayers.

Against

There is no evidence that raising medigap premiums or reducing benefits would deter people from using health services unnecessarily, and most patients can't tell whether a service is necessary or not. But there is evidence that postponing needed services leads to greater health problems that cost Medicare more to fix.

Redesigning Copays and Deductibles

Currently, Parts A and B in traditional Medicare have different copays and deductibles. Some proposals would combine the programs to have only one deductible—for example, $550 annually, and uniform copays for Part A and Part B services, plus an annual out-of-pocket expense limit, similar to employer insurance plans.

For

Simplifying Medicare benefits to make them less confusing could save Medicare up to $110 billion over 10 years. An out-of-pocket cap would provide great financial protection, especially for sicker beneficiaries, and reduce the need for medigap supplemental insurance.

Against

Some beneficiaries might pay less, but others—especially those who use few services or spend longer periods in the hospital—would pay more out of pocket than they do now, unless they have additional insurance.

Adding Copays for Some Services

Medicare does not charge copays for home health care, the first 20 days in a skilled nursing facility—rehab after surgery, for example—or for laboratory services such as blood work and diagnostic tests. Several proposals would require copays for one or all of these.

For

Added copays would discourage unnecessary use of these services. Over 10 years, copays could save Medicare up to $40 billion for home health, $21 billion for stays in skilled nursing facilities and $16 billion for lab tests.

Against

Patients without supplemental insurance could pay significantly more for these services, or might not be able to afford them. This could end up harming patients and costing Medicare even more money if postponing treatment worsened patients' health, leading to expensive emergency room visits and hospital admissions. Also, patients generally follow doctors' orders and do not know which services are medically necessary and which are not.

Critical Thinking

1. What two proposed financial changes would bring in money directly to the Medicare funds?

2. What is the benefit to people who buy Medigap supplemental insurance?

3. What could be done to assure that Medicare would have adequate funds to pay for all services in the future?

Test-Your-Knowledge Form

We encourage you to photocopy and use this page as a tool to assess how the articles in *Annual Editions* expand on the information in your textbook. By reflecting on the articles you will gain enhanced text information. You can also access this useful form on a product's book support website at www.mhhe.com/cls.

NAME: _____ DATE: _____

TITLE AND NUMBER OF ARTICLE: _____

BRIEFLY STATE THE MAIN IDEA OF THIS ARTICLE: _____

LIST THREE IMPORTANT FACTS THAT THE AUTHOR USES TO SUPPORT THE MAIN IDEA: _____

WHAT INFORMATION OR IDEAS DISCUSSED IN THIS ARTICLE ARE ALSO DISCUSSED IN YOUR TEXTBOOK OR OTHER READINGS THAT YOU HAVE DONE? LIST THE TEXTBOOK CHAPTERS AND PAGE NUMBERS: _____

LIST ANY EXAMPLES OF BIAS OR FAULTY REASONING THAT YOU FOUND IN THE ARTICLE: _____

LIST ANY NEW TERMS/CONCEPTS THAT WERE DISCUSSED IN THE ARTICLE, AND WRITE A SHORT DEFINITION:

NOTES

NOTES

NOTES

NOTES

NOTES

NOTES

NOTES